AN IRON CURTAIN BREAKAWAY

With gratitude for your assistance

Maurice

AN IRON CURTAIN BREAKAWAY

From Romania to America

PART I: ROMANIA

Maurice Nachtigal

Copyright © 2014 by Maurice Nachtigal.

Library of Congress Control Number:		2014901454
ISBN:	Hardcover	978-1-4931-6661-9
	Softcover	978-1-4931-6660-2
	eBook	978-1-4931-6662-6

All rights reserved. No part of this book may be reproduced or transmitted in any form or by any means, electronic or mechanical, including photocopying, recording, or by any information storage and retrieval system, without permission in writing from the copyright owner.

This book was printed in the United States of America.

Rev. date: 02/06/2014

To order additional copies of this book, contact:
Xlibris LLC
1-888-795-4274
www.Xlibris.com
Orders@Xlibris.com
542233

Contents

Introduction 11
    Why Memoirs? 11
    Autobiography? 13
    A Resume 15
    Acknowledgments 18

Chapter 1: The First Years: 1933-1941 21
    When and Where 21
    Neighbors 25
    Romania before WWII 26
    The Nachtigals 28
    The Wappners 38
    The Winters 40
    The Bercovici 42
    Childhood: The Good Years 46
    Starting School 49
    Anti-Semitism 51
    Love Affair and Politics 53

Chapter 2: War and Communism: 1941-1951 57
    Father in Concentration Camp 57
    Poverty 60
    Mother's Sickness 63
    First Allied Bombardment 64
    More Bombs 67
    End of War 69
    Death Strikes 72
    Bar Mitzvah 74
    The Best Summer Vacation 75
    My Father under Communism 76

Tuna the Socialite 79
Lyceum 81
Culture and Vacation 91
The "Cockerels" 93
Girlfriend 95
Overview 96

Chapter 3: Medical School: 1951-1959 99
Admission 99
Freshman with a Passport 103
Communism in the Medical School 109
Research and Festival 111
Donald and the Blizzard 114
Military Training 119
Poland and Albert 120
Mona 122
Mother Has Cancer 126
First Year of Medicine 129
Father's Troubles 131
A Warning? 132
Eye Surgery 132
Quarrel with Father 135
Mama Mare Leaves 135
A Life-changing Beach Vacation 137
End of Romance 138
Final Thoughts 143

Chapter 4: The Hospital: 1959-1961 145
Călinești Hospital 145
Friends 149
Life in Călinești 153
In Charge of Pediatrics 156
The Bogați Village Experience 158
Admission to Oncology Institute 159
My Father's End 161
Wrapping Up 164

Chapter 5: The Oncology Institute: 1961-1966 167
    Learning about Cancer 167
    Joe Melnick, My American Gate 172
    Miracle on the Mountain 173
    Good Times 176
    My First International Meeting 176
    Leaving the Oncology Institute 180
    Thoughts 182

Chapter 6: Sidonia 184
    Meeting Sidonia 184
    From Colleague to Friend 185
    Childhood and Youth 188
    Marriage 190
    From Friendship to Love 192
    A Fateful Beach Vacation 195
    Divorce 200
    Happy Marriage 205
    A Dangerous Pregnancy 215
    A Risky Delivery 218
    A Baby at Home 220
    Happiness and Love 221
    A Post Scriptum 226

Chapter 7: The Ciugudean Family 228
    Marius Zeno Ciugudean 229
    Mutis 232
    Mimi 234
    The Vingard Home 237
    Refugees and War 238
    Communist Robbery 239
    The Other Ciugudeans 240
    Sidonia in Vingard 241
    Uncle Ovidiu Visit 243

Chapter 8: The Microbiology Institute: 1966-1971 245
    A Team 245
    Sidonia Surgery and Move 246

Visiting Soviet Union 250
War? 252
A Baby and a Car 253
Privacy 257
West Germany 260
Alina 261
Houston I Come 263
My French Family 264
Baylor College of Medicine 267
Back to Romania 276
Overview 276

Chapter 9: Medical Schools: Craiova and Hershey: 1971-1977 278
Sidonia at Cantacuzino Institute 278
Craiova Medical School 280
Teaching Medical Students 282
Albert 283
Life in Craiova 284
Family life 286
Budapest Congress 291
Hershey, Pennsylvania 292
Jan 293
Another War 294
Ştefan 294
Bad News 295
A Small World 297
A Failed Breakaway 298
Return behind the Iron Curtain 299
Textbook 302
Dinner with a Securitate General 303
Ceauşescu Visit 303
Looking for a Killer 304
Party Member? 306
Earthquake 307
Troubles with Securitate 309
Looking for a Job 311
Wrap-up 312

Chapter 10: The Cantacuzino Institute: 1977-1980 315
    Polio Vaccine 316
    Job Offers 319
    Balkan Nephropathy Again? 321
    Warnings 322
    Family Life 327
    Fight for Passports 329
    Mimi's Death 336
    How to Set Up a Breakaway 336
    Out of Romania 341
    Crossing the Iron Curtain 341
    Jan in Amsterdam 342
    Paris and HIAS 344
    Strasbourg Family 346
    Separation Ordeal 347
    Sidonia the Brave Fighter 348
    Life in Paris 351
    American Visa 352

Introduction

Why Memoirs?

I was considering writing these memoirs for some time, wondering if anybody will be interested to spend time reading something produced by a nonprofessional writer. In the last twenty-six years of my activity, I was a full-time professor of pathology at the University of South Carolina, School of Medicine. In this capacity, I wrote scientific reports and reviews, lecture handouts, and protocols and a good number of grant proposals. None of those would qualify as literature, and they were not supposed to. This is not said to excuse my lack of professional experience, just to explain my hesitation in approaching this challenge. I should add that English is actually only my third language, Romanian being my native language, and French that of my maternal grandmother and the rest of my family in France.

Under these circumstances, the obvious question is why did I write these memoirs? The answer is that after talking to various individuals, I became inclined to think that although written by an amateur, this story would be of interest to such diverse people as Doug, my son-in-law; Charles, the guy that helped us fix the unaccountable loss of water (and dollars); Phillip, a professor of pharmacology at the University of Georgia in Athens, Georgia; and even Donald, my friend and medical school classmate from Romania, now a neurologist living in New York. For Doug, our American-born son-in-law, the reason for these memoirs was that his daughters, Nicole and Sydney, someday would like to know more about their ascendants. I found this line of thought very reasonable. Sydney has started establishing a family tree; and Sidonia, my wife, and I regret that we don't know more about our family history to contribute to this tree.

One of the most important incentives for writing the story of my life came rather unexpectedly from my American medical students. It was 1991 or 1992, one of the years when I used to teach a course of virology at the University of Orléans in France. As it happened that year, I came back from France and decided to have a meeting with the group of medical students from our medical school with whom I worked during the year for what was called Discussion groups. During these meetings, we were reviewing clinical cases and microscopic slides associated with these cases. Being close to the end of the academic year, I was planning to discuss with the students how they felt about the pathology course and their preparation for the final exam and part one of the National Board that followed shortly thereafter. We had a good discussion about the pathology course, and the whole atmosphere was relaxed and friendly. It was getting late afternoon, and I was thinking that it was time to close the meeting so that everyone could go home and have dinner. So I launched the last question, "Is there anything else you would like to discuss?" expecting a wide "no" answer and a rush to the door. But the answer from the students came back as a surprise: "Yes, we would like to know why and how you defected from Romania!"

I was not prepared to give a talk about this subject that obviously would have been a long and rather complicated story. However, I decided that I have to answer the question as best as I could with a short but still reasonable reply. I delivered a brief talk, probably around fifteen minutes, in which I related the essential events. I have to say that in my twenty-six years of teaching at the USC School of Medicine, I never had a class that was so focused and concentrated. When I finished my brief story, the students came to me and thanked me in a very friendly manner. I somewhat felt they were trying to tell me that they understood what I did and were supportive of it. That evening, I went home and told Sidonia what happened. My conclusion was that I probably missed my call in life. Instead of teaching pathology, I should give talks about my life experience.

Thinking more about why such a story might be of interest to some people, I concluded that I lived through a very unusual time in history. This time has seen the Second World War (WWII), the rise and fall of Nazism and communism, the Holocaust and the Gulag, the cold war with its Iron Curtain, the rebirth of a Jewish state after two thousand years, the rise of China as a new superpower, and the expansion of Islam into the world, among many others. During my lifetime, the world went from radio and telephone to computer and television and the explosion of information transmission technology, globalization, extraterrestrial travel, human genome decoding, nuclear energy, and much more.

I watched all these events from two opposite sides of the world. I lived the first forty-seven years of my life in Romania, a country that after WWII became a satellite of the Soviet Union and a totalitarian communist regime. Like the Soviet Union and the other eastern European satellites, Romania was, for almost fifty years, behind the Iron Curtain. The term "Iron Curtain" was used by the former British prime minister Winston Churchill in a speech at Fulton, Missouri, US, on March 5, 1946, when he said, "From Stettin in the Baltic to Trieste in the Adriatic, an iron curtain has descended across the Continent" (Encyclopedia Britannica). This political, military, and ideological barrier was created by the Soviet Union to seal off itself and its satellites from contact with the West. In 1980, I managed to break away from the Iron Curtain and to resume my life on the other side of it, in the United States. Crossing the Iron Curtain from one side to the other by me and my family was a complicated and painful endeavor. By the time the Iron Curtain ceased to exist in 1989, my family and I were American citizens living happily in our adoptive motherland, which is definitely a different world. (Thank you, God).

Autobiography?

When I started writing these memoirs, I had in mind to try to put together an extended autobiography. Under communist Romania, writing an autobiography was almost a routine; they were required by the personnel services of every institution for any job application. The autobiography was serving to establish if the individual had relatives who were exploiters of the working class, if they owned land enough to require hired workers, shops, or enterprises with workers. Also, family members could have been active in politics or could live abroad, all hallmarks of possible affiliation with the class enemy or, even worse, the imperialist camp.

For those readers who may find this bizarre, I will offer just one example. At some point, I was employed by the School of Medicine in Bucharest as an adjunct professor to do a few-hours-a-week laboratory work with medical students. The position was temporary, and for me, it was just to supplement my income and to continue some teaching activity. My full-time job was at the Cantacuzino Institute in polio vaccine production. After a few months, I was told that I am fired from my teaching job. No official explanation was given, but unofficially, I was told that the reason was that I had a relative living abroad. I was not the only one fired; we were several, all having a relative abroad.

In my case, this was my uncle Willy, a brother of my father that left Romania in 1926 and settled in Mexico. We were in 1978, fifty-two years later. How did they know about him? When they hired me, although it was a temporary job, I had to give to the personnel office my autobiography in which I mentioned this uncle. To hide such information could have been dangerous, bringing unpleasant consequences. No doubt there was a red flag on my file from the start. Any of my American readers could rightly say, well, we have to write resume or curriculum vitae also for job search. Yes, you do, but you don't have to write down that your sister moved to Ireland, or took a job in Budapest, unless you think that this will improve your chance for being hired, which is highly unlikely. Yes, the form maybe similar, but the content and its consequences are very different.

Talking about similarities I want to make an important point for my American readers. In this blessed country, the United States, people are put in jail when they do bad things that hurt their community. When I mention people, like my Uncle Jonas or Sidonia's Uncle Ovidiu that ended up spending years in jail or labor camp, I am talking about a different political system, where the crooks were putting the honest people in jail. The concept of jail may be similar, but the content is very dissimilar.

Anyway, from an autobiography, this baby started growing and growing until it reached dimensions that overcame my initial project. It turned out that the best way to handle this eighty-year-long story was to divide it in two parts, a Romanian part and an American one. This seemed to be fair enough. After all, I spend about half of my life in each of these two countries, actually two different worlds, separated for almost fifty years by the Iron Curtain.

The Romanian part of the story is ready, and I decided to release it and not wait to finish the American part. I promise to work on the American part since it is very interesting, but life is unforeseeable, and I am happy to accomplish my initial goal, to provide my granddaughters and hopefully future grand-grandchildren with something in writing in case they wonder who these ancestors that came from far away to start a new life in a new land were. I wish I had something like this from my ancestors that wandered through the world.

There is one important point that I would like to emphasize. I think the story of my life is not different from that of many Romanians who lived in the shadow of the Iron Curtain, under the repressive communist regime, and ended up seeking to leave that country by any means, and take refuge somewhere on the other side of the Iron Curtain. My story, like that of these fellow countrymen, is that of my daily life, with its ups and downs and the personal troubles and deeds, that was many times shaped by the Big Brother. The breakaway from the Iron Curtain is an important part of this story, but not the whole one. I know quite a number of Romanians that have defected, and each one has a different account: crossing the Danube by swimming, crossing the border by walking, joining a tourist group and running away from the Securitate (secret police) agents through the streets of Vienna, Austria, defecting while attending a conference, etc. Behind all those breakouts were years of living under the oppressive communist system. My story is just one example of such a life.

A Resume

I divided my life in Romania in chapters related to different steps of education, training, and professional positions. My life started as that of a child of a well-to-do couple living the good life of a middle-class family. My parents belonged to families that came to Romania from the Hapsburg Empire and France. My childhood and adolescence were unusually troubled. Like many others in those times, I was exposed to the vicissitudes of violent anti-Semitism and the peril of war. Compounding these troubles was the separation and divorce of my parents following an affair of my father. This affair brought him into supporting outlawed communist activity, and he ended up spending the war years in concentration camps. Overnight, we became poor, without any income or financial reserves. My mother managed to take care of my sister and me during these years, but her struggle and its consequences stayed with me for life.

Education has been a dominant pursuit from childhood, and it took me through some excellent schools, in spite of war and racial and social discrimination. From the elementary school to the medical school, I benefited from the first-rate educational system that was still in Romania. I was a bright medical student, but the medical school years were tumultuous. During those years, I was engaged to my first love, and the engagement was broken, possibly for political reasons. My mother developed breast cancer and died as she was fifty years of age. Furthermore, I watched my father going from being the best lawyer to a pauper as a result of his conflict with the communist government.

Medicine and medical research and teaching have been my lifetime dedication. After going through a residency, I was fortunate to enter medical research during a period of détente in the policy of the communist regime. This allowed for productive years in my career and resulted in two stages in the United States, the first one as a fellow at Baylor College of Medicine in Houston, Texas, and the second one as a visiting professor at Hershey College of Medicine in Hershey, Pennsylvania, both world-class institutions. In both instances, I had to leave my family in Romania, and I had to return there. Joe Melnick from Baylor and Fred Rapp from Hershey, whom I proudly call friends, assisted me in this endeavor and are thankfully recognized as having a major role in my life.

Soon after the war, by the time I was a teenager, Romania became a satellite of the Soviet Union, a communist country behind the Iron Curtain. The wealthy family members managed to flee the country; others were not so lucky, and ended up in jail as opponents of the communist regime. From now on, until I defected in 1980, I was going to live under this totalitarian government.

During all these years, my life will be largely depended on changes of the communist dictatorship. I learned fast that one has to watch what you say and with whom you talk. It was a matter of survival. Fear was the main tool of the communist establishment. The other tool was to assign all the important positions to members of the Communist Party who would be obedient individuals ready to strictly follow whatever the party leadership decides. I refused to become a member of the party because I saw it as a corrupt establishment that ruled the people through violence, and sought benefits for its members indifferent of their competence. I saw this happening in my field of medicine and I knew that would destroy the country.

As I progressed in my profession, I reached the level when further advancement in Romania was permitted only to members of the Communist Party. Not being a party member, I was disqualified for any upper-level position in medical research or teaching. Moreover, having a conflict with the Securitate that accused me (wrongly) of passing scientific information to a foreign scientist compelled me to leave the medical teaching career.

After I returned to Romania from my first stage in the USA, I was determined to leave the country. It took me ten years to accomplish that. My first attempt to defect to the United States failed because I did not want to jeopardize my family by risking an endless separation. Nevertheless, I learned that I had to obtain from the Romanian authorities a passport to travel abroad as a tourist, and not with a work-related passport. Also, I knew that I had to have a position waiting for me, to be able to ask the Romanian authorities to be reunited with my family. I defected when I had these two conditions fulfilled.

One chapter of this book is dedicated to my wife. Sidonia has played an overwhelming role in my life. Together we built our family; together we struggled to improve our livelihood under the communist regime and finally to get out of Romania. After my defection, Sidonia had to stand alone the brunt of the fight with the vengeful Romanian communist authorities while taking care of her old father and our two children, and protecting them from dangers they were exposed. The eighteen months separation was an ordeal for Sidonia, our children, and me. Our unconditional love and bonding were a blessing that took us through our separation and the hardships of our life, caused more often than not by the communist regime. We are forever grateful to Sidonia for her sacrifice and endurance.

The reason for having a chapter with the story of Sidonia's family is that it is a good example of how, following the communist takeover in Romania, a middle-class family that had nothing to do with politics was brought to poverty.

At the end of most chapters, I tried to draw a few conclusions, sort of take-home tidbits, that the reader could think about. Everyone's life is special, but general situations involve in one way or another each individual. The Iron Curtain has affected the life of hundreds of millions of people. Its effects are still felt today, more than twenty years after its removal. After all, it is said that history tends to repeat itself, and it is wise to try to learn something from it. As far as I am concerned, the history of my parents and family has been a lesson that I tried to understand and draw the conclusions. Looking back, I think this made me wiser and better prepared for life.

One lesson of this story is that one cannot and should not ignore the political system under which he or she has to live. Sometimes one can help changing it, but many times this cannot be done. The decision is either to stay and survive, or leave. In my case, I tried to stay and make my life and that of my family behind the Iron Curtain. At some point, I realized that I am ruining our lives and jeopardizing the future of our children. I had to move to the other side of the Curtain, and I did it although it was a very risky and painful endeavor. Looking back, I am absolutely convinced I did the right thing, and everyone in my family who were part of this breakup thinks likewise.

Everything that is written in this book is the real story to the best of my recollection. However, the reader should be aware that this is a memory book and not a history book. To respect the confidentiality of some people mentioned in this book, their names and affiliation were replaced with fictitious names.

Acknowledgments

As I was getting closer to finish writing this book, I passed around some chapters. The cheering response that came from Donald Aberfeld, Dan and Bianca Stănescu, Rodica and George Grădinaru, Lew and Judy Johnson, Miki Grecescu, Dana and Norbert Schlomiuk, gave me enough confidence to publish this story, which was meant initially to be only a family affair.

A special contribution came from Mrs. Rita Kale, who volunteered to edit this manuscript. She enjoyed reading the book, which gave me even more support for publishing it. Since my friend Donald speaks English and Romanian he was helpful picking up and correcting those sentences in the book that looked more like English transcript of a Romanian text. A significant help came from Sidonia, my beloved wife, who has organized our collection of negative films, slides, and photos that she managed to ship from Romania after my defection.

This breakaway was the most painful experience in our family life. It was a complicated operation in which I had the help of Ștefan Mironescu and his wife, Donna; Dr. Nicolae Ciobanu; Dr. James Caulfield; and Sidonia's uncle, Ovidiu Ciugudean. In the first stage of our breakaway, we had assistance and support from quite a number of people. I can list only some of them: Mrs. Millo, Mihai Zamfirescu, Andrei Vermont (Romania); Mira and Vlad Pauker, Colette and Jackie Meyer-Moog, Claude Hohnel, Nardi Horodniceanu (Horaud), Radu and Karin Crainic, Luc Montagnier (France); Jan Walboomers (Netherland), and Maria Motz (USA). The Hebrew Immigrant Aid Society (HIAS) and the Immigration and Naturalization Service (INS) have done an excellent job expediting my American entry visa. This was an essential step in our struggle for family reunion, and only the first stage of our breakaway. This part of my life ends with me being admitted as a political refugee to the United States. Thus starts the second and crucial stage of this breakaway, getting my family, the hostages, out of communist Romania.

I wrote most of this story at Sidonia's bedside. Sidonia was the inspiration, love and companion of my life. I dedicate this book to her.

Chapter 1

The First Years
1933-1941

When and Where

Let me get started with the first important event in my life, my birth. I was born at my mother's home during the morning of Wednesday, May 17, 1933. This was done with the assistance of a midwife, Mrs. Blum. My father noted in his daily calendar the hour of my delivery (10:40 AM) and my first name. His first choice was Mauriciu; he then scratched over it and changed it to Maurice, the French version of the name. As is customary in Jewish families, the first name given to a newborn is that of a dead relative. Since my sister had already been given the name Jacqueline, after Jacques, my father's father, and my maternal grandfather, Julius Bercovici, was still alive, I was given the name of a paternal grandfather's dead brother.

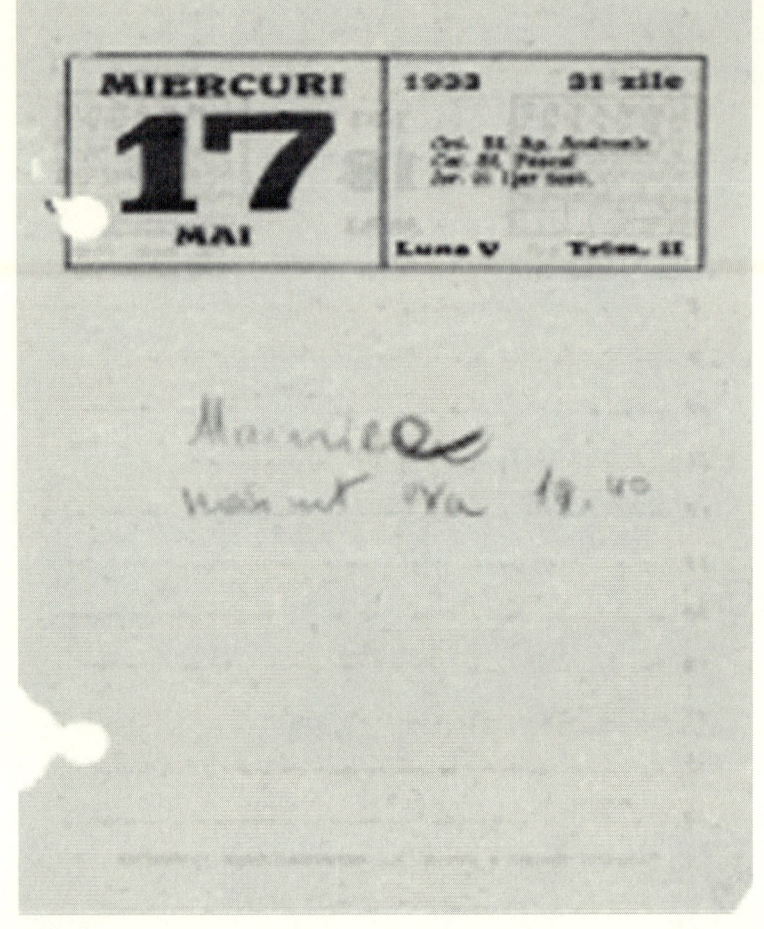

Fig. 1. This is the page from my father's agenda with my name and time of birth.

In Romania, my friends and family called me Burși (boor-schi). I guess this nickname was chosen by Mitzy, who was my nursemaid. She belonged to the German minority established for centuries on Romanian territory as border guards by the Hungarian kings. Over centuries, this relocated population managed to keep its German roots almost intact, and that included their language and religion. In German, *bursche* means "boy," and probably, Mitzy didn't like Maurice and used a German nickname that stuck. So all my friends and relatives in Romania knew me as Burși, but some of my colleagues in the medical school called me Mauriciu. This changed when I traveled outside Romania. My family in Strasbourg and my colleagues and friends in America and France called me by my first name, Maurice.

My delivery took place in Bucharest, the capital of Romania, at Number 19 Bibescu-Vodă Street, on the third floor (this was actually the fourth floor since in Europe, the ground floor is not counted as the first floor), apartment number 10. This was a new reinforced concrete high-rise apartment building that had six floors including the ground floor. The entrance of the building opened into a lobby at the ground floor, which was quite elegant. It had red carpet over a marble floor, a couple of stuffed pelicans (very likely hunted in the Danube delta), and tall Ficus trees. A nice wood-paneled Schindler—brand elevator went up the four floors where the apartments were. A large staircase with marble floors and red carpet also reached the four floors. Each floor had a large hall where wide solid wooden doors would open into the apartments. The building is still standing. It survived not only the bombardments of WWII, but also the major 1977 earthquake, and even Ceaușescu's terrible demolition campaign of downtown Bucharest.

Fig. 2. I was born and lived for thirty-five years in the building on the right side of the Bibescu-Vodă Street.

By the time I was born, the building belonged to Mr. Petre Ștefănescu, an overweight business man who looked like Falstaff. He owned a cheese shop in the central farmers' market. He also owned sheep flocks that produced the excellent feta cheese and kashkaval he was selling in his shop, generating the income spent for the construction of this new building. The building was located in downtown Bucharest within walking distance to the Parliament, the main church of the Romanian Orthodox Patriarchate, and the largest farmers' market in Bucharest, with its huge hall for meat products.

Most importantly for my father, the Court of Justice was within walking distance. I assume that for him, as a lawyer, the vicinity of this place where he spent most of his time was important. This was likely the reason my parents decided to rent this apartment, which otherwise was not really fit for a family of four that included two children. The ground floor of the building was occupied by several shops. Until 1945 or 1946, next to the entrance, there was a confectionery that had a window display of a nice array of sweets, among which crème schnitt and tart savarin prevailed. After WWII, this was replaced by a shop that refilled siphon bottles, which was followed by a tobacco store that also had a public telephone.

The building had four rows of apartments (a total of sixteen): two rows of apartments faced Bibescu-Vodă Street, and two rows faced the buildings behind and a small courtyard. On the east side of the building was a driveway leading to a two-car garage on top of which was the apartment of the concierge. The concierge also served as a mechanic to ensure the constant supply of hot water and, in winter, the central heating supplied by heating oil. Each of the apartments that faced the street had a servant room on the fifth floor that was accessed by a stair used also by producers to reach the back doors of the apartments, to sell their products, such as farm cheese, sour cream, eggs, or fruits.

On the east side of the building, the stair opened onto the driveway, whereas on the west side the stair opened onto the street. The apartments on the back side of the building had their servant room attached to their kitchen. The servant room was meant to be used as a bedroom for the maidservant. In those years in Romania, it was common for middle-income families to have a housemaid who lived in the same building as the family. The room was part of the wage.

Our flat was on the east side of the building, facing the street and consisting of four rather-large rooms, a foyer, one full bathroom, a separate toilet room, a large kitchen, a pantry, and a long and narrow balcony.

During my childhood and even later, I used to spend quite a lot of time on that balcony. It was my window to the world, looking down at the street and having a view even farther. During my medical student years, I used to prepare for the summer exam sessions on the balcony in the morning hours while sunbathing. On that balcony there were a few pots, which were my first garden. That's where I planted lettuce and petunia seeds and watched them grow. Very likely, that was the place where my gardening hobby developed.

Neighbors

The Zaidman family lived on the fourth floor, and they had a son, Beno, who was just eight days younger than me. I don't remember when we became friends, but it must have been very early. During my childhood and teenage years, actually until he migrated to Israel with his wife, Lili; his son, Michael; and his father, Beno and I were such close friends that I considered Beno like my brother. Although we didn't go to the same schools, we spent all of our free time together, either at his apartment or at mine. We shared our books and our friends. Beno now lives with his wife, Lili, their two sons, and several grandchildren in Jerusalem, and they visited us a few years ago.

Fig. 3. Beno with Sidonia, Lili, and Maurice, sharing a cup of tea in Jerusalem. January 1992.

During the war (WWII), when my father was in the concentration camp, the Zaidman family treated me as their son. They loved my mother, and my mother loved them. They were very close friends and tried to help us as much as they could. When Sidonia and I went to Israel in 1991, we stayed at Beno's and Lili's apartment in Jerusalem. This was a memorable visit from many points of view. Among other things, I will always remember visiting Mr. Zaidman in his nursing home. After being separated from him for about twenty-five years, it was like a father-son reunion; that's how I felt. The tears in his eyes told me that was how he felt too.

Very likely, our most famous neighbor was Mrs. Cleo Stieber. For years, Cleo was the national Romanian television anchor. She was petite, very nice looking, and overall a pleasant person. Cleo lived in the same flat with her older sister, Mrs. Felicia Weiss, a beautiful woman, and her husband. This family was living on the same floor with us. Cleo was married to Dr. Stieber, an oral surgeon and, after serving the national Romanian television for years, left for Israel. When the Weiss family left for Israel, my mother bought from them a nice modern desk. This was my first desk and was used even by our son, Noël, when he was in school.

Romania before WWII

By the time I was born, Romania was enjoying a period of rapid economic growth. Romania was one of the top oil producers in the world, and the only European country that had a significant oil reserve. It was also a major producer and exporter of wheat grown on the huge land proprieties in the Danube plain. A few important industries such as a heavy machinery factory in Bucharest (Malaxa), and another in the western part of the country (Reșița), were new developments. The first skyscraper, serving as the national telephone center, was built in Bucharest by an American company in 1932. For the first time in the history of the country, a middle class was emerging.

> Wikipedia. The Kingdom of Romania emerged when the principalities of Moldavia and Wallachia were united under Prince Alexander Ioan Cuza in 1859. Independence from the Ottoman Empire was declared on May 9, 1877, and was internationally recognized the following year. At the end of World War I, Transylvania, Bukovina and Bessarabia united with the Kingdom of Romania. Greater Romania emerged into an era of progression

and prosperity that would continue until World War II. By the end of the War, many north-eastern areas of Romania's territories were occupied by the Soviet Union, and Romania forcibly became a socialist republic and a member of the Warsaw Pact.

Bucharest (Romanian: București pronounced [buku'reʃtʲ] is the capital city, cultural, industrial, and financial center of Romania. It is the largest city in Romania, located in the southeast of the country, and lies on the banks of the Dâmbovița River. Bucharest was first mentioned in documents as early as 1459. Since then it has gone through a variety of changes, becoming the state capital of Romania in 1862 and steadily consolidating its position as the center of the Romanian mass media, culture and arts. Its eclectic architecture is a mix of historical (neo-classical), interbellum (Bauhaus and Art Deco), communist-era and modern. In the period between the two World Wars, the city's elegant architecture and the sophistication of its elite earned Bucharest the nickname of the "Little Paris of the East" (Micul Paris). [5] Although many buildings and districts in the historic center were damaged or destroyed by war, earthquakes and Nicolae Ceaușescu's program of systematization, many survived. In recent years, the city has been experiencing an economic and cultural boom.[6] According to January 1, 2009 official estimates, Bucharest proper has a population of 1,944,367.[2] The urban area extends beyond the limits of Bucharest proper and has a population of 2 million people.[3] [7] Adding the satellite towns around the urban area, the metropolitan area of Bucharest has a population of 2.15 million people.[4] According to unofficial data, the population is more than 3 million.[8] Bucharest is the 6th largest city in the European Union by population within city limits.[9]

Romania is a country rich in Jewish heritage. The first Jews arrived as part of the Roman legions (*Legion Judaica*) that invaded Dacia in 101 A.D. During the middle Ages, Jewish immigrants began settling in Walachia and Moldova, with ever-increasing numbers arriving after Spain's expulsion of the Jews in 1492. By the early 16th century, their number again increased by immigrants fleeing from Cossack uprisings in Poland and the Ukraine. During the 15th and 16th centuries, Polish Jewish merchants set up storehouses, trading posts, and eventually permanent settlements.

During the region's domination by the Turks, the Romanian Jewish Community evolved into a prosperous middle class. Today, there are poignant reminders of Romania's Jewish heritage and roots. The country is unique in Eastern and Central Europe for its scores of well-maintained synagogues (nearly 100, of which half are still used for worship) and more than 800 cemeteries scattered around Romania. (http://www.romaniatourism.com/jewish-heritage.html)

The Nachtigals

Unfortunately, my knowledge of the history of what I consider to be the German branch of my family—the Nachtigals—is short, and I couldn't go further back than three generations. Jews in Romania were not given Romanian citizenship until after World War I (WWI), so it is possible that there were no records made or kept for the older generations although they were living on the Romanian territory. Family members who could help me to fill this gap are no longer alive.

The name of my father's family is of German origin. *Nachtigall* in German means "nightingale." Notably, the name lost the last "l," a change which may help in tracing the family history. I tried to trace the ancestry of the Nachtigal family, but this turned out to be very difficult. As far as I know, in Romania, there were only two families with this name, both living in Bucharest. They were listed in the phone book. Rumor has it that the other Nachtigal family tried to leave the country after WWII and was killed while crossing the border.

Visiting the city of Cluj-Napoca, I found out that, in the church of Saint-Michael, the beautiful wooden pulpit was carved by Johan Nachtigal, who was invited in 1740 to Transylvania, which, by then, was part of the Hapsburg Empire under the empress Maria Theresa. Johan Nachtigal is credited with other artworks in Transylvania such as the sculpture on the front side of the Franciscan church in Cluj, and some sculptures at the Bonțida castle. However, in those years, it would have been unusual for a Jew to have this craft. Moreover, there is no Nachtigal family in Cluj-Napoca that I am aware of, but this does not exclude the possibility that they moved around the country.

Searching Heritage.com, I found a Jewish Nachtigal family in Sambor, Galicia, Poland, consisting of Getzel and Malka Nachtigal. Both were born before 1792 and had a son, Salomon, who lived there between 1810 and

1896. By that time, the town of Sambor was part of the Hapsburg Empire. On another search, that I did on the JewishGen Family Finder, I found a cluster of Nachtigal Jews around the town of Lublin in Poland in the nineteenth century. Persecution of the Jews may have pushed some members of those families to more promising and secure lands. A major migration of Jews from Poland happened during the Khmelnitsky uprising in the seventeenth century, and it is possible that some of them have migrated south into Romanian territories.

It is worth mentioning that the Bukovina Society of the Americas (PO Box 81, Ellis, Kansas, 7637, USA) cites a Nachtigal among descendants of Bukovinians. I would not exclude the possibility that these Nachtigals were Jews because Bukovina was a region where large Jewish communities existed until WWII. Bukovina was, in those years, also part of the Hapsburg Empire. The transition from Bukovina, which is a province in the northern part of present Romania to the southern region of the country, may have taken a generation or two, but considering the mobility of this population, such a migration, is easily conceivable.

My father mentioned that our more recent ascendants had been located in the town of Buzău, which is situated in the center of Romania. It is possible that the town of Buzău was the place where the Nachtigals settled on their migration through the Romanian territory before moving on to Bucharest. Buzău has a long history of a Jewish community with Polish Jewish merchants setting up permanent settlements as early as the sixteenth century.

> Wikipedia. The city of Buzău (formerly Buzeu, or Buzău; Romanian pronunciation: [bu'zəw]) is the county seat of Buzău County, Romania, in the historical region of Wallachia. It lies near the right bank of the Buzău River, between the south-eastern curvature of the Carpathian Mountains and the lowlands of Bărăgan Plain. During the middle Ages, Buzău was as an important Wallachian market town and Eastern Orthodox episcopal see. It faced a period of repeated destruction during the seventeenth and eighteenth century, nowadays symbolized on the city seal by the Phoenix bird. Those destructions are the main reason for which no building older than the eighteenth century exists in the city.
>
> In 1593 Mircea Ciobanul attests the presence of some Jewish inhabitants in Vernesti, a parish in Buzău, in 1575; Mihai Viteazul issues a "document-order" confirming that, in 1593, the Jews were

for a long time on those places, and some pieces of land in Topliceni were attested as propriety of a Jew named Haim . . . Almost one century ago, on an old piece of paper found in Ciolanu hermitage, father Provian, director of the Theological Seminary within the Buzău diocese, found the words written by a monk saying that, in 1794, "a Jewish medicine man from the Jewish community in Buzău town cured his severe illness." The oldest tombstone kept in the old cemetery and also the oldest document that exists in the archive of the community date from 1832. (www.romanianjewish.org)

Although I have very little information documenting the history of the Nachtigal family, it looks like they moved from Germany to Poland, presumably, at a time when the religious persecution became severe in Germany, and Poland was interested in attracting Jews. When Poland became part of the Hapsburg Empire and their condition in Poland became critical, they may have moved within the empire to Bukovina and farther south into Romania.

I have only a few data about my paternal grandfather, Jacques Nachtigal. He was a highly educated person who studied finance and commerce in Istanbul (Constantinople), the capital of the Ottoman Empire (Romania has been a vassal state to the Ottoman Empire). Jacques became an international salesman covering the Middle East. According to my father, after catching a tropical disease in Egypt, where his business travel took him, he died around 1909 at a rather young age.

Fig. 4. Jacques Nachtigal, my paternal grandfather.

Jacques had two brothers, Peter and Maurice. Peter Nachtigal was in the military, which was quite unusual for a Jew in those days. Apparently, he was stationed in Pitești, the capital of Arges County, where he married and had a daughter, Bica. He died quite young, and his widow remarried and had two more children, a girl and a boy. This girl had a daughter named Paula. Paula was married in Pitești to Mr. Marinescu, a Christian and son of a general. They migrated to Israel with their children, a daughter and a son. Paula's husband died quite young in Israel of lung cancer, and Paula moved to Ottawa, Canada, where her daughter lives with her family. Bica, the daughter of Peter Nachtigal, married Dan Aladgem, a Sephardic Jew, and they lived in Pitești until they moved to Israel. They had no children.

Maurice Nachtigal, whose first name I inherited, was also called Mișu (pronounced Mee-shoo). He was married to Jeana and had two daughters, Jacqueline and Luizel. My mother kept good relations with Aunt Jeana, and I remember visiting her while she was living with her daughter Jacqueline.

Both Jacqueline and Luizel were very nice-looking young ladies, real beauties, but different from each other. Both of them migrated to Israel, and we lost contact with them.

My father and his brothers spoke German fluently and were educated in Bucharest, in schools run by German clerics where, most likely, German language and culture was an important subject. I assume that the Austrian culture of their mother played a major role in their education. It is possible that, on their side, the Nachtigals kept their original German culture throughout their migration, and this may have been the background of the marriage between my paternal grandparents, Jacques Nachtigal and Helene Wappner. The four sons had an enormous respect and fondness for their mother.

Losing his father at the age of thirteen, my father, Alphonse, became the bread-winner of his family, which included his mother and three younger brothers, Oscar, Willy, and Rudolf (Rudy). He made a living by tutoring after the school day ended. In the evening and at night, he had to work for his own education. I guess because of this schedule, he became used to working late in the night and having only a few hours of sleep. He kept this habit as long as he worked.

After my parents' wedding in 1926, Willy and Rudy left Romania for the United States. The story in the family says that they intended to go to Hollywood to become movie stars. They made it to United States; at least Rudolph is on record with the immigration office as having arrived in New York. They never made it to Hollywood, and Rudy died in an obscure accident. There were no details about him kept in the family, at least none that I am aware off.

Uncle Willy settled in Mexico, where he married Luz (Lucita), who was of Spanish descent. They lived in Guadalajara, where Uncle Willy died in 1986. They didn't have children, and he made quite a fortune being a successful entrepreneur. He owned a pharmaceutical company that was packaging medications and selling to physicians around Mexico. He also owned land and several apartments that he rented to Americans living in Guadalajara. His last financial interest was running an art and antique store. On some of his trips to Romania, he would stop in Italy and France and purchase antique items such as furniture, icons, and religious paintings that were shipped to Mexico, where they were restored and sold. According to Willy, Lucita was extensively involved in this operation, and they were also functioning as interior designers.

As soon as WWII ended, Willy started sending his mother a monthly allowance of $200, which at that time was a nice sum of money. The money was sent through the National Bank of Romania that was starved for hard currency. Every time she went there to collect her money, she was treated as royalty. She received this allowance until her death in 1960. After her death, Willy continued to give this money to Uncle Oscar.

Willy came to Bucharest for the first time in 1961, and he did so at least every other year until 1980, when he was around eighty years old. During his first visit to Bucharest, he stayed at a hotel; but for the following visits, he stayed at Uncle Oscar's apartment. The only time I met his wife, Lucita, was in 1962, when they came to visit this side of the family. Lucita was afraid of flying, so they took the boat to cross the Atlantic and then drove through Europe to Vienna. By that time, Bucharest probably looked like a very poor town, and she never returned.

One of the high points of their visit was when Uncle Willy and Aunt Lucita invited all of the family to a dinner at the Pescăruș (The Seagull) restaurant. This was a fancy restaurant located on the border of the Herăstrău Lake on the north side of Bucharest, in one of the largest park in the city. By then, I was working at the Oncology Institute and dating a young lady named Geta. She joined me at this dinner. We stayed there late into the night and had a wonderful time with musicians playing Mexican music for us.

On his visits, Willy used to bring gifts, most of the time clothing, that he would buy in New York on his stopover from Mexico to Romania. Most of the gifts were for the Oscar family, but he would also bring things that would fit Sidonia or me. He was very much attached to Oscar who, in his youth, was his preferred brother. For the rest of the family, he had a benevolent attitude.

On one of his visits, he offered to get the Oscar family to Mexico. This was possible then as the Romanian communist government started to actually sell its citizens to whoever would pay the right price in dollars. This idea was rejected by Aunt Jenny, Oscar's wife, and their daughter, Mariana, and probably was of no interest to Mariana's husband, Paul. The only one who would have been happy going to Mexico was Uncle Oscar, but his opinion was not taken into account. Looking back, it's very hard to judge if this was a good or bad decision, as far as they were concerned.

Willy also offered to get me out of Romania. He managed to contact a certain Mr. Jacober, who was the intermediary between the Romanian authorities and the relatives of the Jews from Romania willing to leave the country. The price in dollars was collected by Mr. Jacober and turned over to the Romanian party, which most likely was the Securitate. Rumors were that this money went to Ceaușescu's personal account in a Swiss bank. As far as I was concerned, this deal was never closed. By that time I was already deeply involved in my training and research at the Oncology Institute, and not interested in leaving the country.

Fig. 5. Three Nachtigal generations. Uncle Willy holding my son, Noël, up is accompanied by Uncle Oscar and I. September 1967.

Uncle Oscar, who became a lawyer, married Jenny (Eugenia) Drăgulănescu. This was the first intermarriage in the Nachtigal family. The next one was the marriage between Uncle Willy and Lucita. My marriage to Sidonia would be the fourth one, since it followed my father's marriage to

Dora. It turned out that all the contemporary Nachtigals married Christian ladies and kept their inborn Jewish faith. All intermarriages were successful.

Aunt Jenny was a pharmacist, and Oscar followed her to a village not far from Bucharest, where she ran a pharmacy. This village was in the middle of the Bărăgan plain, which is actually part of the Danube plain. Oscar practiced as a lawyer, and they had a very active and enjoyable social life. He did a lot of gardening, which seems to be a hobby that runs in the family. Their daughter, Mariana, is my only first-degree cousin.

As a child, I went a few times to visit them with my mother, who had a very good relationship with Jenny, a straightforward, no-nonsense person. Our last visit to their home in the countryside was in the summer of 1941, when Romania, allied with Germany, started the war against the Soviet Union. In those days, we were seeking refuge from potential bombardment of Bucharest. Actually, the Soviets sent several planes over Bucharest that made us go to the shelter and stay there for the night.

Our stay at Oscar's house was very soon cut short by the Romanian government's decision to forbid Jews to live in the countryside. We returned to Bucharest together with Uncle Oscar, who, in spite of being married to a Christian lady, fell under the constraints of this anti-Semitic law. During the war, Oscar lived in Bucharest at his in-laws' house and commuted clandestinely to visit his wife and child.

Fig. 6. Uncle Oscar, daughter Mariana; her husband, Paul Burtoiu; granddaughter Andreea. November 1990.

Aunt Jenny had three sisters and a brother. One of the sisters and her husband died young and left a daughter, Sanda, who was raised by the two sisters, Bebe and Coca. Coca was a very nice-looking, elegant lady who was divorced. She was a close friend of my mother, and she died young of breast cancer, a sad fate that left a strong impression on my mother, who would share the same fate a few years later. Bebe never married, worked at the central post office, and dedicated her life to Sanda and her two daughters with whom she lived.

Sanda studied medicine and married one of her colleagues, Ninel Filipescu, who became an oral surgeon. They moved to a coal mining town, and she worked there in the Public Health Department. They divorced, and Sanda remarried Dan Georgescu, an engineer. They had two daughters, Anca and Raluca. The Georgescu family moved to Bucharest, where Dan and Sanda were promoted to good positions.

Sanda defected to the United States in 1981. Most likely, she did it to get out her two daughters from the communist Romania. This was a major sacrifice for Sanda because she had a good position, and she and her husband owned a newly built apartment in a fashionable neighborhood in Bucharest. In New York, Sanda struggled to find a job, and ended up working as a technician in a small food factory with low pay and no benefits. She managed to bring her daughters to the United States, and Anca and Raluca pulled each of their boyfriends out of Romania and got married. They live in New York, where Anca has two sons and works as a librarian at Columbia University. Her husband, Sasha Meret, is a talented painter.

When she had to attend lyceum Mariana moved to Bucharest. There she grew up together with Sanda, who is a few years older; they were like sisters. Mariana enjoyed socializing with the medical students, who were Sanda's classmates and friends, and I suspect this was the main reason for trying to get into the medical school. Although she is one year younger than me, she graduated from the lyceum the same year I did, because the communist government, in its haste to build a new society, had decided that eleven years of schooling were just as good as twelve years. Mariana didn't make it through the written test for admission into the medial school. With only three years of lyceum, there was little chance of succeeding in this very competitive examination.

Mariana was unhappy and decided to go to the mining school where there were unfilled seats. At the mining school Mariana met Paul Burtoiu who was also a mining engineer student, started dating him, and got married in 1959. Paul was a positive, friendly fellow, always ready to help with car, or any other problems. Unfortunately, he was a cigarette smoker and died quite young. Mariana and Paul had a daughter, Ileana-Anca, who married Ștefan Sirbu, and they had a daughter, Andreea. Andreea and Mariana visited us in 1999 in Columbia, and they met our family.

Fig. 7. Uncle Oscar, with his granddaughter Ileana, November 1990.

Over the years, I had a good relationship with Oscar's family. The relationship improved dramatically after they met Sidonia, whom they loved. We were invited to many of the family dinner parties. They were a lot of fun. Oscar, under the direction of Aunt Jenny, was a great cook, and he loved to prepare tasty and nicely decorated dishes. Many times, they would also invite Toto Niculescu and his wife to dinner. Toto was a lawyer and had been a politician before the communist regime. He was the ultimate storyteller, and would make the dinner go on and on until late night with all his stories. He was a natural entertainer and loved to have a public, us, enjoying his show. Aunt Jenny had a special love for Sidonia, they shared several resemblances.

By the time I was born, my parents already had another child. This was my sister, Jacqueline, who was born March 4, 1932, only fourteen months before me. Jacqueline was born with some disorder. I suspect that my parents were told about this at the time of her birth or soon thereafter, and were advised, or decided on their own, to have another child, and that was me. Jacqueline, for as long as she lived, was in the care of Professor Parhon, who was the founder of endocrinology in Romania, a scientist, and a very good clinician. I have no idea what kind of disease this was, but looking at Jacqueline's pictures, I have a suspicion that it may have been either Down syndrome, or a thyroid deficiency, or both. Professor Parhon was a specialist in thyroid disorders, and I think he treated her with thyroid gland extract, which, in those days, was probably produced in his laboratory.

The Wappners

My paternal grandmother, Helene, was born around 1875 into the Wappner family in Miskolcz, a town presently in Hungary, but then part of the Hapsburg Empire. Despite firm evidence of the early presence of Jews in the area that is now Hungary, the ancestors of the majority of Hungarian Jews did not arrive until the eighteenth century from Bohemia and Moravia, parts of the Hapsburg Empire, and in the nineteenth century from Poland and Galicia. Helene was a short-statured woman, used to being treated as a lady, and overly preoccupied by her health. Although she had diabetes and was treated with insulin, she lived to the age of eighty-five and died from complications of breast cancer. She had an Austrian education, and I assume that the spoken language in her family was German. On her nightstand, one could always see books by Schiller and Goethe printed in Gothic German.

Helene had a brother, Joseph Wappner, who was a banker and a sister, Frida, who owned a large appliance shop in downtown Bucharest. Helene had another brother who was a physician in Vienna, Austria, and who had two children, Greta and Oskar. Another sister, Cecilia, married Mr. Hassan in Bucharest. They had a son, Daniel, whose daughter, Yvonne, married Mr. Petre Solomon. They had a son, Alexandru, who lives in Bucharest.

Fig. 8. Helene Nachtigal, my paternal grandmother.

Uncle Joseph, Grandmamma's brother, used to have lunch with us during the war years. It seemed that he kept a normal relationship with my mother even after my parents' separation, and that sufficed to put him on my good list. Joseph Wappner was a big man with white hair, somewhat resembling Spencer Tracy. He had two daughters, Stefi (Stephanie) and Margit. Stefi was married to Mr. Weissman and had a son called Burşi (pronounced boorschee), the same nickname I had. Margit was married to Mr. Metzinger and had no children. Both couples were wealthy.

I remember one summer accompanying my father on a visit with the Metzinger family at their luxurious villa in the mountain resort town of Predeal. By the time the communist regime took over Romania, they left the country for some place in South America. After they left Romania, we had no contact with them and never heard of them again. The Predeal villa was no doubt taken over by the communists and used most likely by party leaders and their families.

My relationship with Grandmamma was never very deep. I used to visit her, usually following instructions from my father or mother, and these were always sort of semiformal visits. I was doing it without much enthusiasm. My feelings toward her were strongly influenced by my understanding that in the separation of my parents, she took the side of my father against my mother. As far as I was concerned, this was enough to put her on my little black list. She was always preoccupied by her health problems. Usually, at the end of my visit, she would give me some money, but this did not change my feelings about her. Money doesn't buy love. She was buried at the Jewish Giurgiu cemetery in Bucharest, and Uncle Oscar, with financial support from Willy, built a beautiful marble monument.

The Winters

My maternal grandmother, Hortense Winter, was born and grew up in Goersdorf, a village near Strasbourg, presently in Alsace, France. Her family can be traced in Alsace at least to the seventeenth century. By the time Hortense was born on December 12, 1877, Alsace was part of the German empire following France's loss of the 1870 war with Prussia, and remained German until the end of the WWI in 1918, when it was returned to France.

It is interesting how the family name of Winter was acquired. The Emperor Napoleon had asked the Jews in France to replace their Hebrew family name, which went like "X son (Ben in Hebrew) of Y," with French family names. Our ancestor, Samson, "son of Levy," on his way to the town city hall to get a new family name, met a friend who was just coming back from the town city hall with a new family name. He asked him what his new family name was, and the man told him "Sommer," which means summer in German (the Alsatian dialect is close to German language). On the spot, Samson decided his family name would be Winter, which has the same meaning in German as in English.

Hortense was one of five daughters and one son, children of Nahum Winter, the son of Samson Winter. The way she got to Romania from Alsace is quite remarkable. It all began when her father, Nahum, lost his wealth. According to the family story, his business associate took off with all their money and went to America. This was the end of Nahum's business and the beginning of major trouble for him. He had five daughters to marry off, and he was supposed to give each one a decent dowry in order to get a decent son-in-law. To alleviate this problem, the oldest daughter, Jeanne, went to Paris and became a nursemaid to one of the aristocratic Romanian families, who preferred to spend their life in Paris instead of Bucharest, and wanted their children to speak fluent French.

At some point in time, this family returned to Romania, and Jeanne Winter went along with them. For reasons that are unknown but can be presumed (loneliness, potential for marrying without dowry), Jeanne brought her sister, Eugenie, to Bucharest. Eugenie married Mr. Carol Suliţeanu, who ran a barber shop near the Bucharest Central Railway Station (Gara de Nord, or the North Railway Station).

It happened that Mr. Julius Bercovici, who was the owner of a major retail shop La Spiridon (Spiridon is a Romanian first name) in downtown Bucharest, traveled for his business, often going abroad to purchase merchandise for his store. On one of these trips, he stopped at Mr. Suliţeanu's barber shop, and was shown the picture of Hortense, the younger sister of Mr. Suliţeanu's wife. He was impressed by her figure, and probably attracted by the idea of having a beautiful French lady as his wife. Julius decided that she should be his bride. Obviously, he was well off enough not to care about a dowry. Hortense traveled from Alsace to Bucharest and became Mrs. Bercovici. The couple lived happily in Bucharest and had one child, my mother.

Fig. 9. Hortense Bercovici née Winter and her daughter, Adine.

The Bercovici

Before leaving Romania, while putting some old papers in order, I found the citizenship certificate for Julius Bercovici, the father of my mother, whose ancestors, at least for one generation, lived in Romania where he was born. Romanian was the only language that his sisters, Sofia and Ana, and brother, Jonas, spoke. Bercovici was a common family name for the Romanian Jews, and it would be impossible to trace its origins. Sofia was married to Mr. Elias, and they lived with her mother in a small house with a garden close to our apartment. They had no children. We used to go quite often to visit them, and I remember my grand-grandmother who was living with them. She was a short, bent, old woman. She was always kind to my sister and me, her grand-grandchildren. She must have been well over ninety years of age when she passed away.

Aunt Ana was a widow by the time I knew her. She had a son, Marcel, who used to visit us in the company of his girlfriend, a beautiful woman named Rodica. I remember the family commenting about Rodica being Christian, because in those years, the Jews were a persecuted minority, and it took a lot of courage and love for a Christian lady to get romantically involved with a Jew. Toward the end of WWII, an outbreak of typhus spread by lice occurred in Bucharest. Rodica was instrumental in providing the vaccine to protect my sister and me from this deadly disease. A few years later, I learned that Marcel had developed a nasal infection that had propagated to the brain and killed him.

A few months after my birth, while my mother and grandmother were spending their summer vacation with us (the children) in Poiana Țapului, a resort in the Carpathian Mountains, my grandfather joined them. According to the family story, he got sick there and in a short time died. I could not reconstitute what might have been the disease; it sounded like something that had to do with the liver, either an acute hepatitis, or a complication of a gallstone. He was in full health, and then he was gone. His grave is at the Jewish Giurgiu cemetery. I visited it once a long time ago, but when I went back after the 1989 revolution, the alley to the grave was blocked by the outgrowth of vegetation.

Fig. 10. Julius and Adine Bercovici.

The death of my grandfather must have been a serious blow for my grandmother, but she was a very strong woman, as proven repeatedly over the years, and managed to resume her life, largely linked with my mother and us, her only grandchildren. I should add that, paradoxically, although she was French, I used to call her with the Romanian Mama Mare, which in Romanian means "great mother." The other grandmother, Helene, on my father's side, was called Grandmamma, which is French. Around the time that my parents separated, Mama Mare moved in with us, and she took care of me lovingly and devotedly up to the time when she left for France in 1959. She was like a mother to me.

Every day Mama Mare read the newspapers religiously and was up to date with all of the political events. Her Romanian was always with a French accent, and her grammar was not very good. She was loved by every one of our neighbors. My mother and Mama Mare kept some Jewish traditions. They lighted candles on Friday evening and said prayers. They also kept the Yom Kippur day (Jewish Day of Atonement) by fasting, and Mama Mare would spend the entire day at the synagogue. At the end of the long fasting day, she looked, and probably was, exhausted but seemed happy to have fulfilled the old tradition and hopeful that a good new year would follow.

My mother's maiden name was Bercovici, and her first name was Aline, although when she was young, she was called Ada or Adele. Most people who knew her called her Adine (with the French pronunciation in which the letter "e" at the end of the name is not pronounced). She was born in Bucharest as the only child of Julius Bercovici and Hortense Winter. According to the new calendar, she was born on May 1, 1907; according to the old calendar, which was followed by the time she was born, her birth date was April 18.

Fig. 11. Adine Bercovici eighteen years old. August 1925.

My mother grew up as the daughter of a wealthy businessman. She attended the prestigious pension (boarding school), Notre Dame de Sion, where daughters of the wealthy and aristocratic people in Bucharest used to learn to speak fluently French. In 1926, when she was nineteen years old, she married my father, Alphonse Nachtigal, who was about thirteen years older and was a rising star among the Bucharest lawyers. At her marriage, her dowry was one million lei ("leu" is the Romanian currency, "lei" is the plural), which in those days was a fortune.

Fig. 12. Alphonse and Adine Nachtigal just married. 1926.

Fig. 13. This picture was taken about the time my parents got married. My mother is in the middle, wearing a light-colored dress; she is surrounded by the Nachtigal-Wappner family. Behind her, wearing a bowtie is my father. On her right is my grandmother Helene. On the left of my father is Uncle Oscar, who is also wearing a bowtie.

Childhood: The Good Years

Those were the good years of my childhood, when my father was still part of our family and was taking good care of us. Petre Pandrea, who was a lawyer and a friend of my father, in his autobiographical book, (*The Memories of the Valach Mandarin*, Albatros Publishing House, Bucharest 2000, page 179), mentions that my father told him that, in 1936, he earned from the Câmpeanu brothers, who were oilmen, 2.5 million lei. In those days, this was a fortune. In the same year, for the Ana Pauker trial, he was paid 120,000 lei. His reputation was expanding, and he could consider himself wealthy.

We, the children, had a nursemaid named Mitzy, who, being of German ethnicity, was probably hired by my parents to teach me German. This goal was never reached. The best of what I got were a few words like butter, bread, and good-bye. Moreover, I could not learn German even in high school, when I had a very good teacher, Mr. Eckert, who gave me excellent grades. I suspect that Mitzy's presence, combined with the German behavior in WWII, contributed to my distaste for this language, which otherwise would have helped me in my studies. Mitzy used to take my sister and me to the Carol Park, not far from our apartment, where we played with other children from the neighborhood.

Fig. 14. Maurice and Jacqueline, walking to the Carol Park. January 1939.

In those years, we used to spend one month in the summer at the Black Sea, renting a room at Perla Mării (the "Sea Pearl"), a villa with a large veranda overlooking the beach in Mangalia. After the sea vacation, we would spend a month in a mountain resort in the Prahova Valley called Bușteni. This is where I received my first bicycle and learned to ride it. Once when we were in Bușteni, my father came, and he and my mother went hiking for several days in the Bucegi Mountain. This may have been the last time they went anywhere together. My father loved the mountains, and I probably inherited this leisure pursuit from him. I think he spent some of his childhood vacations in the same resort, Bușteni, and that's why we, as kids, would go there for the summer, away from the hot weather in Bucharest.

Although my parents were Jewish, they would celebrate Christmas and put up a beautiful Christmas tree, and we, the children, would receive gifts. In fact, in my childhood, we would always observe Saint Nicholas day, which is December 6. During the night of December 5, as the tradition in Romania goes, Saint Nicholas would come and fill the shoes of good children with candies and other goodies. So my sister and I would put our shoes at the door and the next morning would find all kinds of nice things in those shoes.

The last Christmas celebration of my childhood was complete with a nicely decorated tall Christmas tree and a Santa Claus, who, in Romania, is called Old Man Christmas. He came loaded with toys and asked my sister, my cousin, Mariana, and me the usual questions about being well behaved and so forth before distributing the gifts. After that, the adults, which included my parents, Uncle Oscar, and Aunt Jenny, set out for their dinner, and we, the children, started enjoying our gifts.

Among the gifts I received was a beautiful fabric-bound book, which contained the stories of Ion Creangă, a classical Romanian story writer. This was most likely the first book that I read, having learned to read before going to school. My appetite for reading was just beginning. Throughout my younger years, until I reached the medical school, I read everything available in Romanian but also a lot in French. I used to read while lying in bed, and late at night. In fact, there was no other place where I could read besides the dining room table, which was not comfortable. Even so, I used to read while eating, which horrified Mama Mare, who was telling me that this would make me sick.

In my readings, I went from Mihail Sadoveanu (a well-known Romanian author of novels, some of them referring to the Romanian history), to Anatole France or Eugen Ionesco (in French). This range included Jules Verne (I still like to read it now!), Alexandre Dumas, Conan Doyle, Edgar Wallace, Agatha Christie (thrillers), Erich Maria Remarque, Ștefan Zweig, Kipling, Cronin, etc. I didn't care too much for poetry, either Romanian or foreign. Among the American authors that I became familiar with and loved were Jack London, Upton Sinclair, Sinclair Lewis, John Steinbeck, and Ernest Hemingway.

After I retired in 2006, I started reading literature, something that I did very little during the working years. Again I enjoyed reading Jules Verne books, the story of the count of Monte Cristo, etc. As I have aged, I think I have a different understanding of these stories. I read all seven Harry Potter books just to find out what the young generation appreciates.

This was the last Christmas celebration for my family. What followed were years of extreme hardship. For us, this was no time to celebrate Christmas or anything else. I resumed the Christmas celebration only after I married Sidonia and we had our son Noël. After that, we had a Christmas tree every year as long as we were in Romania, and we resumed this tradition in America. In Romania, the celebration of Christmas starts on Christmas Eve with a special dinner. During this time, Santa Claus arrives and unloads the gifts under the Christmas tree, which was always a natural fir tree. We used to trick the children into making them believe Santa Claus was coming. We would distract the kids while one of us would put the gifts under the tree.

In America, we kept the Romanian tradition until grandchildren came on board. In the years that followed, we still did the celebration on Christmas Eve, but the dinner was replaced with a luncheon, and the gifts were laid under the tree days and weeks before Christmas. I was used to the Romanian way of Christmas celebration and felt that our granddaughters were missing a nice tradition that has some mystery to it.

Starting School

My formal education began when I entered the primary school, the equivalent of the American elementary school. At that time, 1939, the school system in Romania consisted of four years of primary school and eight years of lyceum, divided in two parts, each being four years. To pass from the first four years of lyceum to the next four years required an examination which was called *capacitate* (competence exam). At the end of the eight years of lyceum, one would have to pass a comprehensive examination called *baccalaureate*. Passing this examination conferred the title of "baccalaureate," which opened the door to higher education or, eventually, to some job that could be fulfilled by people with this degree (some clerical work for instance).

In the fall of 1939, I was considered by my parents ready to go to school. The problem was that admission to the primary school was for seven-year-old children, and I was only six years and three months old. I recall accompanying my father to some office, most likely at the Education Ministry, to acquire permission to attend the school since I was under age. I don't recall the details. Most likely I would not have understood the arguments, but I remember the scene, at some point, becoming rather violent. My father probably wouldn't take no for an answer while the bureaucrat behind his desk was doing what he was supposed to do and just kept saying no.

I don't know what the follow-up to this meeting was. The fact is that the next step was my father taking me to the Sfântul Andrei (Saint Andrew) School. This was a school run by German Catholic monks. My father knew the principal of the school who was his teacher when he attended Saint Joseph, another school in Bucharest run by the same order of monks. He was warmly received by Bruder (brother) Anthony, and my admission at the school went as smoothly as one could wish. For the first grade, I had Mrs. Ionescu, a middle-aged overweight woman, as my teacher. At the end of my first school year, I was awarded the first prize. In those years in Romania, at the end of the school year, students in each grade were awarded three prizes, first, second, and third, the first prize being the highest. In addition, several mentions were usually added. This tradition was maintained during the years our children were enrolled in the Romanian schools.

As an extracurricular study, the Saint Andrew School offered English classes, and I was enrolled by my parents. I still remember my first English textbook, which had, on the first page, a picture with an open mouth showing the tongue protruding between the front teeth. This was to be an exercise to pronounce the "th" sound, which does not exist in the Romanian language and requires special training to articulate it correctly. This was the beginning of my English speaking education, and I am thankful for the wisdom of my parents to enroll me in this class.

As a matter of fact, I continued to take English lessons during the following years. One of my teachers was a British officer who stayed in Romania after WWI. He had a wonderful British accent, which unfortunately I didn't pick up. Nonetheless, the knowledge of the English language proved over the years to be a very important asset for me, and I am grateful that my parents, particularly my mother, understood that and supported it. Among other things, this has allowed me to write these memoirs. It may not be perfect English, but I wish and hope it is not too hard to read.

Anti-Semitism

The summer of 1940 came, and I was looking forward attending second grade at the St. Andrew's school. The school year began as usual in September, but for me it was not going to last long. A major political change occurred in September for Romania. On September 4, 1940, the Legion of the Archangel Michael, a fascist movement built after the example of the German Nazi party, formed an alliance with General (later Marshal) Ion Antonescu to start a National Legionary State government. They forced the abdication of King Carol II in favor of his son Mihai and leaned Romania strongly toward the Axis. Romania would formally join the Axis in June 1941.

Once in power, from September 14, 1940, until January 21, 1941, the Legion ratcheted up the level of already-harsh anti-Semitic legislation and pursued, with impunity, a campaign of pogroms and political assassinations, not to mention showing their own skill at outright extortion and blackmail of the commercial and financial sectors. Their violence was not limited to the Jewish population. They had previously assassinated two prime ministers, and more than sixty former dignitaries or officials were executed in prison while awaiting trial. Historian and former prime minister, Nicolae Iorga, and economist Virgil Madgearu, also a former government minister, were assassinated without even the pretense of an arrest.

The Legion imposed legislation that eliminated Jews, students and teachers, from all the schools. Therefore, after a few days of school, I was out of St. Andrew School. The Bruders said, "Sorry, but we cannot do anything." Not to miss a school year, my parents decided to enroll me with Mrs. Moscuna, the lady who was my sister's teacher. My sister never attended a public school but took private lessons with this lady who specialized in teaching handicapped children, so my second class was private at Mrs. Moscuna's home, where I accompanied my sister daily.

After I spent my second grade with Mrs. Moscuna, my sister's teacher, I was admitted to the third grade at the Elementary School of the Sephardic Jewish Community. The school was close to where we lived and had outstanding teachers such as Mr. Eugen Campus, who became the principal.

Fig. 15. My class, at the Elementary School of the Sephardic Jewish Community. 1942.

The anti-Semitic legislation has affected us in other ways too. For instance, Jews were not allowed to own a radio; therefore, our excellent Phillips radio with shortwave bands was transferred to the Trandaburu family, our Christian neighbors. Jews were also no longer allowed to have a telephone, so we lost our telephone. It took twenty-two years until I had again a telephone in my apartment.

On January 1941, the Iron Guard became disenchanted with the policy of Marshal Antonescu and tried to take the power through an armed rebellion. In the process, the members of the Legion, known as legionnaires, started a pogrom in Bucharest, hunting and killing Jews and burning synagogues. I vividly remember being awakened that night in January by my mother who took me to my bedroom window to look outside. It was a typical quiet, frigid winter night, with snow covering the roofs, making everything look brighter. Not far from our home, I could see a large fire burning like fireworks. It was the synagogue of the Sephardic Jewish community that was less than a mile from our home; it was set on fire by the green shirts (the uniform of legionnaires consisted of green shirts).

That night, we didn't sleep but kept the lights off. After a while, we heard the sound of voices and steps on the service staircase. Fear for our lives was overwhelming. The next day, we learned from Maria, our Christian maid that a group of legionnaires came to our building. Since the main entrance was locked, the legionnaires went through the door getting to the driveway that was open and climbed the service stair all the way to the fifth floor. There they were met by Maria and her husband, Petre, who were awakened by the noise. The green shirts asked them if there were any Jews living in the building. Maria and Petre assured them that there were none, and they left in search of other victims. In reality, twelve of the sixteen apartments were rented by Jewish families. Later on, we learned that on that night, hundreds of Jews were killed in Bucharest, many of them hanged at the slaughterhouse under the writing "kosher meat", or taken to a forest on the outskirts of the city and shot. Maria and Petre saved our lives and those of our neighbors.

Love Affair and Politics

By the time I was born, my father was already a well-known lawyer in Bucharest. His office had a few younger lawyers functioning as secretaries. Around this time, a young lawyer, Ita Lerner, nicknamed Tuna, joined his office as another secretary. This woman had been married at least twice before and apparently was interested in becoming involved with men who had a potential for rising in their profession. According to Ema, (a daughter from his second marriage), Tuna's first husband, a young doctor, caught her in bed with Lucrețiu Pătrășcanu. After WWII, Pătrășcanu was a leader of the Communist Party and Ministry of Justice. The doctor divorced Tuna, and she married Mr. Athanase Joja, who, under the communist regime, became president of the Romanian Academy. However, by then, Mr. Joja ended up spending time in jail for his leftist political affiliation. Tuna divorced him and apparently resumed her search for a successful man whom she could eventually marry and thus move up on the social scale, which seems to have been her ultimate goal.

My father succumbed to the magic of this woman and became involved with her. For my father, this was not to be a simple affair. By the time he became involved with her, Ms. Ita (Tuna) Lerner was a high-ranking member of the outlawed Romanian Communist Party. In his book, *The Memories of the Valach Mandarin*, (on page 179, Albatros Publishing House, Bucharest 2000), Petre Pandrea quotes my father, stating that Tuna was a member of the legal office of the Romanian Communist Party. She was not only trying to get my father to marry her to become husband number three, but she also engaged him in her political activities. Thus, he acted as a defending attorney for some leaders of the Communist Party who were caught and put on trial for their illegal political activity.

One of the most famous trials in which my father was a defending attorney was that in which the main defendant was Ana Pauker. Ana Pauker was one of the most important members of the illegal Romanian Communist Party. She had strong connections with the Soviet Communist Party since she may have been the Komintern representative for Romania. After the communists took power in Romania, post-WWII, she became the Foreign Ministry and a leading figure of the Communist Party.

In a biography of Ana Pauker, (*Ana Pauker: The Rise and Fall of a Jewish Communist*, University of California Press, 2001), Robert Levy describes how my father acted during this trial, which took place in the city of Craiova in 1935. "On one occasion the tensions exploded during a dispute between the prosecution and defense attorney A. Nachtigal as recorded by a journalist covering the trial. Nachtigal was ordered by the chief magistrate to leave the hall. The attorney refused. Screaming, the judge again ordered him out. Refraining from screaming, the attorney again refused. Uproar ensues: the defense attorneys rise to their feet in protest; the people in the hall rise to their feet, protesting the protesters. The judge orders royal commissioner Stavrache to physically remove the lawyer. The proceedings are suspended, the judges withdraw, and officers and troops enter the hall. The royal commissioner demands that the attorney leave the building. The other attorneys form a circle around Nachtigal, in solidarity with their colleague. All hell breaks loose. In the face of such force, there's nothing that can be done says the lawyer. He leaves the hall together with the other attorneys, surrounded by sentinels in military uniform, bayonets drawn."

It is likely that my father had liberal political views before he met Tuna. During WWI, as he was taking refuge in the city of Galați, he put out a newspaper that was of liberal orientation. He told me that, after WWI, he had been a member of the Iunian party, a small political party with liberal orientation. As documented by the Romanian historian, Stelian Tănase, my father was associated with a well-known politician, N.D. Cocea, who had leftist and antimonarchic views. According to the October 16, 2005, issue of the newspaper *Informația Zilei* (Daily News), Alphonse Nachtigal was listed as a freemason, and this seems to be confirmed by the statement of the first grand master of the Grand National Lodge of Romania, Nicu Filip, grand master ad vitam (for life), who was put by the communists in the maximum prison in Bucharest. When asked, "Why were you put in jail?" he declared, "I wonder myself. I was together with Franciscan monks. For political prison they gave no explanation. They jail you and if you were lucky, you come out after many years; if not, your bones stayed there. We were three lawyers who were rising fast and we were helped by the Jewish Union vice president, the greatest lawyer of his time, Alphonse Nachtigal." My father's activity as a sympathizer of the outlawed Communist Party brought him severe retaliations. In 1939, he was kept, for several months, in a concentration camp for political prisoners at the town of Miercurea-Ciuc. He was freed from there but not for long, and things got worst thereafter.

As a very young child, I was never told or had explained to me what was going on with my parents. However, I felt that something wrong had occurred and that my mother was terribly upset. I remember a time when my mother took the two of us, my sister and me, and went to have a talk with her mother, who was living not far from us. When we got there, she sent us to some neighbors who had a girl, Thea, of our age, to play with her. This was unusual, and I knew that something very bad was going on, but I had no idea what it was. My understanding is that Tuna came to ask my mother for a divorce. Apparently, my mother refused, but nonetheless, my father seemed to be totally in the hands of this woman. He was no longer living at our home as he had moved to Tuna's studio.

Evidently, this extramarital affair of my father had severe consequences on his marriage, our family, and my life. The political implications of his affair compounded enormously their effects on our family life. Throughout my life, I found it indefensible that my father had left us, his children and his wife, without showing any concern for our well-being. No one could blame him for the general political conditions, but he didn't seem to care about the consequences on his family. This did not diminish my admiration and respect for his professional accomplishments. On the contrary, I think that his ability should have served him better in what were his private life judgments.

The fact remains that from this age, I have little remembrance of my father except that he taught me to play chess. This happened while he was still having Sunday luncheon with us, his family. After luncheon, he used to ask me to play chess with him. In the beginning, for quite some time, he always won, and I used to go into the bathroom and cry; but the day came when I won a game, and I cannot say how happy I was. Except for that, there is a complete emptiness in my memory regarding my father at this age.

Thus has ended the first chapter of my life, the early years of my childhood. They began under wonderful circumstances and ended with my father disappearing from our family life. What followed were the toughest, roughest, and most dangerous years of my life under the worst circumstances. My memories of those early childhood years are overall mixed. I have very good memories of our vacations at the Black Sea and in the mountains, our last Christmas celebration, and my interaction with the children in my neighborhood, either in Carol Park or on Saint Catherine Street, where I practiced riding my bicycle. The shadow of what was going on between my parents was there, and without understanding much, I felt it.

One significant event of those years was acquiring the Jewish identity. Until I was put out of Saint Andrew School, I had very little or even no recognition that I was Jewish. The brutal anti-Semitism that I was exposed to has imprinted a strong lifelong bonding with the Jewish people and my faith. On a much larger scale, one could argue that the violent anti-Semitism during WWII helped the creation of the state of Israel and the migration there of the survivors of the Holocaust. It was a dreadful price to be paid, but after two thousand years, the country and its people are back and there to stay.

One important lesson to be learned from this story is that political events in which one is not involved can have tremendous consequences on one's life. During my childhood, Romania went from a budding democracy to dictatorship and fascism. Like most people, my parents didn't recognize what was going on, and they paid a very heavy price. The consequences of this error on my life were huge and long lasting.

Chapter 2

War and Communism
1941-1951

Those were the years when I finished primary school and went through lyceum (the equivalent of American middle and high school) while experiencing war and poverty. This was the time when, from a fascist-military dictatorship, Romania became a satellite of the Stalinist Soviet Union behind the Iron Curtain. As a child, I saw violence and desolation, and I experienced poverty and fear for my life. I witnessed serious illness and death in my family. I witnessed and understood the hardships of my mother. All these came on top of being without my father, practically a temporary orphan.

Father in Concentration Camp

One night in April 1941, secret police agents and soldiers came to our apartment to arrest my father and to search for subversive papers. My sister and I were awakened by all the noise and lights. Obviously, they didn't find my father since by then he was sleeping at Ms. Lerner's studio. Apparently, at the same time, a search went on at Ms. Lerner's studio, where they got both of them and also found some compromising papers. They ended up in a military prison called Malmaison ("bad house" in French) and were put on trial by a military court.

My father was put in a jail cell, having as company several leaders of the Communist Party. Petre Pandrea, in his book, *The Memories of the Valach Mandarin*, published in Romania in the year 2002, relates this episode, quoting my father: "There were in prison: 1} Nachtigal, 2} Chişinevschi, 3} Georgescu and others, in a very crowded cell. Nachtigal was sleeping next to Teohari who in summer had the habit of sleeping naked without a shirt, in Adam's suit. I (my father says) had an extreme nausea. He had a body with feminine skin. I told Ioşca (Chişinevschi), a smart boy, cultivated, who spent eight years in Prague, knows literature, we discussed about Anatole France. Not to offend him I played chess till late at night until Teohari slept and then we moved another one in my place that could bear the close proximity of his white feminine body." (From: The Memories of the Valach Mandarin by Petre Pandrea, page 178, Albatros Publishing House, Bucharest 2000). After the war, when the Communist Party took the power, these men were part of the leadership and government. They ruled the country.

> Wikipedia. Chişinevschi was born to a poor Jewish family in Bessarabia, then part of the Russian Empire. Largely self-taught and a high-school dropout, he joined the PCR in 1928. Arrested that year (since the PCR had been banned in 1924), he went to the Soviet Union upon his release in 1930. He had personal connections within the Soviet secret police, of which he was an agent (which he remained through the 1950s), infiltrating the PCR hierarchy's upper ranks.[2] A devoted Comintern man, he was unconcerned with Romania's cultural and political history and context. Reconfirmed as a member of the PCR Central Committee in 1940, he was arrested that year, spending World War II in the Caransebeş penitentiary and the Târgu Jiu camp, where he was among the closest associates of Gheorghe Gheorghiu-Dej, especially after 1942.

My father's trial took place in a military court, and he was acquitted. Nevertheless, he was sent to the concentration camp for political detainees in the town of Târgu Jiu. There he was locked up with other political prisoners, some of them members or sympathizers of the Communist Party or just plain democratic leaders. The camp at Târgu Jiu was originally built to accommodate the Poles refugees. When they left, Marshal Ion Antonescu populated the camp with people who opposed the regime: Jews, rebellious intellectuals, and communists. Among those were personalities such as the poet Tudor Arghezi, and Gheorghe Gheorghiu-Dej, and Nicolae Ceauşescu, future leaders of communist Romania.

On June 22, 1941, Romania joined Germany in its war against the Soviet Union. The German and Romanian armies advanced quite rapidly and occupied a large portion of the western side of the Soviet Union. The Romanian army occupied what is now the Republic of Moldova and Ukraine and accompanied the German army all the way to Stalingrad. On July 18, 1941, the Romanian dictator Ion Antonescu announced his intention to have all Jews who were not born on Romanian territory deported to concentration camps in a region called Transnistria.

Transnistria, which was a backward piece of land with highly productive agriculture beyond the Nistru River, was part of the Soviet Union in 1940. The living conditions there were, to say the least, primitive, even in normal times. The fate of the deportees was quite obvious; very few survived. Since Ita Lerner (Tuna), my father's mistress, was born in Hotin, a small town in Bessarabia, part of Soviet Union in 1940, she was due for deportation. To avoid her fateful deportation, my father, who was with her in the Târgu Jiu concentration camp, decided to marry her, therefore granting her Romanian citizenship. He asked my mother for a divorce, and my mother accepted it. Ironically, this did not prevent the deportation a few months later of the newly married couple, my father and Tuna, along with the other Jews who were detained in the Târgu Jiu concentration camp, to the Wapniarka concentration camp.

> Wapniarka. Ukrainian town attached to Transnistria for most of the war, and site of a detention camp established by the Romanians in October 1941. The first prisoners brought to the camp were Jews from Odessa. In 1942 Jewish prisoners arrived from Bukovina and Romania. At the end of that year, Wapniarka became a concentration camp for political prisoners under the direct control of the Romanian government. The camp was actually designated for Jews, since no other "political prisoners" were held there. There were 1,179 Jews in the camp, including 107 women. The inmates established a camp committee to help each other survive the terrible conditions. The camp also had an underground. The prisoners overcame typhus by keeping

the camp immaculately clean. However, they were fed horse fodder, which caused hundreds to contract a paralysis-inducing disease that affects the bone marrow. The inmates demanded medical help; the authorities permitted the Jewish Aid Committee to provide medicine, and finally stopped feeding the Jews animal food. As Soviet troops approached in October 1943, the authorities decided to liquidate the camp. Some Jews were sent to ghettos in Transnistria, but most prisoners were moved to another Romanian camp until the National Legionary Government toppled in the summer of 1944. Shoah Resource Center; www.yadvashem.org.

My father was elected the leader of the camp committee that tried to take care of the prisoners. They successfully enforced a cleaning operation that avoided lice and, implicitly, typhus contamination that was raging in the region. Unfortunately, some of the prisoners refused to follow instructions not to eat the horse fodder that was provided to them as food. They developed lifelong leg paralysis as the toxin in this food attacked the spinal cord. As Soviet troops approached in October 1943, the Romanian authorities decided to close the camp. Together with other prisoners, my father and Tuna were returned to the concentration camp in Târgu-Jiu. During the retreat, some of the detainees were killed by the retreating Romanian army.

Poverty

After my father's arrest and deportation, we, the children, never heard from him or about him. For all practical purposes, we were orphans. In a way, I didn't feel a major loss. Father was not part of our daily life before. Between his profession and his mistress, Tuna, there was not much left for us. Nevertheless, the consequences on our material life were considerable. My father was the breadwinner of our family. My mother had no income, and apparently, there were no financial reserves set up. She never had a job, had no training or professional skills, and there was nobody else to pay the rent and provide the necessities for the three of us.

My grandmother Mama Mare, who had moved in with us, owned shares of some oil companies. I recall actually seeing shares from the Steaua Română (the Romanian Star) Company, one of the major oil companies. They impressed me because they looked like some very fancy diplomas. Before the war, she was probably doing well financially, having money invested in what was supposed to be safe securities. She was living independently in a small rented apartment. When Romania entered WWII, these shares became useless since all belonged to British or American oil companies (Standard Oil, etc.). Consequently, moving in with us did not help us financially, just added one more body to our impoverished group. In order to survive, my mother started selling everything that had value in our household: her jewels, my father's books, her beautiful nutria fur, the Rosenthal China services, paintings, linen, rugs, etc. Almost overnight, once a wealthy family, we became poor.

After a while, to generate some income, my mother started repairing socks. It was the beginning of nylon socks, and women preferred to have them repaired instead of throwing them away. There was a small shop not far from our home that took these damaged socks from customers and passed them on to my mother, who worked day and night to return them repaired to the shop. This must have generated some income, although I doubt it was enough to cover all of our living expenses. Later on, Mom learned typing and shorthand. She bought a typewriter and started typing manuscripts and other documents. She had a few writers who gave her their manuscripts to be typed. This created some income and helped her find a job after the war ended.

Still the financial problems were overwhelming, and Mom decided to rent the room that used to be my father's office. This decision had long-term implications, but I assume there was no other way for us to survive. We had to pay the rent. From then on, for as long as I lived in the Bibescu-Vodă apartment, I lived in a shared apartment. For me, this total lack of privacy was the most definite sign of poverty, and it was worse than not having enough food or clothes. For instance, Mr. Cristescu, who lived in our apartment for several years, felt obliged to participate in my education. By then I was a teenager, and I didn't appreciate his educational input. There were several encounters between us that were not carried on in a diplomatic fashion.

Altogether, this experience left me with a strong desire for privacy and for living independently. This was a time when I really learned what privacy means and how precious it is. The lack of privacy bothered me a lot and during my childhood, adolescence, and my young adult age I never had a private place. I slept on a couch in the same bedroom with my grandmother,

Mama Mare. The only girl that I invited to my place was Mona, and that happened only a long time after we were friends.

Ironically, what my mother started as a way of generating some vital income became, under the communist system, a way of life. By that time, all apartments that were nationalized were administered by the state. Instead of paying rent to the landlord, Mr. Ştefănescu, we were paying rent to the state. All this real estate was under the control of a state agency, the Office of Inhabitable Space, which was following the rule that each individual is entitled to seventy-two square feet (eight square meters) in which to live.

This childhood in poverty would leave a mark on me for the rest of my life. Those were the years when I learned that food is precious. The lesson that I was repeatedly told was that food should never be thrown away unless it is spoiled. Even now, as we live in this land where food is abundant, I have the tendency to store food more than we need. We have never been hungry. We, the children, always had enough food, but this was probably accomplished through sacrifices from my mother and Mama Mare. It was not only for lack of money, but during those years, basic food items like bread, milk, and meat were rationed, and more could be obtained only on the black market, which was expensive. We never had overweight problems. These years in poverty had set up what I would describe as an inferiority complex. Throughout my childhood and adolescence, I carried with me the feeling that I belonged to a poor family, and this was not something to be proud of. Having to live in a shared apartment enhanced this feeling.

The end of the war and the return of my father alleviated the financial problem but didn't change it fundamentally. My father provided child support, but this was probably calculated for the two of us, my sister and me. It was enough to cover the cost of food, which was and still is a big expense in Romania. However, the other items in the budget such as rent, utilities, etc., didn't seem to be covered, and they had to be provided by my mother.

Those years taught me the lesson of yearning for financial safety. All my life, I've tried to make sure that I have a financial reserve available, which means savings. I started saving as soon as I had my first salary as a physician, although I was single and didn't have to provide for anyone else. Even during the time spent under the communist regime and when I married Sidonia, we tried and managed to have some savings.

Mother's Sickness

The winter of 1941 was severe over all of Eastern Europe. It probably saved Moscow and the Soviet Union from the German invasion. The cold weather came early, and the fall rains made the Russian dirt roads unusable by the heavy tanks and trucks of the German army. Most of the roads in the Soviet Union were dirt roads meant to be used by wagons or sleds pulled by horses. Then the snow and the ice covered the land, and that stopped the German army in its tracks. Starting from the clothing of the soldiers to the oil of the trucks, the army was not prepared for this kind of weather.

By January of 1942, my mother developed pneumonia. By then the only treatment available was sulfonamides, and they had significant side effects. She was treated by our family physician, the old Dr. Schwartz, and was probably saved by him. Dr. Schwartz had been my father's family's physician since my father was young. He was an old man, with white hair and a big moustache looking like the typical old-fashioned family doctor.

I remember one night when my mother's condition became life threatening. In the middle of the night, my grandmother (Mama Mare) went to our neighbors, the Zaidman family, for help. Mr. Zaidman went to fetch Dr. Schwartz. The snow was several feet high; there was not a soul on the street, and no vehicle could move. Mr. Zaidman had to walk several miles in high snow to Dr. Schwartz's home, and he and the doctor had to walk back in the snow. This may have saved my mother's life. The disease lasted quite a while because of complications, but in the end, my mother recovered. I will always remember those people with a deep feeling of love and gratitude.

The disease must have left my mother weakened since a few months later, she fell in the kitchen and badly broke a leg. One of our neighbors, Dr. Tomescu, an orthopedic surgeon, put her leg in a cast. After several days, it became obvious that he didn't align the bones properly; my mother had terrible pain. She called on Dr. Cooper, another orthopedic surgeon. Dr. Cooper came with his small team that included a technician named Calin. Dr. Cooper operated on my mother's leg and put on a new cast, and everything went smoothly from there on. I met Dr. Cooper again as a student in the medical school where he was our professor of orthopedics. A wonderful man!

First Allied Bombardment

For the summer vacation of 1943, my mother decided to send me to Târgoviște, a beautiful town situated in the foothills of the Carpathian Mountain, close to the oil fields of Ploiești. My uncle Ionel (Jonas Bercovici), a younger brother of my maternal grandfather, Julius Bercovici, lived there. Uncle Jonas was a kind person. His wife, Rachel, was a wonderful, motherly woman. They had two children, a son, Armand, and a daughter, Lala. Both were older than me. Lala must have been around twenty, and Armand was probably eighteen. Uncle Jonas was a brush maker. He had a small workshop at his home, where he made all kinds of brushes. He also had a small shop in downtown Târgoviște, where he sold these brushes along with all kinds of other household items, a sort of mini Home Depot. I enjoyed going to his store on Main Street and watch people come and go.

> Târgoviște is the capital city of the Dâmbovița county România. It is situated on the right bank of the Ialomița River, at 80 km far from Bucharest, the actual capital city of România. There are about 90,000 inhabitants. First attested in 1396, in the Travel Accounts of Johannes Schiltberger, Târgoviște was the capital city of the Wallachian voivodship between 1396 and 1714 when the Royal Court ("Curtea Domnească") and the Chindia Tower ("Turnul Chindia"), now the symbol of the city, were built. It is known as "The city of 33 voivods" as there were 33 princes who ruled the whole country from Târgoviște when it was the capital city. Among them we can mention Vlad Țepeș (known as Dracula from the horror novel "Dracula" written by the Irish novelist Bram Stoker). Chindia Tower was added to the Royal Court during the regime of Vlad Țepeș.http://www.scuolerignanoincisa.it/foodforthought/foodforthought_partner_romania.htm.

An unexpected event happened during my visit there. Uncle Jonas went to Bucharest for some business by train, and about the time he was expected to come back home, I went to the railway station to wait for him. As I was in the railway station on the platform waiting for the train to come, I saw some huge planes flying very low above the station. One could see them very clearly as they flew almost at tree level. They looked like huge black birds flying in a V formation, making a loud noise. Many years later, I learned that this was a mission called Tidal Wave, and those planes were part of the fleet of 160 Liberators, huge four-engine bombers that flew from their air base in North Africa and were going to destroy the oil field of Ploieşti, the main source of gasoline for the German Army.

The crowd in the station understood immediately that those planes were ready for bombardment, and panic arose. The crowd ran berserk for the exit, which was just a regular door, allowing only two persons at a time. Realizing that this wouldn't work, the crowd turned like a herd of frightened animals to find other exit and ran from one side of the railway station to the other while the airplanes kept flying over the station while the train that I was expecting to come from Bucharest was already approaching the station. Luckily, the bombers were not interested in the railway station; they were concerned about reaching the Ploieşti oil fields nearby because those were their target. Of course, in the panic, nobody figured that out.

I don't know how I got out of the station, but I know I found myself running at full speed away from the station on the tree-lined boulevard that led from the railway station to the city. Much later, I recognized that I had witnessed the first American bombardment of the Romanian oil fields. The following day, I watched one of the American fliers who had been taken prisoner being paraded in the city farmer's market. This was the first American I had seen, a tall young fellow who looked rather worried. The crowd was looking at him with curiosity, but no manifestation of hate or otherwise occurred. Nobody cared about the Ploieşti oil fields.

> Wikipedia. The United States Army Air Forces (USAAF) began planning for a buildup of American air power in the Middle East in January 1942 in response to a request from the British Chief of the Air Staff. The initial unit to arrive was given the codename HALPRO. It was under the command of Col. Harry A. Halverson and consisted of twenty-three B-24D Liberator heavy bombers with hand-picked crews. It had initially been assigned to the China Burma India Theatre to attack Japan from airfields in China, but after the fall of Rangoon the Burma Road was cut so the detachment could not be logistically supported in China. In June 1942, 13 B-24 Liberators of the "Halverson project" (HALPRO) attacked Ploieşti. Though damage was small, Germany responded by putting strong anti-aircraft defenses around Ploieşti.

Luftwaffe General Alfred Gerstenberg built one of the heaviest and best-integrated air defense networks in Europe. The Germans would be ready to protect their refineries from the American B-24s.

Europe's largest oil production and refining complex was at Ploeşti (ploy-ESHT), approximately 35 miles north of Bucharest. Ploeşti was also among the first sites in the world to commercially exploit oil, having put its first refinery into operation in 1856. By the late summer of 1941, Romania was allied with Hitler, and was set to become Germany's largest single source of oil. Petroleum from Ploesti soon provided a third or more of Germany's requirements. This fact was not lost on the Allies. In fact, British Prime Minister Winston Churchill declared that the Romanian refineries were the "taproot of German might." A commitment to the destruction of Ploesti was one of the many decisions made when Churchill and President Franklin D. Roosevelt met at the Casablanca conference in Morocco in January 1943. The planning for Ploeşti's demise began almost at once. War history on Line Ploeşti was Hitler's oil supply so it had to burn. November 25, 2012, Jay A. Stout.

Wikipedia. Operation Tidal Wave was an air attack by bombers of the United States Army Air Forces (USAAF) based in Libya on nine oil refineries around Ploieşti, Romania on 1 August 1943, during World War II. It was a strategic bombing mission and part of the "oil campaign" to deny petroleum-based fuel to the Axis.[5] Colonel Jacob E. Smart planned the operation, based on HALPRO's experiences. HALPRO had encountered minimal air defenses in its raid; so the planners decided Tidal Wave would be executed by day, and that the attacking bombers would approach at low altitude to avoid detection by German radar. [citation needed] 310 air crewmen were killed, 108 were captured by the Axis, and 78 were interned in Turkey.[1] Three of the five Medals of Honor (the most for any single air action in history) were awarded posthumously.[1] Allied assessment of the attack estimated a loss of 40% of the refining capacity at the Ploieşti refineries,[1] although some refineries were largely untouched. Most of the damage was repaired within weeks, after which the net output of fuel was greater than before the raid.[1] Circa September, the Enemy Oil Committee appraisal of Ploieşti bomb damage indicated "no curtailment of overall product output"[8] as many of the refineries had been operating previously below maximum capacity.

I should mention the history of this branch of our family because it's so typical for those times. Armand, the son of Uncle Jonas, took advantage of the porous borders immediately after the end of WWII and left the country, crossed into Hungary and farther until he reached Austria. Armand enrolled as a student at the medical school in Graz, Austria. After finishing his medical studies, he migrated to Israel and began practicing medicine. He never returned to Romania and had no connection with us. I heard that he changed his family name from Bercovici to a Hebrew name.

His father, Uncle Jonas, was not so lucky. After the war, when the Communist Party was on its way taking absolute power, the party aimed to dismantle all the political parties that were not under its orders. One of these parties was the Social Democrat Party, an old small party in which Uncle Jonas was a leading member. Together with other leaders of the party who did not submit to the communists, he ended up in jail where he spent several years. When he was released from jail, he came to visit us. By then he was a weak old man who was very silent, completely changed; he looked and acted like a zombie. With his wife and daughter, Lala, he migrated to Israel. There Lala married Mr. Haimovici and had two daughters. She returned to visit Romania, and so we met again.

More Bombs

On April 1944, the Allies started a campaign of systematic bombardment of Romania with the oil fields and refineries of Ploiești as their main target, but also including Bucharest. Before WWII, Romania had been the fifth oil producing country in the world and the only European oil producing country. During the war, Romania was the main source of oil for Germany. In 1944, the Allies occupied Italy and built air bases there, and Romania became a reachable target for the Allied Air Force. Between April and August 1944, bombardments took place almost daily.

It all started on Tuesday, April 4, 1944. Alarms began to sound throughout the capital. We heard the siren, which was on the top of a high-rise building across the street, going on while we were having lunch. Since an alarm exercise had previously been announced, nobody paid attention. However, after a while, some suspicious sounds were heard. They were not very clear, but they were ominous. We had not heard the sound of falling bombs before, but we quickly learned what they were. We decided to descend to the lobby. Apparently, almost all our neighbors had the same idea. By the time we were gathered in the lobby, it was clear that a bombardment was ongoing. Later, we found out that over two hundred bombers were involved. Not far from our home, a bomb fell in a trench built as a shelter and killed several dozen people who sought cover there. Many never reached shelters, becoming innocent victims.

Bombardments became an almost daily and nightly routine. British pilots attacked only at night. The British planes arrived around midnight. For this reason and also for the sound they made, they were called mosquitoes by the Romanian population. The night of 2 to 3 May was the first recorded night attack made by the British, when seventy bombers that departed from southern Italy had reached the sky of Bucharest. They came back with a hundred heavy bombers on the night of 6 to 7 May.

We would go to bed at 8:00 PM, and around 11:00 PM, the siren would sound the alarm. We would wake up, dress in a hurry, and descend to the shelter. The shelter was a rather large hall in the basement of our building, which had been furnished with wooden benches that could accommodate up to one hundred people. To get to the shelter, one had to descend a steep stairway of at least twenty steps. At night, for camouflage purposes, we had to keep the lights off, and that made it more difficult to see the steps. The door to the shelter was built like a very solid armor of steel about two to three inches thick. With six floors of reinforced concrete above us, the shelter was supposed to offer some protection against bombs.

Usually, many people were waiting in line to descend into the shelter, and a few times, we were still outside, waiting to descend into the shelter, when the sound of the antiaircraft guns could already be heard. People seeking refuge were not only the families living in our building, but also people from neighboring old brick homes, and people who were walking on the street. Once in the shelter, families would sit together, usually in silence. When the bombing was getting closer, the silence was absolute; one could hear only the sound of the bombs falling and the antiaircraft guns.

The same routine occurred around 11:00 AM, when the American planes would arrive. The difference was that it was daylight, so it was easier for us to see the steps that we had to descend. The American planes would arrive over Bucharest around 11:00 AM, as they probably had left their air base in Italy around 6:00 AM. On May 7, 1944, a total of seven hundred aircraft (five hundred B-24 bombers and two hundred fighter planes) were over the city, just ten hours after the British night attack. Our neighborhood seemed attractive to both, maybe because in the large piazza behind our building, there were several batteries of antiaircraft guns.

During these months in Bucharest 3,456 homes had been destroyed, 3,473 were partially destroyed, 401 were damaged, and 2,305 had been burned. Several bombs fell within 100 yards of our building. One bomb destroyed an old house, and another fell in the street and left a hole in the ground that could easily hold a truck. When these bombs hit the ground and exploded, the shelter was shaking like in an earthquake or a boat on a stormy sea. I was frightened and even as I grew older, I react to sounds that resemble those of the bombs exploding or antiaircraft firing.

I remember one morning when the shelter was full with many people who had been walking on the street when the siren sounded. The sound of the falling bombs was getting louder and so was that of the planes. People in the shelter became very quiet; nobody was talking. Then a priest or pastor of some denomination started praying loudly. We were all there together sharing the terror and asking for heavenly protection. The sound of the prayer, which was not specific for any religious group, mixed with that of the falling bombs nearby, left a strong impression on me. In those days in the shelter, I was praying too. As children, we were living with the reality of daily bombardment to the extent that we started playing war, imitating it. Beno would come to my place, and we would construct buildings with my toys and then start dropping "bombs" and watching them crash. We were aware this was not a game.

End of War

The bombardments continued almost daily through the months of April, May, June, and July and then all of a sudden stopped. We didn't know then but realized later that Romania was trying to reach an armistice with the Allies. By August 23, around 10:00 PM, King Michael came on the national radio and proclaimed that Romania was breaking its alliance with Germany and siding with the Allies. Although I was only eleven years old, I was awake and very excited by this historical event that would no doubt affect our lives, hopefully for the better.

Wikipedia. On August 23, 1944, King Michael joined with pro-Allied opposition politicians (who included the Communists) and led a successful coup with support from the army. Michael, who was initially considered to be not much more than a "figurehead," was able to successfully depose the dictator Ion Antonescu. The king offered a no confrontational retreat to German ambassador Manfred Freiherr von Killinger, but the Germans considered the coup "reversible" and tried to turn the situation around by military attacks. The Romanian First Army, the Romanian Second Army (under formation), the remnants of the Romanian Third Army and the Romanian Fourth Army (one corps) were under orders from the king to defend Romania against any German attacks. The king then offered to put Romania's battered armies on the side of the Allies.

The next day, Bucharest became the target of the German army that was located outside the city. The Germans were trying to get into the city from the north side, and there were some fierce fights with the Romanian army, helped by civil volunteers. A major difficulty was that the Germans had taken over the Băneasa Airport at the north of Bucharest. They started precision bombardment of Bucharest with their famous Stuka planes that could drop bombs while plunging straight onto the target.

The bombs hit the Royal Palace, a revenge for the king's coup. They also hit the central phone building, the tallest building in town built before the war by an American company, and the municipal emergency hospital where they killed hundreds of people. For three or four days and nights, we stayed in the shelter, going out only for food. And then one morning, around 11:00 AM, we got out of the shelter and looked up and saw the American Liberators, shining like little silver toys, flying high in the sky. We could hear the sound of the bombs they were launching over the Băneasa Airport, and we knew that this was the end of the German bombing. We didn't know then that the Liberators would never come back to assure our life in liberty.

Across the street from the building where I was living was the Theology Seminary, a sprawling complex that extended farther along the Sfânta Ecaterina (Saint Catrine) Street. In normal times, this was a place for educating priests for the Romanian Orthodox Church. During WWII, this complex became the prison camp for the captured Allied airmen. By August 1944, when an armistice between Romania and the Allies was signed, the Theology Seminary camp hosted about 1,500 prisoners, including Americans, Canadians, and British airmen. They were served by Russian prisoners and were guarded by Romanian military.

Our balcony was across the street at the level of the second floor of the Theology Seminary dormitory. From my bedroom or the balcony, I could actually look into their common bedrooms and into the garden between the building and the fence, where the prisoners spent their time all day long. Besides evidently being bored to death, the life of the prisoners was something resembling a vacation. They were very well treated by their Romanian guards, and there were rumors of some wild parties that the prisoners had together with the Romanian officers. The confectionery from the ground floor of our building had a very active business providing cakes to sweeten the boring life of these prisoners. On Sunday mornings, a few prisoners could be seen walking to church accompanied by a Romanian soldier.

When German soldiers were walking on the street, they could be seen from the second floor dormitory of the camp, and the prisoners would jump to the windows and start shouting "Hitler Kaput." There were never reprisals, and obviously, the prisoners enjoyed doing it, while the Germans walked away trying to ignore it. I guess that by then, summer of 1944, they knew that they had lost the war. The only thing that scared these prisoners was the Allied bombardments. While we were in the shelter, under six floors of reinforced concrete, the prisoners were in their old two-story brick building that would have been knocked out by one of those bombs, and maybe they knew that they were in a target area.

The day Paris was liberated by the Allied forces, my mother wrote this news on a big sheet of paper and displayed it from inside our apartment so the prisoners would see it from their dormitory and know that their captivity was getting close to the end. Later we learned that they had radios and could listen to BBC or VOA. The Romanian guards were very tolerant with those prisoners. After August 23, those prisoners were freed and were given guns. They came to visit with families in our building. Several came to visit us, and I remember one of them being reluctant to try the homemade sherbet that my mother offered. Practicing my English, I got the address of two airmen; unfortunately, I didn't keep them. One prisoner became engaged to one of our neighbors, Ms. Braunstein, who was a beautiful young lady and, soon thereafter, left the country, taking her with him.

After the Allied prisoners left the building, they were replaced by German women who were taken prisoners and were guarded by Romanian soldiers. Apparently, Soviet soldiers found out about them and one night tried to enter the building. A firefight broke out with the Romanian guards that lasted several hours. We never found out how it ended, but very likely, they were not able to enter the building.

Discipline was not the hallmark of the Red Army; it soon became clear that the soldiers would attack people on the street and forcefully take their wrist watches. *Davai cias* ("Give me your watch" in Russian) became a popular slogan. One could often see on the street patrols of the NKVD (some sort of Soviet military police) soldiers who would pick up the Russian soldiers who were drunk or behaved strangely. The rumors were that they would be shot immediately.

My father was freed from the concentration camp in August 1944 and returned to Bucharest. Soon after he arrived in Bucharest, he came to visit us, but without seeing him or having news from him for so long (more than four years), my feelings toward him were not those of a child meeting his dad. Our reunion had nothing of what would be expected. There was no hugging or joy; for us, the children, he was like a visitor. He moved to Tuna's studio, which, during the war, was occupied by his mother. Tuna was freed a couple of weeks later and joined him in her studio. In retrospective, I think that, although I was just a kid during all these years, I had a feeling of what was going on with my parents and that my father had basically abandoned us. Through my adolescence and actually throughout my entire life, this feeling stayed with me.

Death Strikes

A major blow to my family and me occurred in the winter of 1945 with the death of my sister, Jacqueline. By January 1945, she became ill with diphtheria. Having gone to a private teacher, she did not receive the vaccinations that were mandatory in public schools. Her early symptoms that looked like a sore throat (angina) were misdiagnosed by a young physician who was a family friend. The disease progressed to the point of threatening to choke her, and then an experienced pediatrician was called and diagnosed diphtheria. Treatment was immediately started with antidiphtheria serum. The disease began to improve, but unfortunately, as often happens, the toxin from this microbe had already attacked her heart, and she died of heart failure. I was at school on the morning of February 7, 1945, when she died. I came home at noon and was led to her room where she lay with her eyes closed like she was quietly sleeping. I kissed her on the forehead and left just at the time when my father arrived with a famous cardiologist, Professsor Danielopol, who confirmed her death.

Jacqueline's death shook me profoundly, and the sorrow and grief of my mother that lasted a long time was overwhelming. It was a terrible loss because Jacqueline was part of my childhood, and she was very much attached to me. My parents loved Jacqueline immensely. She was an affectionate, kind, and gentle child whom both tried to help, and were hopeful she would improve. For my father, this was an awful blow. He had a particular love for her, and I had never seen him so distressed. He put together an album about her, but unfortunately, it was lost. I have read it, and the way he expressed his love for her was very impressive. I had the feeling that something had broken inside him and that he would never recover from it. My mother found the strength to stand up and move on; I don't know where she got her strength. I am sure that my presence helped; that was about all that she had left. She was also surrounded by good friends.

It was not my first encounter with death. During the 1944 bombardments, from the balcony of our apartment, I had seen a truck carrying the bloody body of a young woman. But this time, death was within my reach, and by night, when I was sent to sleep at one of our neighbors, I stood awake a long time, wondering how irreversible death was. I didn't cry, but I was awed by the mystery of death. I still am. I felt the emptiness that comes with it. I never learned to accept it.

The war years were a very tough life experience for me, but by far, the most traumatic event of those years was the death of my sister Jacqueline. The pain of losing someone so close, the physical disappearance, the emptiness that follows stayed with me. It left a deep scar that I have carried with me over the rest of my life. The fact that this was probably the result of a medical error would follow me through my teaching of medical students and my medical practice. Many years later, when I could return to Romania, I went to the cemetery and had no problem finding her grave. It was there, and I felt a feeling of reunion. To my major chagrin, my attempt to have some repair done to her grave, which has deteriorated over time, was unsuccessful.

Bar Mitzvah

Approaching my thirteenth birthday, my mother and Mama Mare decided that I should make bar mitzvah. I went for instructions to rabbi Gutman, and was trained for the ceremony. My religious background was indeed very weak. After I had two years of religion at the Sephardic Elementary school with Mr. Rabinsohn, I knew only one prayer—the Shema—and a few habits such as washing the face in the morning and washing hands before eating. The rabbi managed to teach me how to dress the religious items and to say the required prayer. My knowledge of Hebrew was not very strong; by then I knew how to read the Hebrew alphabet and had a limited vocabulary of common words. I never practiced what the rabbi taught me, and with time, I almost forgot the Hebrew alphabet. Nonetheless, my mother and Mama Mare were happy about the ceremony, and I was happy to please them.

My father did not attend the ceremony and did not refrain from telling me what he thought about it. Following this event, I used to fast on the day of Yom Kippur as an expression of solidarity with my mother and Mama Mare, who were fasting on this day, and also as a token expression of my Jewishness. Again, my father did not agree with my practice, but I continued to do it as long as my age and health allowed. However, my total lack of religious education was a major obstacle in attending any synagogue. This was not a problem in communist Romania, where few people went to religious services but was a problem when I went to visit my relatives in Strasbourg who practiced the traditional religious services. When they took me to the synagogue for the Sabbath service, my understanding of the prayers was very poor, and that applied also to the religious routine at the dinner table concerning the blessings. I have to say that my relatives understood perfectly what had happened and accepted Sidonia and me with much love and total support.

Wikipedia. Bar Mitzvah (Hebrew: בר מצוה) (plural: *B'nai Mitzvah*) and Bat Mitzvah (Hebrew: בת מצוה) (plural: *B'not Mitzvah*) are Jewish coming of age rituals. Bar "בר" is a Jewish Babylonian Aramaic word literally meaning son (in Hebrew, it is Ben "בן.") Bat "בת" is Hebrew for daughter, and Mitzvah "מצוה" is a commandment and a law. While this literally translates to "son of commandment" or "daughter of commandment," the rabbinical phrase "bar" means here "under the category of" or "subject to," making "Bar Mitzvah" translate to "an [agent] who is subject to the law." According to Jewish law, when Jewish boys become 13, they become accountable for their actions and become a Bar Mitzvah.

The Best Summer Vacation

The end of WWII happened during my summer vacation in 1945. On that August day, I was in the countryside staying with friends of my father, the Arion family. I still remember the newspapers with the large titles and the pictures of the atomic bomb explosions in Hiroshima and Nagasaki. In all honesty, I don't think that, by that time, I was impressed, mostly because I did not understand what that meant. By then I was too preoccupied to enjoy my special vacation with the Arion family.

Professor Arion was a university professor of entomology (the scientific study of insects) at the Agriculture University in Bucharest. He was married to a lady who was divorced from Prof. Traian Săvulescu, a national authority in agriculture. My father was the attorney in this divorce, I guess on the side of Mrs. Arion, and they remained on very good terms. He was probably her lawyer.

Mrs. Arion owned a very large piece of land, probably thousands of acres, not far from Bucharest in the village of Stoenești, and they had a beautiful large villa not far from the village. The home had a rose garden that was cared for by Mrs. Arion. On the grounds, there was a separate house for the servants and the keepers of horses and cattle, and barns for these animals. Immediately outside the large courtyard, there were twenty-five acres of orchards with plum trees of various kinds that were in the care of Professor Arion.

The Arions had a son, Mimi, who was about five or six years older than me, and we had known each other since he used to come and repair my electric toy trains. He was also the driver of the old car that the Arion family was using to get around and to shuttle to Bucharest, where they were living.

By the time I went there for my summer vacation, a large land reform had just taken place, and the land owned by the Arion family was reduced to about three hundred acres, which was very little compared to what they had before. In the Bărăgan Plain, where this land was situated, the boyars had thousands of acres of fertile land that was used to grow grains, particularly wheat and corn. These wide land areas were fit not only for large production of wheat for internal consumption, but also for export. The first communist land reform, giving small parcels of land to peasants, resulted in small producers who barely had enough for their needs and had nothing to give to the state or to sell on the market.

Next, the communists started to force the peasants to put their land in cooperatives, the collective farm Soviet model. This model didn't work in the Soviet Union, and it didn't work in Romania either. The peasants were not convinced that, in the end, they would get something for their work, so they just refused to work. Moreover, with the emphasis on industrial development, many peasants went to work in the new industry and villages became inhabited by older people, women, and children. At harvest time, the government had to send students and soldiers to do the work.

This summer vacation developed in me a taste for living in the freedom of the rural setting. I loved to be free to wonder in the plum tree orchard, or just to sit there in the shade of a tree. I was the only child there, but this didn't bother me as long as I was free to walk around and explore the territory. I used to take a book with me and just lie down and read. I loved the dawn and the evenings when the cows were going back to the barn, and there were all those noises related to preparations for the night. When harvest time came, I enjoyed the excitement of the machines running day and night to take advantage of the days without rain. I also went fishing with an old gentleman, a friend of the Arion family, who woke me up very early in the morning and took me with him to the Argeş River, which was within walking distance. There we spent the day catching fish.

Unfortunately, I learned that the communist regime had succeeded in destroying this wonderful outlet. The Arion property was confiscated like all the other land properties, and I suspect the Arion family ended up in poverty, if not in some concentration camp or jail. The yearning to live in the freedom of nature stayed with me over the years and, by the time I was approaching my retirement, made me decide to build a home outside the city and to have land where I could do some gardening.

My Father under Communism

It is interesting to note that, in the years that followed his return to freedom, it became clear to me, and very likely to others too, that my father had completely rejected his support of communism. Having to live for so long with the communist comrades had allowed him to better know who they really were. These comrades were selfish and interested in their own well-being. For the rest of his life, my father remained strongly anticommunist. As far as I know, he refused to be appointed minister of interior affairs, but he also refused to be hired as the lawyer of the US embassy in Bucharest. Either way, he would have ended in jail or worse.

Sometime after he returned from the concentration camp, my father decided to start a new political party to represent the rather large Jewish community. He invited me to come to a meeting that was held at a movie theater close to the main Jewish neighborhood in Bucharest. There, he and a friend of his, Dr. Cajal, a well-known pediatrician, would deliver talks. I think his subject was the French Revolution. I went there and was seated.

As the theater was filling up with people, my father and Dr. Cajal walked onto the stage. As they were getting ready to speak, suddenly, from different parts of the hall, hecklers stood up and started shouting slogans against my father. It was obviously an affair organized by the Communist Party that was in the process of eliminating the old traditional political parties and did not care to see new parties, that were not under its control, being set up. The meeting ended as my father and Dr. Cajal walked out, thus avoiding any violence that these fellows were obviously ready to engage in. Later, we learned from Mrs. Moscuna's children, who were involved with the Communist Party that it was indeed set up by them. For me and very likely for the other people who were in the hall, it was a frightening experience. We experienced firsthand the taking over of the political power by the Communist Party.

After the takeover of Romania by the Communist Party imposed on the country by the Soviet Union, my father's hope was that "the Americans will come, and we will be free again." He lived many years with the expectation that the Americans will free the country from communism. He was even telling me that he will then buy a Lincoln car. Dreams!

Obviously, my father, like many others, was not aware of the deal between Churchill and Stalin and approved by Roosevelt, according to which Romania should be under Soviet influence in exchange for leaving Greece free of communism. I should add that he was not alone in this hope, which, of course, has never materialized.

> Wikipedia. The Percentages agreement (also known as the "Naughty document") was an agreement between Soviet premier Joseph Stalin and British prime minister Winston Churchill about

how to divide southeastern Europe into spheres of influence during the Fourth Moscow Conference, in 1944. The agreement was made public by Churchill. No confirmation has ever been made by the Soviet Union or Russia, or from the American side, which was represented in the meeting by Ambassador Averell Harriman.

During all the years that he practiced law, my father was quite openly against the communist regime and fought it in court, defending a good number of people who were victims of this regime. A famous trial in which he was involved as a defense attorney was that of Zionist leaders who stood accused of treason, conspiracy against the state, etc. One trial that he lost and which greatly affected him, was that of the engineers who were building the Danube-Black Sea channel. Apparently, the mechanical equipment that was provided by the Soviet Union didn't work, and they were blamed for it, tried, and executed.

As soon as he resumed his professional activity after the war, my father became one of the most renowned and sought-after attorney in the country. During those years, his reputation as an outstanding lawyer reached the top. His income was estimated to be very high, and people wrongly believed that I was a beneficiary of this wealth. In spite of his rather large income, my father was providing us with a weekly allowance, which was just enough to cover the living expenses of my sister and me. Although the financial situation was never discussed with us, the children, or in front of us, my understanding is that this child support was enough to cover only the food expense. In reality, between Tuna and mistresses, there was not much left for us, but that is probably how I learned the value of earning a good living. In order to cover all the expenses, my mother had to work. She had learned typing and shorthand and was hired as a secretary at the Institute for Foreign Cultural Relations, where she worked until she was diagnosed with breast cancer in February 1957 and died one year later.

Judging from my father's reputation as the best and most expensive lawyer in town, people would have thought that I was living in luxury. I remember being invited to dinner by Professor Teodorescu, who was the best oral surgeon in the country and an acquaintance of my father. He had a son of my age and was probably looking to find some good friends of similar social standing for him. His home was something that, until then, I had seen only in movies. After dinner, Professor Teodorescu showed me his home museum, a nice collection of antique objects worth probably a fortune. Obviously, for me, there was no way to reciprocate and to have his son at my home; he would have been shocked to see how I was living in a shared apartment.

Tuna the Socialite

As far as Tuna is concerned, I suspect that she was either expelled from the Communist Party or she resigned while she was in the concentration camp. After being released from the concentration camp, she never tried to go back to her profession or to her political activities; she had reached her goal. She now played the role of the rich wife of a very successful attorney, going out daily at the most expensive cafes, giving parties, and playing poker (and losing money) with other ladies of the same social standing. Money was not an issue for her since my father was quickly becoming one of the most expensive lawyers in the country, and she enjoyed showing this to her friends.

To make sure that money was coming her way and is spent correctly, Tuna started collecting stamps and jewelry, particularly diamonds. She learned quickly that "diamonds are a girl's best friend," and she collected as many as she could with my father's money. When she migrated to Israel in 1959, she managed to ship all these valuables there through the Israel embassy in Bucharest. Since this was illegal, after her departure, Uncle Oscar was interviewed by the Securitate about this transfer. Interestingly, they never called me; they were well informed about who would know what.

It may sound strange, but I believe Tuna made it into the Romanian literature. Let me explain. Not long ago, I read a book written by Vlad Muşatescu. He was a Romanian author of thrillers; some of them parodies of Conan Doyle's books, the stories of the well-known detective Sherlock Holmes. The title of Muşatescu's book, translated into English, is *The Extravagant Conan Two*. The book, in two volumes, contains several novels. I started reading the first one, and after several pages, I was shocked. One of the main characters of the novel was a lady, Marita Nachtigal. I said to myself, *What a coincidence: to use, in a Romanian story, a name that, in Romania, was almost nonexistent!* To the best of my knowledge, in the entire country, there were only two Nachtigal families, both in Bucharest, one being my family and the other a medical doctor.

So was this character inspired by Tuna? My answer is absolutely, yes. Further in the novel, the author describes Mrs. Marita Nachtigal as an avid cigar smoker. Well, I saw Tuna smoking cigars many times, my father's cigars, and I don't think there were many women in Romania smoking cigars. She must have been unique at least for one thing. Moreover, her first name in the book, Marita, contains her first name, Ita. Mrs. Nachtigal, in the book, was definitely inspired by Tuna (this was her nickname). Now I have no idea how and where the author, Mr. Vlad Musatescu, met Tuna, but her social encounters were quite wide. On the other hand, according to his Wikipedia biography, Mr. Mușatescu worked in Bucharest starting in 1946, the same time when Tuna started her social activity and became an active socialite, and his characters were inspired or taken directly from his life.

> Wikipedia. Mușatescu Vlad (born May 4, 1922, Pitești, d. 4 March 1999) was a Romanian writer and humorist. He has written numerous books for children and adults, especially parodies detective, and translated from Kipling, London J., Cronin, Dylan Thomas Caldwell. His books are often written in first person and the facts, places and other characters are inspired or taken directly from the writer's life.

Having plenty of free time and money, Tuna bought a piano (Beckstein) and started taking piano lessons. After not too long, she decided that she had no chance of becoming another Liszt. However, she suggested that I should start taking piano lessons. So unexpectedly, I got a piano and started lessons with her piano professor, who was an elderly lady, Mrs. Solomonoff. As a matter of fact, I enjoyed playing the piano and continued to take piano lessons until I entered medical school in 1951. Mrs. Solomonoff was quite pleased with my performance and, at some point, suggested that I should consider getting into the musical conservatory. I liked playing, but I have never spent the required time practicing, a condition without which one could never reach a higher level of piano playing. I found repeating the same exercises again and again boring. In general, I am not good at repetitive actions, and this exercise meant repeating things many times.

Moreover, since I was eleven or twelve, my mind was firmly set on becoming a medical doctor, so her chances of pushing me into a musical career were close to zero. The piano itself came in handy when I needed money. I sold it after I graduated from medical school to a neighbor living in the same condo. Dr. Epurescu was an oral surgeon, and he bought the piano for his daughter. I believe it helped me using all fingers and not just the index finger typing on my typewriter and later on the computer key board.

As soon as the postwar situation become stable, my sister and I started visiting our father every Sunday morning. It was a fifteen-minute walk from our apartment to the studio where he now lived with Tuna. I continued this routine for as long as he lived there. All I recall is that the general atmosphere was tense with Tuna being around. I continued going there after the death of my sister.

After my father moved to an apartment where he had a waiting room for his clients, I started visiting him on Friday evening. This was the time when I was supposed to receive my weekly allowance and child support. I would arrive usually around 7:00 PM, and most of the time I had to wait till 10:00 PM. He would then finish seeing all his clients, and we would have a late dinner and a short talk. After that, I would go home, and he would go out for a walk before coming back around midnight to start preparing the papers for the trials on the following day.

Tuna was there only when she had guests. These were ladies who were either married to some important persons like herself or relatives of some of the old aristocracy. They were always playing cards, and sometimes I had nothing else to do but watch them play, as I was waiting for my father to get out of his office and give me the money. I remember only one of these ladies whom I liked. Mrs. Bumbescu was the wife of a theater director who had defected to the United States. She was a nice, friendly lady. She died from a heart condition not long after I met her.

Lyceum

By the fall of 1943, after graduating from the primary (elementary) school, I was ready to go to the lyceum. There were several of them run by the Jewish community in Bucharest; the problem was that they all required tuition since the state would not fund them the way it did with the public schools where Jews were now excluded. With my father in the concentration camp, my mother did not have the means to support my tuition. The solution to this problem came from the lyceum that allowed me to take an examination to see if I would qualify for a scholarship. I took the test, passed it, and was enrolled in the first class of the lyceum Cultura B, which was located in a private house on Ioan-Vodă Street. The school year started as usual in the fall of 1943 but ended early at the end of March 1944. That was just a few days before April 4, when the first massive bombardment of Romania by the Allies started. I don't think it was a coincidence.

Fig. 1. Maurice (left) and Juliu Barill (right) at Physical Education in 1st grade at Lyceum Cultura B.

By the fall of 1944, Lyceum Cultura B moved to a better building, and I resumed my studies of second grade, which would be the equivalent of the sixth grade in the American middle school. The following school year, 1945-1946, I continued my studies for the third grade at this lyceum. By the fall of 1946, my father insisted that I should move to a prestigious lyceum, a national college. I accompanied him to visit the principal of the Gheorghe Lazăr lyceum, a certain Mr. Stoicescu, who happened to have been my father's professor of mathematics at the Matei Basarab lyceum. The reunion between the teacher and the former student, now a famous lawyer, was warm. I was accepted to start the fourth grade (the equivalent of the eighth grade in the American system) at this prestigious lyceum. At the end of the fourth grade, I passed the competence examination and entered the fifth grade (the equivalent of American ninth grade).

> Wikipedia. The Gheorghe Lazăr National College (Romanian: Colegiul Național Gheorghe Lazăr) is a lyceum located in central Bucharest, Romania, at the southeast corner of the Cișmigiu Gardens, on the corner of Bulevardul Regina Elisabeta. One of the most prestigious secondary education institutions in Romania, it was named after the Transylvanian educator Gheorghe Lazăr who taught at the Saint Sava College. Founded in 1860, it is the second oldest high school in Bucharest.

My transition from the Jewish lyceum to the Gheorghe Lazăr lyceum was not smooth. Several classmates and professors were openly anti-Semites, and I was the only Jew in my class. Under the new political regime, anti-Semitism was forbidden by law, but that did not change the opinion of some Romanians who were anti-Semites before, and that included both professors and students. This is not to say that all my classmates were anti-Semites. On the contrary, some of them were friendly; and from those years, I had some lifelong close friends such as Ştefan Mironescu, Mihail Grecescu (Miki), Andrei Aubert-Combiescu, Paul Galbenu, and Nicolae Ştefănescu-Gyon.

Fig. 2. The Gheorghe Lazăr National College
(Romanian: *Colegiul Național Gheorghe Lazăr*).

Throughout those years at this lyceum, Miki was by far the best student. He was bright; actually, I believe he is one of the brightest individuals I have met in my life. He was endowed with a sharp mind, an excellent memory, and an outstanding intelligence. Moreover, he had a wonderful personality. I am still proud that, of all my classmates, I picked him to become my good friend. It turned out that we had a lot in common. He was orphaned, and like him, I was raised by a single mother. His grandmother, who was helping out in his household, was French like my Mama Mare, and they resembled physically and, in their accent when speaking Romanian. Miki lived in the same neighborhood, so we used to walk home from school together. In the last three grades, we shared a bench. I think the fact that we shared some family features helped our friendship. Our friendship continued after we finished our graduate education and even after we got married. We even played bridge together.

Miki was an honest individual and was outstanding in his profession. Romania, irrespective of political regime, should have promoted him at least as a university professor or a director of some research institute. Instead, the Ceaușescu regime demolished his beautiful family home and moved him and his family into a peripheral small apartment. I guess this was the time when Miki and his wife Aura decided to leave the country and seek asylum in Switzerland. The loss for Romania was huge. Is there any question as to why this country is what it is, even today?

Fig. 3. The interior court of Gheorghe Lazăr National College (Romanian: *Colegiul Național Gheorghe Lazăr*), where we played in the break time and during the physical education hours.

In physical education, we had a teacher who insisted that we learn and play a Romanian national game called *oina* (pronounced o'eena). When I came to America, I realized this game resembled baseball. Basically, it was a game of batting and running for bases, the difference being that, instead of a ball, it was a piece of wood. In addition, I became a member of the lyceum chess team. Our lyceum team was very competitive. At least two of the team members achieved national recognition, and one was, for several years, the national champion.

In addition to what I was learning at school, my father thought that I needed more education. He hired a private French teacher, Mrs. Ionescu, a young lady who was quite nice-looking and who had tried, along with her husband, to get out of the country by crossing the border. They were caught and put on trial, and my father was their defense attorney. My teaching may have been part of some deal to pay my father's honorarium. I would go weekly to her apartment, which was in a nice villa downtown, and have my French lesson.

Mrs. Ionescu tutored me in the French language, but she also instructed me quite methodically in French history and literature. Although at that time, I didn't appreciate this tutoring too much, I have to admit that I learned a lot about French history and literature. I became familiar with the great classics of the French literature such as La Fontaine and Rabelais, Corneille, Racine, Voltaire and Molière, and history, the French revolution and Napoleon. This definitely enhanced my knowledge and made it easier for me to understand many things when I traveled to France, notwithstanding the facility to speak French, which became my second language. I am still reading French literature. As I got older and wiser, I learned that every foreign language opens new horizons worth exploring.

When I finished the fifth grade, the communist government, which in the meantime had acquired absolute power in Romania, passed a so-called education reform that completely changed the education system. Among other things, it drastically reduced the number of lyceums, which were considered elitist, and created so-called technical schools, which, instead of the last four years of lyceum, would provide four years of technical training in different specialties. This was supposed to generate the manpower required by the intense industrialization planned for Romania. For instance, in technical sanitary schools, students were prepared for health care professions to become either nurses or to go into medical schools.

In order to enter the new lyceum, one had to pass a competitive examination, which I did. In the process of reform, the old Gheorghe Lazăr lyceum for boys was closed. The building, which was and still is, a hallmark of downtown Bucharest, located near a nice park, became a lyceum for girls. We, the former students of the Gheorghe Lazăr lyceum who had passed the examination, were admitted to a new Lyceum No. 9, which was located in the building of the former Spiru Haret lyceum. This is where I would be starting the tenth grade (which was the equivalent of the sixth grade in the old structure).

Fig. 4. Lyceum No. 9 (previously called "Spiru Haret") where I spent the grades 10 to 12.

I must admit that the change turned out to my advantage. The size of my class was unusually small; there were only twenty-four or twenty-five students in this class. Almost all of the professors were outstanding. The most remarkable, as far as I am concerned, was the professor of chemistry, Mr. Constantin Rabega. We had him for three years (grades 10 through 12), and I needed almost nothing in chemistry when I went on to medical school, even though we had Professor Mezincescu and he was a demanding character. Mr. Rabega covered inorganic and organic chemistry and even some biochemistry. His lectures were of perfect organization and clarity. In addition, he would assign some of us topics on which we had to write a review. For instance, my subject was about the application of radioisotopes in medicine. We were in 1949-1950, and this area was, by then, on the frontier of medicine. This was one time when I missed not knowing Russian because one could find a lot of the most advanced American scientific knowledge translated into Russian available at the Russian bookstore in Bucharest. This happened after having several classes of Russian in the lyceum and in the medical school. It followed the way of the German language. Lack of interest and rejection of the aggressor led to a psychological block.

In natural sciences, which included biology, zoology, human physiology and anatomy, we had as professor, Mr. Sanielevici, who was the author of textbooks covering these subjects. His lectures were concise and clear, easy to follow and to learn. Under these circumstances, my preparation for medical school was excellent. I enjoyed his lectures on anatomy and physiology and listened quietly to his lectures on biology. The communist government, implementing its ideology on education, was promoting the Soviet science, which was claiming new revolutionary scientific findings, all fake but fitting into the communist ideology or Stalin's ideas.

Mr. Sanielevici, the old professor, was required to teach this nonsense and he was not comfortable doing it. One day, he interrupted his biology lecture and began accusing me of being reactionary since I was smiling and therefore deriding what he was saying. This was completely false; I was not smiling. There was nothing funny to smile about. His outburst was very likely an expression of his own guilt feelings. Anyway, this did not prevent him from giving me the highest grade at the end of the course.

The last three years of lyceum, spent in a class of only twenty-four or so students and being exposed to outstanding teachers, prepared me for the studies that were to follow. The chemistry that I learned from Mr. Rabega is still with me as I am getting old. Also, Professor Sanielevici taught me the basics of anatomy and physiology. Those were the pillars on which I managed to build further studies and my professional skills. By summer of 1951, I passed the baccalaureate examination and graduated from lyceum. I received the maximum grade of ten in all subjects except mathematics, where I got (unjustly) a nine. I remain grateful to all those wonderful teachers that I had, and I probably appreciate them now more than I did then.

Also, I had exceptional classmates, some of whom remained friends for life: Andrei Aubert Combiescu, who later became the direct supervisor of Sidonia and me; Miki Grecescu, one of the brightest individual I have ever met; Ștefan Mironescu, who was my colleague, not only during the lyceum and medical school, but also during our training at the Oncology Institute and was instrumental in helping me come to Columbia, South Carolina; Paul Galbenu, who became the best pathologist in lung diseases of Romania. So in addition to education, those years were a time when I forged friendships that lasted for lifetime.

By the time I was in the lyceum, all students became enrolled in the new political youth organizations that were set up by the communist government. They changed their names from the progressive youth, to the union of students, or the union of the working youth. Everyone had to be enrolled; refusing meant trouble. However, children of former wealthy people, landowners, industrialists, or war criminals were not accepted into those organizations.

I have to admit that, at that age, neither I nor my colleagues understood the significance of these political activities. We were as credulous or gullible as one can find even in adults with more life experience than ours at that time.

My father tried to tell me to stay away from those organizations, and this made no sense to me. Of course he knew better; his experience in the concentration camps taught him a lot about the true ideology of the new masters. In my class, I was assigned to coordinate a group of students studying a book about the life of Joseph Stalin. We would get together every couple of weeks and discuss chapters of this book about the "wonderful" life of Comrade Stalin. Everyone was supposed to study the book about his life and learn what an absolute hero he had always been. Those were the years when Stalin personality cult reached its peak, and this was reinforced in all the satellite countries behind the Iron Curtain.

In 2001, we celebrated the fiftieth anniversary of our lyceum graduation. The planning was done by Andrei Combiescu, George Teodoru, and Paul Galbenu. Since Andrei was then the director of the Cantacuzino Institute, they met at his office. As I was in Bucharest, I was invited to attend their meeting. The anniversary meeting took place at the Spiru Haret lyceum, but we went to visit our alma mater, the Gheorghe Lazăr National College.

Fig. 5. Andrei Combiescu, Paul Galbenu, George Teodoru, and I, at the organizing meeting of our lyceum graduation, fiftieth anniversary.

Fig. 6. Survivors of our class of 1951. In the middle of the lower row is Mr. Ionescu who was our class headmaster, now 90 years old in perfect physical and mental condition.

Fig. 7. We sat in the same bench in class as we used to. I am sharing my bench with Miki Grecescu.

Culture and Vacation

Those were the years when I got a taste of going to the opera, ballet, and concerts. For the first time, my mother took me to the opera. It happened to be *Der Fledermaus* (*The Bat*). I enjoyed it at that time, and I still do. I continued to go by myself to the opera, the theater being within walking distance from our apartment. I got to see many of the major operas—*Rigoletto, Tosca, Faust, Madame Butterfly, La Traviata, Eugene Onegin, Boris Godunov,* and *Prince Igor*—sung by great artists. I enjoyed each one of them. I also loved classical ballet shows such as *Swan Lake* and *Scheherazade*, and they were of excellent quality.

This was also the time when I started going to concerts that were held Sunday morning at the Romanian Atheneum, an impressive historical building in downtown Bucharest where the national philharmonic orchestra played under some outstanding conductors such as George Georgescu and Constantin Silvestri. The concerts included some excellent soloists: on piano, Valentin Gheorghiu, Mândru Katz, Silvia Șerbescu; on violin, Ion Voicu; on cello, Radu Aldulescu and Vladimir Orlov, just a few names that remained encrypted in my mind for their outstanding performances.

Fig. 8. The building behind the bridge was the Opera house. It was a rather small hall that was previously a theater. In the next block behind the trees was the City Hall where we got married. The bridge covers the Dâmbovița river, which runs through Bucharest.

Over the years, Romania has produced several opera singers and ballerinas of world reputation. Recently, after singing at La Scala in Milano, Angela Gheorghiu sang at the Metropolitan Opera in New York, and Alina Cojocaru was prime ballerina in the United Kingdom with the Royal Covent Garden Ballet and in New York with the Metropolitan Opera. Among the outstanding soloists is Radu Lupu, one of the greatest piano musicians of our times. I am grateful to my mother for opening up this wonderful world of musical art to me.

Those were the years when I also started going to the theater. There were several theaters in Bucharest, and they were all outstanding. From Shakespeare to Romanian writers like Caragiale or Mihai Sebastian, the program covered a wide range, and the actors and actresses were terrific. I continued to go to the theater and to concerts, even while I was a medical student.

In March 1945, I joined my father at the Diham lodge in the Bucegi Mountain. It was soon after my sister, Jacqueline, had died, and my father badly needed to get away. Snow was still on the ground in the mountains as we hiked for about two hours the trail to get to the Diham Lodge. The lodge was run by a family of Romanian-Germans named Roth. They loved my father since they spoke with him in German; they felt like "Herr Doktor," as they called him, was one of them. This was my first vacation spent in a mountain lodge.

The group at the lodge included Dr. Harden Ashkenazi. He was a neighbor of my father and one of very few neurosurgeons in the country. He was trained as a neurosurgeon in France under Drs. Marcel David and Clovis Vincent, and in the States, at Johns Hopkins under Dr. Walter Dandy. He was married, but his wife looked snobbish. They didn't have children, and I accompanied him on several hiking trips. This man's personality impressed me so much that he became my model. I just wanted to be like him, and when years later, I got into the medical school, the first hospital that I went to was the Gheorge Marinescu Hospital, which had the only neurosurgery ward in Bucharest. By then, Dr. Ashkenazi had emigrated from Romania to Palestine. He ended up in Cyprus (many immigrants were imprisoned there by the British), and was smuggled into Israel, where he became one of the founders of neurosurgery. I watched several operations performed by the chief of neurosurgery, Dr. Arseni. The entire thing seemed to be more like butchery and was painstakingly slow, each surgery lasting many hours. The whole experience was on the negative side, and the dream of becoming a neurosurgeon disappeared for good.

In August 1947, I accompanied my father and Tuna on my second vacation in the Bucegi Mountain. We went to the same lodge at Diham. The Roth family was still there and doing everything to make everyone comfortable. I passed my time doing some hiking with my father on the wonderful trails close to the lodge, or sunbathing on the large deck in front of the lodge. I was the only child among the guests at the lodge; everyone else was adult seeking relaxation and a break from their busy life.

I had no interaction with the teenagers who were busy helping the Roth couple to smoothly run their operation. However, one day as I was coming down the stairs from my room, a girl of the Roth family stopped me and kissed me on the mouth. The girl was about sixteen years old and was pretty. We never talked, and I don't know her name. I think this was my first, what I call love kiss and I remember it although at the time, it didn't mean much to me. I was just fourteen years old.

The "Cockerels"

We were close to the end of our vacation at the Diham Lodge when the communist regime proceeded to mandate a so-called stabilization. By then, the country was running on a terrible inflation with prices getting into the millions. What the communists did was to cancel all the money. People, including my father, lost hundreds of millions of lei (the Romanian currency was always called *leu*, which in Romanian means "lion"). The only currency accepted by the national bank in exchange for the new currency was gold coins. These gold coins had been put on the market by the previous government, and since a rooster was on the coin, they were called "cockerels."

> Wikipedia. On August 15, 1947, a revaluation took place, with a new leu replacing the old one at a rate of 20,000 old lei = 1 new leu. This revaluation, called a *monetary reform* or stabilization measure (*mica stabilizare, marea stabilizare*), was carried out by the Communist authorities with absolutely no advance warning and without the possibility to exchange more than a fixed amount of money for the new currency. This was done in order to depose the former middle and upper classes of their last assets, after

nationalization, to prepare for collectivization and to finalize the installation of communism. At the time of its introduction, 150 new lei equaled 1 US dollar. The Romanian currency is Leu.

We continued our vacation at the Diham Lodge, and the Roth family gave my father credit for all of his expenses for food and lodging, being sure they would get paid. I still remember vividly that, after we returned to Bucharest, my father came and gave my mother a gold coin, instead of the child support he used to give her for me so that she could exchange it at the bank for the new money.

My respect for gold relates to those days that have remained well imprinted in my memory. Although I was a child, I understood that, overnight, money can disappear, and one can go from being wealthy to being poor. Is there a lesson to be learned there? I should think so. I should add that, soon thereafter, the Diham Lodge was confiscated (nationalized) by the communist government, and the Roth family disappeared. I revisited the lodge several times while it was under government ownership, and it was no longer what it used to be when the Roths were running the place. I recently learned that it burned down, a sad ending to a beautiful place.

In those years, I used to spend summer vacations at the public swimming pools and lakes. I tried almost all swimming pools in Bucharest and liked to go to some of them like Ștrandul Bragadiru or Ștrandul Tineretului. These were very large swimming pools and for the price of admission, one also got a little cabin the size of a closet for undressing and storing clothes and also for food brought for lunch, which for me usually consisted of tomatoes and feta cheese.

One special place that I had access to in the summer of 1946 and 1947 was the club of the Association of Judges and Lawyers. My father subscribed as a member of the association but never went to the club. Family members had the right to use it, and I took advantage of that. It was a beautiful place on the border of the Herastrau Lake on the northern side of Bucharest. A public bus ran from my home to the club, which was very convenient for me. The Herastrau Lake was quite large, and the club had tennis courts, a pool in the lake, and an excellent selection of rowing boats of all kinds, skiffs, gigs, etc. There were very few people visiting the club, so I was almost alone there. This is the place where I learned to swim, and I also took some tennis lessons. What I liked most was rowing a skiff or a gig. Unfortunately, like with almost anything else in Romania in those days, the communist government took over the club, and that was the end of my vacations there. I have never found a place as nice as that one for spending my free time.

Soon after lyceum graduation, I went on a hiking trip with my friends Miki and Beno in the Bucegi Mountains. As we hiked from one lodge to another, we met a group of our colleagues who were doing the same thing. On one of the last nights, I joined a party at the Diham Lodge, and I drank beer mixed with rum. I am not going to describe what happened to me the rest of the night, but I certainly will never have that mix again. I was young and ready to experience life. It was part of the learning process, I suppose.

Girlfriend

Before beginning my preparation for the admission exam to the medical school, I decided to enjoy the summer vacation and went swimming and sunbathing at the Bragadiru swimming pool, which was not too far from our apartment. Going there daily, I noticed a very pretty girl about my age that came, like myself, every day and was always accompanied by a skinny girl who was a few years younger, probably eleven years old.

One day I approached her, and we began chatting. It turned out that her name was Georgeta Marinescu, but she was used to being called Geta as was common in Romania. Geta was blonde with beautiful blue eyes and a gracious slender body. She told me that she was an orphan; her parents were killed in the first American bombardment of Bucharest on April 4, 1944. She was being raised by an aunt and uncle. She came to the swimming pool chaperoning the younger girl, Rodica, who was her neighbor.

Some days I would walk her and her younger companion to their home, which was in a high-rise condominium and which happened to be on my way home. I liked Geta very much, and from talking to her, I got the impression that she was fed up with living with her relatives and was interested in getting married. Unfortunately, this was a time when I was getting ready for my medical school admission exam. For me, getting ready for the medical school was my priority and a major challenge, and marriage was not a consideration. After all, I was only eighteen years old. Regrettably, our relationship was very short; it lasted just for that summer.

But this is a small world. In 1955, when I started dating Mona, she told me that her brother's girlfriend was none other than Rodica. Rodica told Albert how my behavior had hurt Geta and depicted me as some kind of a monster. I really didn't appreciate at the time how hopeful she was in that short-lived relationship. I felt very sorry for hurting Geta. I am sure she would have made a wonderful wife, but this was not the time for me. In those days, medical students in Romania got married only when they graduated from medical school, which lasted six years, or thereafter, when they had obtained a position as a physician.

Sometime in 1962 or 1963, when I was working at the Oncology Institute, I was riding the bus home when Geta stepped onto the bus. I wouldn't have recognized her as she had changed from a pretty girl to a beautiful lady, but she recognized me. She told me that she had gotten married, but her husband left her while she was pregnant with a daughter whom she was now raising. I was stricken by how bad the destiny of this nice girl was, first orphaned of both parents and then abandoned with a child by her husband. I still believe that she would have made a wonderful wife. She may have been the right person but at the wrong time. My destiny was keeping me in store for someone else.

Overview

Those years were some of the toughest of my life. As a child and a teenager, I was exposed to violence of all sorts, to poverty, and to the embarrassment that comes with it. I lost my privacy, and I had to share my lodging with people with whom I had nothing in common. This constant invasion of privacy was, for me, an unceasing reminder of our condition and a source of humiliation that was not over until Sidonia and I succeeded moving to another apartment. Those were the years when I lost my sister, and I learned about death. This was a very sad event that stayed with me for the rest of my life.

A few bright spots happened when I went on summer vacations to Târgoviște and at Arion's farm and when my father returned from his deportation in the concentration camp and resumed some financial support. In a paradoxical way, the anti-Semitic laws pushed me into some excellent schools. Likewise, the communist education reform had certainly benefitted my instruction. My encounter with the American prisoners of war had left a trace of a dream for a faraway land. Back then, I never thought that one day this would become my homeland.

The serious illness of my mother had definitely left a long-standing mark on my young and impressive mood. It enhanced my attachment to my mother and my resentment for not having my father with us under those difficult circumstances. The long hours of terror in the bomb shelter have emphasized what I would probably inaccurately describe as my religious outlook.

As I am now at the end of my life, or close to it, I can look back over all those years and identify several miraculous events that affected me personally. The wonder that bombs fell hundred yards from our apartment and we survived unhurt and with our living quarters undamaged were, for me, one of them. There were several other instances in my life that would deserve this description. Unfortunately, on other occasions, when I would have given anything to have a miracle happen, it didn't occur.

Those years have been of major importance since I believe the education that I got then was to play a paramount role for the rest of my life. Those were the years when I acquired the basic knowledge, what used to be called in Romania "general culture.", a round education. This involved not only the lyceum curriculum, but also the literature, learning about the arts, getting into the habit of attending a concert, an opera, or a ballet, and enjoying them. All of these habits have endured the test of time; they stayed with me through the years, through profound changes in my environment. I like listening to Beethoven's "Moonlight Sonata" now as much as I did when I was a teenager and was even trying to learn to play it. The same goes for the opera Tosca and many others. I am grateful to my mother who encouraged me to develop a taste for art and to my friends who have shared everything they had with me.

The history of my father and his life left me with the yearning to have a family, with an understanding of the accountability toward those close to you, the importance of having the financial stability and the strength that a united family can bring to its members. From his life experience, I learned what a life mate means. When my pathway crossed Sidonia's pathway, I recognized it and decided, through my free will, to take what my destiny offered. I have no doubt this was the best decision of my life.

One important lesson of those years is that nobody in our times could or should ignore the political environment. If anyone thinks that he or she can live in his or her community like in a cocoon, isolated from what takes place on the large scene of political life, it could turn out to be a major mistake with very serious consequences. I am tempted to say that if something can go wrong in the political arena, it will happen more often than in any other area.

Today like never before, we live in a global world. We find out instantly what happens around the world. We communicate around the globe. The economy has become global, and events that happen elsewhere can have significant consequences on our lives. I am looking back at my family members and how their lives were shattered by political events that they did not foresee or expect. My grandmother, Mama Mare, who was a wealthy lady, with what was thought to be a reliable source of income from dependable oil company stocks, lost everything; Uncle Jonas, who went from owning what appeared to be stable small business, to spending years in a frightful jail and losing everything he owned; my father, who barely survived several years of concentration camp, and was the best lawyer in the country, ended up being disbarred and left without a pension or any other source of income, a pauper. And the list goes on and on. It seems to me that one must learn what is going on in the world and be ready to take life-changing decisions. Missing that could prove to be very costly.

As a teenager, I saw Romania fall behind the Iron Curtain. Did I realize then what that meant for my life? Not really. For me, it took years to understand what was going on. Later on, when in the late '70s, our family life in Romania seemed to be stable and good, I had enough signals to make me decide to go through the ordeal of family separation and the difficulties of starting a new life from scratch, just to be on the other side of the Iron Curtain. Looking back, there is no doubt it was the right decision.

CHAPTER 3

Medical School
1951-1959

Admission

By the summer of 1951, I finished the lyceum. I passed the baccalaureate, which was an exam on several subject matters (mathematics, Romanian language, etc.) with excellent grades, all 10 (grades were from 1 to 10) with one exception in mathematics (only 9), and I was ready to try to enter the medical school. My decision to become a physician started when I was probably eleven or twelve years old, and I never considered any other profession. This was enhanced by reading novels such as *El-Hakim* by John Knight, *Disputed Passage* by Lloyd C. Douglas, or *Martin Arrowsmith* by Sinclair Lewis, describing life of physicians that made me wish clearly to follow this career. When time came to decide my profession, my father tried to talk me to study law and follow his steps in what was a glorious career. However, he also told me that when he was young, he wanted to be a physician, but his financial situation at that time did not allow him to do that. He decided to enter the law school when he watched a play in which a young woman who was unjustly accused was saved by her lawyer. Moreover, becoming a law school student would have allowed him to continue to support financially his family. Attendance of courses was not mandatory.

Admission to the medical school in Romania required passing a competitive examination for the limited number of students admitted. For this year, the size of freshmen class at the Bucharest School of Medicine (presently called Carol Davilla University of Medicine and Pharmacy, then it was called the Institute for Medicine and Pharmacy) was 250. Usually the competition was about 6 or 7 candidates per one student enrolled. The examination involved a written test, and candidates that passed the written test were admitted to the oral examination. The topics that were tested included human anatomy and physiology, biology, zoology, botany, and chemistry.

The admission included a very important social-political screening. Children from family of workers or peasants were favored against children from family of bourgeois origin that included former merchants, owners of small or large businesses (by now nationalized), or land owners (by now many were in jail or concentration camps, and their land was seized). The professionals (physicians, lawyers, engineers) were sort of graded in the middle, better than the bourgeois but still not as high as the proletariat kids. This meant that a larger proportion of the seats was assigned to the favored candidates while what remained of available seats were assigned to the less-favored category. Obviously, this increased the competition in the group I belonged through my social origin.

Social origin meant the financial and political situation of the parents or close relatives. Individuals whose parents belonged by their financial situation to the bourgeoisie who has owned any business with employees (factory, shops, etc.), or had land property requiring hired work, were considered enemy of the people, or class enemies. Also individuals whose parents belonged to the traditional political parties that existed in Romania before the communists took power, were in the same basket, enemies of the people. These individuals were labeled as having a "rotten or unhealthy social origin" and were treated accordingly. They had a hard time being admitted to university, and I know a few that went to work in a factory acquiring thus a healthy social origin in order to be admitted to college. Industrial workers or peasants, with little or no land, and their children were considered to have a healthy social origin and were accepted in any position even when they were not qualified. Having a parent member of the Communist Party also bestowed a healthy social origin. This "social origin," which was contained in the ubiquitous autobiography, was like a genetic marker that stays with you for life with consequences.

Now my focus was the admission exam. I felt that my lyceum education has provided me with quite a strong background. In addition to that, I decided to attend some preparatory classes that the medical school provided free of charge to all the candidates. I remember quite vividly our first class meeting. It was held in a small amphitheater in the medical school building. A professor came as we, a group of about thirty to forty candidates, were seated. He was a rather short guy, wearing eyeglasses and having a curved spine that made him have a shoulder higher than the other one. Later I learned that he was Dr. Marius Fahrer, an orthopedic surgeon, who was also assistant professor of anatomy. After running the attendance catalog, he put his first question to us. His question was about the spontaneous formation of cells in the test tube. As it happened, I had the answer. I raised my hand and told what I knew about this subject.

It turns out that by that time a Soviet scientist, Olga Lepeschinskaya, was claiming that she had successfully grown cells in the test tube in a broth that contained only inorganic stuff. One has to be aware of the fact that this was the period of the Cold War, when the Soviet Union was in competition with the capitalist world, and was striving to prove its superiority in all areas, including science. The imperialist science was wrong, and a new science was created in the Soviet Union. This included biology, where so-called scientists, such as Michiurin and Lysenko, were promulgating new laws in biology that overturned the classical genetics founded by Mendel, Morgan, and Weissman. Romania, as a satellite country of the Soviet Union, was submitted to the same ideology. The new Soviet science was propagated in all education and research Romanian institutions.

One way of propagating these new scientific ideas was through a publication called the *Romanian-Soviet Annals* published by the Romanian Association for Relations with the Soviet Union (ARLUS). My mother, who at the time was working as a secretary at the Institute of Foreign Cultural Exchanges, brought me this publication, which she would get free from her institute. It happened that one issue of the annals contained a detailed description of the experiments of Olga Lepeshinskaya. I read it, found it interesting, but never dreamed how important this will be for my life.

So here I was in the preparatory class, telling Dr. Fahrer about the cell formation realized by Lepeschinskaya. Several weeks later, I had the opportunity to sneak a quick look into the attendance catalog and saw under my name column the rating "exceptional." The grade in the attendance catalog didn't really matter for the admission, and little did I know at that time that Olga Lepeshinskaya will open for me the door to the medical school.

> Wikipedia. Olga Borisovna Lepeshinskaya born as Protopopova (1871-1963), was a Soviet biologist, academician, a personal protégée of Lenin, later Stalin, Trofim Lysenko and Alexander Oparin. She based her career on claims to observe *de novo* emergence of living cells from noncellular materials, and she was infamous for supporting such claims by fabricated proofs. Actually, she filmed the death and subsequent decomposition of cells, than projected these films reversed.

The day of the written admission test came. We were about 1,500 candidates competing for 250 seats. I was seated in the large amphitheater of the medical school, and we received the test. There were two subjects: one, the formation of cells from inorganic material, and the second, the anatomy and physiology of the kidney. Here I went again with the Lepeshinskaya story. I filled up about one page with the description of her experiments with formation of cells from inorganic material. The second subject was straight from the Sanielevici textbook of anatomy and physiology. When the list with admitted candidates for the oral examination was posted, my name was there. It took many years and a strange link of events to find out that at the written test, I was the first among all the 1,500 applicants; I am convinced that very few candidates knew anything about the Lepeshinskaya story because this subject was never covered in the school textbooks.

The next hurdle was the oral examination. I still remember entering the examination room, which was in the medical school library, a large room with high ceiling and a row of tables, each of them with an examiner. At the first table was a man looking awful: completely bald and with a Mongol figure, looking more like Genghis-Khan. Later I learned that this was Dr. Alexandru Caratzali, a man that played a significant role in my life. Also at that time, I didn't know that he was the one who graded me first in the written examination.

In 1961, when I started my employment at the Oncology Institute where Dr. Caratzali was the head of the laboratory of genetics, he introduced me to his assistant Sidonia as a bright medical student and the first at the admission examination. Sidonia told me that years after we got married, but I don't think this played a major role in her decision to marry me. Now he asked me a few easy questions about Michiurin. Very likely, his decision about me was already made a fact, that I was not aware at that time.

I moved to the next table where I met Professor Teitel, the chairman of the Department of Pharmacology. He asked me what I knew about "lilac." In Romanian the same term ("liliac") is used for bats and for the lilac flower. My knowledge in zoology was strong, thanks to Professor Sanielevici, so I jumped to answer the first option. However, Professor Teitel was more interested in the lilac flower, and my knowledge of botany was close to nil. I had it in the lyceum third grade (the American seventh grade), and I didn't like the professor or the matter. Who cared about all these families of flowers? He asked me nicely if just walking in the park surrounding the medical school building I didn't notice the lilac bushes. On a humble voice, I said yes, which was not true but just good enough to satisfy his inquiry. Thus ended our conversation, and I moved to the next tables and examiners where everything went fine, and I was through the admission exam.

Interestingly enough, that evening, while visiting my father and telling him about the exam, he asked me what happened with Professor Teitel. I was a little surprised, to say the least, finding out that he knew people so close to the admission committee. Obviously, with his standing as the best lawyer in town, my performance in the examination was a matter of gossips that extended beyond the committee itself. In any case, my admission to the medical school was a success, but up to this day, I still don't know to what family the flower lilac belongs to. As a matter of fact, I don't think this would matter for anyone involved in medicine, but I can hear the comment, "Can you believe the Nachtigal's son didn't know anything about the lilac flower?"

Freshman with a Passport

The fall of 1951 started in a very exciting way. I was a medical student and thrilled to be. Being a medical student was, in Romania, in those days a prestigious title. We, the medical students, considered ourselves at the top compared with other students. The students at the architecture school were the only ones that claimed to be close to us because they had something to do with arts.

Dissection had something mystical for generations of medical students before us and was, without doubt, the most exciting part. In our medical school, it was performed in large halls with very large windows and rows of stone tables, each one displaying a human body ready to be dissected. For us, the thrill of being dressed in white coats, using surgical instruments such as scalpels and forceps on human bodies, gave us the tangible feeling that we were doctors. The smell of formalin added a special touch to our ego.

In reality, more than learning of anatomy, this experience gives the medical student the harsh feeling of what death is and what medicine is all about trying to prevent it. Much later, we learned that the cadavers we were studying came from jails filled by the communist government with their political opponents. They were emaciated, looking very much like the survivors or the dead of the concentration camp of Auschwitz or Dachau. This made them suitable for our anatomical studies because there was no fat tissue left, and thus dissection of muscles, blood vessels, and nerves was easy to do.

Fig. 1. The medical school, in Bucharest.

Soon after I started the first semester, I received a postcard inviting me to come to the police station to pick up my passport. What happened was that in May, after I have celebrated my eighteenth birthday, with my mother's approval, but without informing my father, I applied for a passport and visa to migrate to Israel. The rationale was that if I fail to enter the medical school, I would have to be conscripted for at least two years in the Romanian army, as was mandated for all eighteen years old that were not students admitted to a university. Learning about the new criteria of admission that involved the social origin made me doubtful about my chances to get into the medical school. Conscription would have been for two or three years and would have put me out of any chances to study medicine.

So one sunny day, I went to the central police station, filled up the application form, and then completely forgot about it. During the following months, I was preoccupied with the preparation for the admission exam to the medical school. After being admitted to the medical school, any interest in following this application was gone. The postcard was the reply to this application and informed me that I was awarded the passport and visa to migrate to Israel. The passport was ready to be picked up at the local police station. Since such a passport was extremely difficult to obtain, usually requiring major bribes or pressure from outside the country, to get it without any special intervention was almost unbelievable. However, it happened; and at that time, I had no idea why and how it did.

As I said, my father was not aware of the whole story, so it was about time to let him know. He was not happy, came to our apartment, and had first a talk with my mother, and then with me. He was strongly opposed to me leaving the country. His argument was that I should go ahead with my medical studies. Going to Israel would have meant immediate enrollment in the army for several years, and it would have been very unlikely that afterward I could resume any studies. My mother, who had no intention to migrate, was pleased not to lose me, so there was no opposition on her side, and he didn't have to argue too much with me either, since with my admission to the medical school, any reason to leave the country became senseless. So I never went to pick up this passport, and up to this day I have no idea what happened with it. My first and maybe last chance to migrate to Israel was gone.

Many years later, I found out what happened. As I was shopping downtown Bucharest, I was looking at stamps in a large Philately shop, which was and still is, behind the Royal Palace and the Congress Palace. A tall and thin old man came to me and introduced himself with a warm and strong handshake. He was Otto Hecht, a lawyer that did his apprenticeship in my father's law office by the time I was born in 1933, and he knew me since I was a baby. Moreover, his sister, Rosy Goldschleger, was one of the best friends of my mother, and her son did tutoring in mathematics with me when I was in the lyceum.

We started our talk with the usual recollections and questions about family, and then completely out of the blue, he mentioned my passport. Actually, he was surprised to see me in Bucharest since in his mind I should have been outside the country for a long time. He obviously knew that the passport was issued, but he didn't know that it has never been collected and used. This was for me an absolute shock. Besides my parents, nobody knew about this passport, and I was sure they didn't tell anyone about it. How did he know? Simply, he was the officer of the Interior Ministry who was in charge of approving passport applications. During those years, Mr. Otto Hecht functioned as a superior officer (I think he told me he was a major) with the Interior Ministry. In this capacity, he changed his name from Hecht to Holban. He told me that he was the one to issue this passport. His explanation sounded like, "How could I refuse my master's son application?" Of course he had no idea that my father, "the master," didn't know anything about this application and most likely would not have approved of it. He just assumed that this was my father's decision. By the time, neither my mother nor I knew what his new function was, and that it will all rely on him. Obviously, these positions were not advertised; most of the times, not even close relatives knew about them.

The first semester in the medical school was probably the most difficult. Anatomy was the main subject and was taken very seriously. The professor was Emil Repciuc, a rather tall man with blue eyes, a blond-red hair, and fair face, speaking Romanian with what seemed to me a German accent. He had a sort of emphatic style of lecturing. Anatomy in those years was considered the foundation of medicine, a concept that probably goes back a few hundred years and has been abandoned. We had to learn everything about the bones, the muscles, the joints, an amazing amount of information that had to be memorized.

Each of the over one hundred bones of the human body had minute details, little holes, grooves, or spikes, each with its own name. Now the names were different, depending on the textbook one used. At that time, it was a trend to globalize the nomenclature and to introduce Latin names for all these anatomical details. That would fit very well the German textbooks that were already using it, but not the French ones that had their names in French and many times used also proper names. The rumors among the students were that Professor Repciuc was an all-Latin-name person and that he actually was using German textbooks as a reference for his course. For me, German text was not accessible (where were you Mitzy?), and I could use them only for looking at the figures and trying to learn the caption, the names that were in Latin. I had the *Gray's Anatomy*, two large volumes translated in Romanian by Prof. Grigore T. Popa that had the Latin names. Popa was a Romanian anatomist that did research in England before becoming professor of anatomy in Romania. I also bought the French Testut anatomy textbook just for the sake of it.

The first oral examination at the end of the first semester was about bones. The professor that examined me was Dr. Robacki, who was associate professor of anatomy. One had to recognize and describe every bone in the body including those small bones that form our wrists, feet, fingers, and toes. I passed it successfully, and during the winter vacation, which was several weeks long, I managed to do more dissection on my own with a couple of my colleagues at the Institute of Forensic Medicine. My father was a friend of the director of the institute, and through this connection, I obtained access to the body of an unidentified woman for dissection. Thus, I spend this vacation in the basement of this institute, studying anatomy together with my friends Paul Galbenu, Doru Sbenghe, and Ștefan Mironescu. We had an interesting company in a group of plastic artist students who were studying human anatomy for a totally different goal. By a strange turn of destiny twenty years later, Professor Robacki would be my colleague when I joined the Craiova Medical School faculty, where he was professor and chairman of the Department of Anatomy.

The second semester went by smoothly as we were getting somewhat deeper into medicine. We were being exposed to some wonderful professors, the quality of which I appreciated only later. After I finished the first year in the summer of 1952, I did some voluntary work in the surgery ward of the Coltea hospital. My first contact with the hospital atmosphere was useful, and I learned several things. Most of all, I saw human disease and suffering. I remember the case of a woman that came from the countryside complaining of sterility. She was married for more than a year, and the couple wanted to have children. It turned out that "she" was actually a hermaphrodite.

Later on this summer, I went on a hiking trip in the Bucegi Mountains with my friend Beno and a group of his classmates. Beno was a student in chemical engineering, and most of the people in the group were from this faculty. We slept for several nights at the mountain lodge Padina in the Ialomița Valley, high up in the mountains. At that time, there was still armed resistance in the mountains waging a guerilla war against the communist regime, and the lodge has been attacked just before our arrival. In the following days, as our group was hiking and doing some rock climbing, we met a group of soldiers that stopped us. Since our identity papers were at the lodge, they accompanied us back there to confirm our identity. I guess it was an opportunity for the soldiers to stop wandering on the mountain trails and have some warm meals and possibly a drink.

We took pictures of us looking like war prisoners surrounded by armed guards. At this age, everything was fun, and this was just another fun event. What resistance? None of us gave a second thought to those poor people that were fighting for their survival opposing the occupation of the country by a foreign force and an alien ideology, or at least nobody made any comment. We all know well our lesson.

I remained for a while part of this group and dated one of the girls, Yvonne. We went to classical music concerts at the Romanian Athenaeum, and we also joined the others in what was called tea parties (nothing to do with the Tea party). These were parties where we listened and danced to American music, Duke Ellington, Glen Miller, and the like. I don't remember drinking tea at those parties, but nobody got drunk. We all behaved nicely, and it was a good feeling of comradeship.

Fig. 2. Summer vacation in the Bucegi Mountain with Beno and some of his friends. 1952.

Communism in the Medical School

The takeover of the political power by the Communist Party was like a disease invading every aspect of the life in Romania, and that included the medical school. When I entered the medical school, some of the faculty were already party members, but some were not. That was going to change. In addition, what was going to change was the student population. Besides the candidates that were admitted to the medical school through the selection process of the admission examination that I described and went through it, there were about fifteen to twenty students that were admitted without any examination. These were communist activists, factory workers that have graduated a two-year special school instead of lyceum or technical school. Not only were they admitted in the medical school without any examination, but also with one exception (Ioan Costică) throughout the years, this group took their exams separately from the other students. Obviously, the professors were persuaded to give all of them passing grades. Behind the closed doors, they never failed. All our exams were oral examinations.

These colleagues were running the political show in the medical school. We were all members of the student organization (it was called the Union of the Association of Students, and then it changed the name to the Union of the Working Youth) that was one of the organizations set up and ruled by the Communist Party. We had meetings where these comrades would pick on some of our colleagues that either were of bourgeois origin, or expressed some feelings that were not in line with the party ideology. "Cosmopolitanism," meaning submission to the influence of the western culture, was one of such points of attacks. These meetings would last until late hours in the night, and were obviously intended to brainwash us and to instill in us fear and submission.

A few years ago, a couple of friends called and told us that they have friends from Bucharest visiting, and they wanted to show them what Romanians can achieve in America. We built our home a few years before my retirement, and it turned out a rather attractive construction. The home looks nice outside and inside, and we have received compliments from almost everybody that came to visit us or do some work. We invited the couple and their friends to come and have dinner.

They came, and I took the ladies for a tour of the home and the garden. After the tour, we sat down and had dinner. As we were talking at some point, the visiting lady said that her brother was a physician, and he was associate professor of internal medicine at the Colentina Hospital, the best teaching hospital in Bucharest. This is the hospital where as a medical student I did my training in internal medicine, infectious diseases, dermatology, and neurology. In each of those clinics, the faculty was of outstanding quality. So out of curiosity, I asked who her brother was. Her reply came as a shock: His name was I. E. Vow! I. E. was my classmate. He was one of the party activists enrolled as a medical student and was not the brightest of them either. As I was recovering from the shock, she was saying that in spite of his position and everything else, "poor" I. E. was living in a small two-bedroom apartment. After the tour of our house, she had new standards to relate to which triggered her last comment "What an injustice!" Obviously, she was referring to the fact that her brother and I have started from the same baseline, and I was enjoying this home while he, in spite of his position and all, was living in a sort of rat hole. Provided of course by the Communist Party!

I felt that the notions of right and wrong would require some clarification. There was indeed injustice, but the injustice was that after graduation, the best and the brightest of the medical students were sent away from the medical centers, and the academic positions in teaching and research were occupied not based on professional criteria, but on political connections. I didn't want to explain that to her, seeing that this would have been probably useless, and after all, she was my guest. This was just the way of thinking that prevailed after fifty years of communism. Moreover, I was grateful that things happened the way it happened, and in the end, I choose America instead of spending the rest of my life and my children's life in Romania. For us, this policy turned out to be a blessing!

By the time I graduated, the Communist Party started to replace the faculty of the medical school. In a few years, all the old professors, even those that were party members, were substituted with younger comrades. A new faculty was installed, and they played according to new rules: Bribery, corruption, and nepotism became the rule of the game, and as far as I know, it still is even though the communist regime has been dismantled. As I was told by Romanians and probably it is true, one could change the rulers, but the ethics stay the same. Corruption is a disease that can last for centuries. A joke describing this situation in Romania is: "They changed the bed sheets, but the girls are the same."

Research and Festival

The second year started, and we were learning some very interesting subjects. Histology, the study of tissues and cells, was one of them. The professor was Ion T. Niculescu, a renowned scientist that has done fundamental research in France and coauthored a classical book about the human brain. A big man with a round figure, his lectures were a joy to attend. For the laboratory, my group was instructed by an assistant professor, Dr. Goldstein. He was an urologist who was outstanding in teaching histology. His textbook written together with Dr. Rivenzon was excellent for the laboratory studies. The figures showing the tridimensional tissue structures that were essential in the study of histology were a novelty at that time and extremely helpful for our learning. Like many other outstanding physicians, Dr. Goldstein and Dr. Rivenzon have ended up in the United States. However, when I visited Romania in 1994, I was told that this textbook was still used in the Department of Histology at the medical school. They were kind enough to make a photocopy of the book and give it to me. I still have it on my shelves together with other medical textbooks, and I used it preparing protocols for my medical students. Some good things never die.

I still remember the final examination in histology. After taking the practical exam, I went to have the oral examination with professor Niculescu. It happened that one of my exam subjects was about the object of his studies. When I mentioned that, he graciously replied, "Maurice, you flatter me," which of course I was, but he didn't seem to mind it. He was one of my great teachers, and I owe him so much. Parasitology and physiology were other major courses given by outstanding professors, Nitescu and Proca. The school year ended with me taking outstanding grades at most of these subjects.

Overall, we used to take detailed notes at the lectures, and these were the basis for preparation for the exams. There were few textbooks available, and in general, professors were interested to make sure that we learned what they were telling us in class. However, we had access to the library of the Romanian Academy, which in those years was quite well supplied with foreign medical textbooks and journals, predominantly American. One of my favorite was the physiology textbook of Best and Taylor. This was a comprehensive and massive volume I was using to complement the lecture notes. To my surprise, when I taught in the medical school in South Carolina, I found out that this textbook is no longer used. In the American medical school, physiology was a semester course, whereas in Romania, we had it for two years. The result was obvious; our American students had to be lectured on elementary physiology, which they were missing.

The contrast between our training in Romania and that which we carried on was very sharp when it came to the interest for textbooks. There is no doubt that there are excellent American classical textbooks that are translated in many foreign languages. The paradox is that, in my experience, the American medical student doesn't use them, preferring to rely on some notebooks that are useful to take multiple choice exams but cannot serve as a broad education tool.

My explanation for this situation is the fact that almost all American medical schools are two years shorter that the Romanian and other European medical school programs. To squeeze in four years, all the information required for a practicing physician is impossible and imposes a terrible strain on the student. Even with the extremely favorable technical conditions that these students have, it is practically impossible to have them learn and retain all the concepts and data that a physician needs.

I was told that the residency is the time when the student, who is by now a medical graduate, learns the craft of medicine, but I don't think this is true. The resident is far too busy covering all of his or her duties in the daily hospital activity and in the process learning the practice of medicine. These wonderful American textbooks remain to be used by foreigners and by professors that have to prepare their lectures, and most likely are not used by the medical student. This is true at least for the textbook that we used in the pathology course over the twenty-six years that I lectured at the University of South Carolina. Every edition of this textbook was so detailed that it would have been totally unrealistic to believe that the medical student would end up learning this massive textbook. Our task as professors was to select from this textbook the basic and transfer it to the students. I should add that the use of computers is changing drastically the learning process. It remains to be seen if this change is an improvement.

During this second academic year, a student scientific group was organized by Prof. Emil Repciuc in the Anatomy Department. I enrolled in this group, and once a week in the afternoon, we would get together, and Professor Repciuc would introduce us to a scientific project that consisted of studying the blood vessels connecting the pituitary gland with a certain area of the brain, the hypothalamus. With each session, we were learning methods of research, gross and microscopic examination of tissues, etc. Our group lasted as long as we were in the medical school, and results of our studies were published in Romanian national medical journals and won awards at the annual competition between different student scientific groups. I believe that this training, with its focus on research, has influenced me for life. This was the first instance when I had to present in public scientific results, and it was a good preparation for the future.

This introduction in basic medical research as an undergraduate medical student was followed by a clinical research that I did when I was a fifth year medical student. During a rotation in internal medicine, I was asked by Dr. Lucian Buligescu, who was my instructor, to help him write a review on the use of corticosteroids in blood disorders. At that time, this topic was something rather new in clinical medicine, and he had a few cases that he has treated with these hormones. My knowledge of English was a major asset for reading the important articles covering this topic, which were mostly published in English and had to be included in this review.

Our review paper was published in the *Romanian Journal of Internal Medicine*, which was the main publication covering internal medicine in the country. Soon thereafter, the Spanish journal of blood disorders *Sangre* (Blood) requested to publish the article in Spanish. In addition to the national exposure, we also got an international exposure in a language of large circulation. For me, besides getting credit for two important publications, it was an excellent practice for writing clinical medical papers.

By summer of 1953, Bucharest hosted the world congress and festival of youth and students. This event was sponsored and organized by the Romanian government and gathered a large number of organizations from all over the world, most of them leftist or openly communists. A previous year, as a freshman with familiarity of English and French, I have spent a short vacation with a group of French students in the mountain resort of Sinaia. My name was probably added to some list that was cleared by the government. Bureaucracy works always the same; once on a list you stay there unless something special happens. The fact that my father has spent all these years in concentration camps as a political prisoner was probably helpful.

Now I was asked to participate as a guide and translator for some of the foreign delegations. For the congress, I ended up escorting the Siamese (Thailand) delegation consisting of three people, a lady and two men. The job was quite easy. These were very nice people, and I would go with them to visits, talks, and meals. I was impressed by their habit of eating very hot meals; they were asking always for the small hot green peppers and would add huge amounts to their meals. For the youth festival, I was assigned as an interpreter to the British delegation. This was a rather large group, very diverse, including Scots wearing the traditional kilts. I slept in the same building with the delegation, and it was a nonstop party. For me it was an excellent opportunity to practice my English, and I took full advantage of that, but I never got paid for this job.

Donald and the Blizzard

Fall of 1953 marked the beginning of my third year of medical studies. This academic year included the first courses of real medicine: anatomic pathology, physiopathology, introduction to internal medicine, introduction to surgery, microbiology, etc. We started participating at rounds in the hospital, and we learned how to examine sick people. This was what we all wanted—medicine. I think this year was probably the most important in terms of our medical education since this was the time when we built the foundation on which everything else was added later on. Like in previous years, we were fortunate to have some outstanding teachers, such as Emil Crăciun in pathology (worked at Johns Hopkins Medical School), Ionescu-Mihăiești in microbiology, and Teitel in pharmacology.

One way for the communist regime to introduce the so-called Soviet science was to insist that all major discoveries were done by Russian scientists. In medicine, it was Pavlov, a Russian scientist who, at the beginning of the twentieth century, has done some interesting studies on the function of the nervous system for which he was awarded the Nobel Prize.

Our course, of physiopathology, which was delivered by Professor Şaragea, was based entirely on what became to be known as Pavlovism. This was a severe distortion of the medical science, and poor Pavlov had nothing to do with it. The result was that medical students hated the subject and the professor, and made it a matter of ridicule. Luckily, we had access to some good textbooks on the subject, who is very important for medical practice; nonetheless, it shows to what extent the political leadership was willing to go to show its submission to Stalin and company.

One of my closest companions in the medical school was Donald Aberfeld. We have been classmates in the Sephardic Jewish elementary school, but then we separated and lost track of each other. Donald was the son of a highly regarded physician in Bucharest, and his mother has been a colleague of my mother in the Notre Dame de Sion boarding school. Unfortunately for us, we had in common the memory of a very sad event. Like me and at about the same time, Donald lost his sister because of a medical accident. His parents had later another daughter, but I am convinced that he remained with the same scar I had.

In January 1954, after we finished our exam session, I went with Donald to the Bucegi Mountains. We took ski equipment with us and climbed the snow-covered trails. The first day we stopped at the inn at 1,500 meters (about 4,500 feet), and the next day we climbed to reach the highest plateau at over 2,000 meters (about 6,000 feet). The mountain was covered with deep snow, and that markedly slowed our hike. The night caught us hiking. Fortunately, it was a quiet night, and the moonlight reflecting on the snow, made it for a quite luminous night. At some point on the trail, we met a group with a guy who apparently just broke his leg. While his friends carried him along, we helped carry his ski equipment and backpack, but that slowed us even more. It was around midnight when we reached the lodge, and after a late dinner, we went to bed. The following days, Donald did some skiing, and we had fun with other people at the lodge.

After we returned home, Bucharest had the worst blizzard in anyone's memory. It snowed abundantly for about three days, and the snow piled up so high that on the street where I lived it reached the level of the first floor (this would be the second floor in the US). One evening, Donald came to my place, and we went for a walk to see the city completely covered with snow, and of course, all transportation, public or private, totally blocked. It was indeed a memorable sight!

Fig. 3. This was the worst blizzard of the twentieth century of Romania: the snow reached fifteen feet in some places. To open the tramway tracks, people, had to dig by hand day and night as shown here in downtown Bucharest. The government asked all the people to volunteer for snow cleaning.

One thing that Donald and I did while we were medical students was translating foreign medical textbooks. These textbooks were impossible to buy in Romania, and in those days, there were no copy machines available. In the second year, we translated a textbook of biochemistry, which was a French book written by Polonowski. Biochemistry was and still is a very important course in medical education. We had two professors, one who was a political appointee (Simion Oeriu), and the other Mrs. Eugenia Soru, an excellent teacher and outstanding scientist. Biochemistry requires chemical formulae, and those were difficult to write down during the lectures, so the translated textbook covered this omission. Also, biochemistry was progressing rapidly, and we were anxious to get the latest discoveries in this field, which were included in the foreign textbook.

Another textbook that we translated was an English textbook of neurology by Russell Brain, which we used in preparation for the exam session at the end of the fifth year. The neurology course was given by

Professor Sager, an outstanding scientist trained in the United States, but not a very good teacher. We had to supplement his lecture notes with a textbook. We worked almost nonstop, day and night, as Donald was typing on his typewriter. He loved to use it.

My relationship with Donald resumed after we settled down in the US in 1981. In 2007, it was the fiftieth anniversary of our graduation from the medical school. Sidonia and I went to New York, and we had a celebration with several colleagues including Donald. When we visited his apartment, he took us to the roof of the skyscraper where he lived to enjoy the view. We had a delightful dinner with Sidonia and his wife, Louie.

Fig. 4. Celebration of the fiftieth anniversary of our graduation from the medical school was shared with (from left to right) Relu Zenker, Donald Aberfeld, Daniel Constantinescu, Constantin Iliescu, and I in NewYork, August 2007.

Fig. 5. Dinner with (right to left) Donald, Sidonia, and Louie, in a New York restaurant. August 2007.

Fig. 6. Louie, Donald, and Sidonia on the roof of the skyscraper where they live in New York. August 2007.

Military Training

In the summer of 1954, we had our first military training. Since students were not required to do the two-years conscription, we had to do the military training during our medical studies. Once a week, we would spend one morning receiving instruction from military physicians. They would teach us the organization of the military medical service. In addition to this theoretical instruction, we were supposed to have two months of practical military training; so by the summer of 1954, we had the first month of instruction.

It all started in the Bucharest North Railway Station, where we were embarked in train cars that were supposed to be used for cattle and not for people. The train left in the evening, and by morning we disembarked in the town of Caracal. This was and probably still is a dusty, sleepy town in the middle of the Bărăgan plain, which extends along the Danube and is very good for growing wheat but not as a tourist attraction. It is very hot and dusty in summer and very cold and windy in winter.

We were taken to a military casern, given military dress and equipment. We became soldiers and met our military instructor, a drill sergeant named Popuța Vasile, who was a living proof that the Neanderthal race has not vanished. He had all the physical traits and behavior of what is supposed one of this race to have. It is true that we all grinned when he introduced himself because his name *Puța* means in Romanian something like "small penis." There were a few spontaneous questions like "What?" or "What did you say?" and he didn't appreciate that. So it was a bad start, and things didn't improve thereafter. He was not a friendly guy, had all the inferiority complexes possible facing medical students, and didn't hesitate to use his authority to prove that he is the boss. Luckily, the officer of our company, a certain Lieutenant Blănaru, was a nice man, and that helped.

For a month we trained like regular soldiers, learning how to run fully dressed and with a rifle that was probably used during WWI and weighed twenty pounds or so under a heat that was over one hundred degrees Fahrenheit. In spite of everything, we took it in stride. After all it lasted only a month, and we were young and medical students. This was the only time in my life when I fired a rifle and a revolver with live ammunition doing target shooting. Every Sunday afternoon, we were allowed to go downtown. The town of Caracal had nothing to show, but it had a small central park with a lake, and we used to go there and walk around. We were happy when it was over, and we could take a regular train to go back home.

Poland and Albert

Fall of 1954 with the new academic year followed. This was MIV, and there were now more specialized courses: ob-gyn, pediatrics, more internal medicine, and surgery. The mornings and some afternoons were spent now in the hospitals, accompanying the attending physicians who were also our instructors. As we were advancing in our study, we were also regarded differently by the physicians. We were now more like younger colleagues than students and were treated accordingly. Some of the professors were just awesome. I remember Prof. Radu Păun in internal medicine. His lectures were so well thought; they were just a flow of well-organized essential information. These were outstanding physicians that have played a crucial role in my professional development. Their influence was long lasting; I could say lifelong.

After we finished classes by summer of 1955 I was sent, together with a group of my classmates to Ploiești, a city about thirty miles north of Bucharest, for two months hospital training in obstetrics and gynecology. We were lodged in a lyceum dormitory and had our meals at the municipal hospital. We were exposed to the routine of medicine, seeing patients under the supervision of the attending physicians. One of the most memorable occurrences for me was when I was asked to examine and clean a uterus after a delivery. The goal was to make sure that after the placenta was expelled, which occurs soon after the delivery, there are no remnants of the placenta left in the uterus that may create complications. It was a very strange feeling to introduce the hand and the forearm almost to the elbow in the uterine cavity and to use the fingers like a small rake to remove any debris that would be left there.

This summer training ended for me sooner than it was planned. I was recalled to Bucharest, and sent as an interpreter to the International Youth Festival to be held in Warsaw, Poland. In this capacity, I traveled by train going through Hungary and Czechoslovakia. The special train stopped in several towns along the road, and the Romanian delegation was met by the local youth organizations. The trip took about three days as we stayed on the train, sleeping and eating there. Living in these rather small quarters, I met my fellow travelers. I befriended one of them with whom I found an easy communication and a very pleasant companionship. By the time, I never dreamt how important role he would have in my life.

This was Albert Niculescu, a guy that I knew from the lyceum. He was two years younger than me, but well known in the lyceum for his outstanding ability for giving public talks and reciting poetry, a feature that he kept into adulthood. He was the son of one of my medical school professors, Florin Niculescu, who lectured to us on Microbiology while we were in the third year.

Florin Niculescu graduated as an MD from the Cluj School of Medicine and trained and worked for about twenty years at the famous Pasteur Institute in Paris. In those days, he was one of the pioneers in Microbiology. In 1939, Florin Niculescu was invited to return to Romania. He accepted the invitation and came to Romania. After his return, he was appointed member of the Romanian Academy, a very prestigious position.

After WWII, as the political power passed in the hands of the Communist Party, Florin Niculescu became a member of the party and was appointed deputy in the National Assembly and, at some point, even vice-president of this institution. He succeeded to create a Microbiology institute.

One of the assistants of Professor Niculescu was Ion Şerban. The fate of Ion Şerban was not good. He ended up spending some time in jail for being the son of a politician, a prominent member of the Liberal Party who provided support to King Michael I in preparation for the action of August 23, 1944. His father was arrested on the night of May 5 1950 (called "night of officials") and led, along with all the group of former officials, in prison in Sighet, where, in 1952 or 1953, he was tortured to death.

After Dr. Şerban was released from jail, he got a position in the Microbiology Institute, was allowed to do research, and was the leader of one of the few remarkable research groups in the institute. After many years, he was allowed to leave Romania and migrate to Greece, probably because his wife was of Greek nationality. In 1980, after I defected from Romania and while I was waiting for my American visa in Paris, I met him at the Pasteur Institute, where I was working, and he was visiting as a member of the Pasteur Institute in Athens, Greece. We were both happy to meet outside the communist Romania.

On this trip to Poland, I became friends with Albert Niculescu. Among the members of the Romanian delegation that very likely, most of them were agents of the Securitate and/or governments officials, we were quite isolated. We did our job as interpreters of speeches that were delivered as the Romanian delegation met delegations from other countries. These speeches were more or less repetitions of the government propaganda. Albert was a charming companion, knowing lots of people and gossips. He was a student in chemistry and apparently a bright one. We enjoyed each other's company, and at our return home, we promised to keep in touch.

Mona

It was one day in the fall, after the school has already started, when I called Albert. He invited me to his home for a Sunday afternoon chat and I decided to go. Instead of Albert, I was received by one of his sisters. She introduced herself as Mona, made some excuses for her brother, and promised that he will show up soon. In the meantime, she will try to replace him. We sat down in Albert's room and started chatting. I learned that she was also a medical student two years younger than me. After what she told me, she got into medicine to please her father, but she was more interested in literature, particularly poetry. She was acquainted with several young poets and writers, and a movie director was apparently trying to become her friend.

As she was playing the nice host, I recalled that I have seen her before. It was at one of the manifestations for a communist holiday, either May 1 or November 7, when all the students, along with all the working people of Bucharest, moved in columns organized and managed by party activists, to demonstrate their allegiance and support of the communist system and leadership. These processions lasted hours; we gathered usually early morning, and started the long walk to the tribunes, a place that we reached around midday, where the party leaders were standing to watch us, as we were passing in front of them, carrying pictures of the communist leaders, Lenin, Stalin and the local leaders. Medical students from every year were in the same column together.

Now as I was looking at Mona, I realized that she was the one person that I noticed on one of these occasions. I remembered that as we were stopped on the main boulevard leading to the tribunes, she was sitting on a small stone fence on the sidewalk. What I found noticeable then, and that happened many times thereafter, was how out of place she looked. She did not seem to belong to the rest of the people surrounding her. With her outstanding auburn hair arranged in a knot on top of her head, and the way she was showing her boredom, she was asking for the classical question, "What is a nice girl like you doing in a place like this?" At that time, I didn't know who she was; I didn't ask her this question and anyone else about her, just noticed how out of place she looked.

The afternoon hours passed by swiftly, and at some point, I realized that Albert is not showing up, and I am getting to enjoy Mona's company a lot. By dinner time, I left with some vague understanding that I may call back. However, on my way home, I realized that I have met "the very special one," but I also had a strong feeling (a premonition?) that all will end up hurting me badly. The difference in our social condition was huge. She belonged to an upper rank and I to a lower one.

The following days, I was involved with the new courses of the fifth year of medical school: more ob-gyn, pediatrics, internal medicine, infectious diseases, surgery, neurology, hospital rounds, etc. Soon I recognized that Mona's image would not go away, something that never happened to me before. Although I have no regrets about what followed, I should have thought more about my "premonition." In the long run, it turned out to be fulfilled. I guess I was just following my destiny.

By the end of October, I did what I never did before. I called and asked her to go for a walk. She agreed, and we met late afternoon somewhere close to the medical school. Being in the third year, she was still having lectures and laboratories in the medical school building. She was wearing a brown leather jacket that somewhat matched her beautiful long golden-red hair set up in a knot on top of her head. The day was October 26. We celebrated this day as long as we were together, it was our anniversary.

We started walking on the streets not far from the medical school. It was already getting dark as the days were shorter. On the tree-lined streets, there were a lot of dead leaves, and she enjoyed stepping and crushing them. Then we reached a short street were there were no more dead leaves. There was no traffic and no one in sight. We stopped under a street light, and I took her in my arms, embraced her, and kissed her. This moment I felt like we were bonded. I knew then and there I will belong to her for life if she wanted. This feeling of bonding was coming back every time I hold her in my arms, which I loved to do. The intensity of fondness that I developed for Mona was such that I thought it would be unbreakable and would survive in spite of time, space, and everything else, if it would be shared. For me it was a desire of sharing and of absolute trust. I was then twenty-three years old, and she was my first love. The thought that she will be my only love lasted longer than four years.

I had a record with the song "Autumn Leaves" I received from a French medical student that I met in a mountain resort. Soon after we met, I gave it to her as a reminder of our first walk together, but also for the words of the song that in a certain way foretold the story of our relationship, which started with autumn leaves. By then, I wouldn't know that it will end four years later. Although our relationship ended up the way it did, I consider myself fortunate to have these four years of my life with Mona. As long as I live (and even beyond if there is something like this), I will be grateful to her for each day that we have been together and for each memory of her that I carried with me through my life.

From that day on, my life changed drastically. I just couldn't stand not to be with her. I started meeting her and visiting her very often. I became a permanent guest of the Niculescu family and was invited to dinner as often as I happened to be there, which was almost daily. The family seemed to like me. Her father was somewhat distant, as would be normal, considering that I was a medical student and he, professor and more. With time, I realized that he was also reserved with his children. His children had a respectful love for him, and Mona was particularly attached to him. I suspect that she was his preferred child.

Mrs. Roxana Niculescu, Mona's mother, was a dominant personality that could easily go from rage to tenderness. Mrs. Niculescu spoke Romanian with a special accent, but this did not prevent her to be very active in supporting and taking care of her family, her husband, and their three children.

Beside her brother, Albert, Mona had also a younger sister, Tina. Tina was studying Chinese at the university. I got along very well with Tina and her parents. At some point, they introduced us to playing bridge. Neither Mona nor I had ever played this game, but her parents seemed to find it a pleasant way to spend some evenings. Since they needed another couple of partners, they recruited us, and we ended up spending evenings playing bridge with them.

Mona and I were quite busy with the medical school, but we found the way to spend our free time together. We listened to music, read books, poetry, and shared everything we thought will bring joy to the other one. Mona introduced me to the *Little Prince,* a book by Saint-Exupery that she loved, and to Wagner's opera *Tristan and Isolde.* We listened to Rachmaninoff's and Beethoven's piano concerts, and Grieg and Chopin, and many more. We enjoyed going to the Nestor Coffee Shop and have their special coffee with cream. What was special between us was probably our desire to share everything. She was not only my love, but also my friend to whom I would open my heart. This was a time when Mona has replaced all my friends; for me she was all that mattered. Mona had a special beauty; she was looking different, with her sparkling blue eyes and long auburn hair. She was generous, she was selfless, and she had an outstanding emotional response to beautiful things from poetry to music.

One summer, we went hiking in the Bucegi Mountain, just the two of us. Mona was not used to hiking, and I was happy to introduce her to this hobby. I don't think she enjoyed it, and after we split, I doubt that she did it again; but on this occasion, she did not complain and was a brave and trustful companion.

Mona loved the beach, and we decided to go and spend a week at the Black Sea. Going there meant that we were going to share a room, something that her parents wouldn't probably found acceptable. She preferred to tell them that we were going to the mountains and staying in lodges, where there were only common dormitories with numerous beds. The first move was to get her beach apparel out of the house, which we did by throwing her stuff from the first-story balcony of her bedroom to me to catch it in the street. A modern Romeo and Juliet setup!

We took the train and arrived in Constanța, the major town on the Black Sea, and we rented a room in a modest house somewhere in downtown Constanța. We decided to go to the beach in Mamaia, which is a few miles north of Constanța. I have never been there. In fact, this was the first time since my childhood that I was at the beach, but Mona had been there before since the academy had a villa in Mamaia that could be used by family of the academy members. There was a public bus going to Mamaia from Constanța, and we used it.

Today Mamaia is a major vacation resort with many high-rise hotels build on the beach, which is almost gone. In those days, Mamaia was a beautiful place. It had a wide beach with very fine sand, small dunes, and just a few nice villas spread around. There were very few people on the beach, and we thought we have it all for ourselves. We were wrong! I think it was the second or the third day on the beach when, to our big surprise, not far from us, we saw a good friend of Mona, Jean, the son of a well-known member of the Romanian Academy. It was too late to avoid him, and he was as shocked to see us there as we were. He was staying in the academy villa, and we had a nice chat on the beach. As far as I know, he has never mentioned our encounter to anyone, a true gentleman. This trip to the beach remains one of my best memories from these years. This was my return to the beach where I used to go as a very young child with my mother and my sister. This time I was with whom I thought will be the love of my life. I kept coming back whenever I could. Seven years later I returned there with Sidonia, the true and only love of my life.

Sometime by the end of 1956, Mona told me that her parents would like me to express my intentions, which as everyone knows means that it was time to ask for her hand. To me this idea seemed pointless because I was so devoted to Mona that life for me meant her and only her. Anyway, I asked for a sort of formal appointment with Professor Niculescu, and I told him that as soon as I finish the medical school I would like to marry Mona. He asked for a few days to think about my request. After several days, his answer was positive. He didn't seem to have any reservations on his part, but no enthusiasm either.

Our "engagement" was followed by visits of my father with Tuna and, separately, of my mother to the Niculescu family. We (Mona and I) were concerned about the meeting of our fathers because of their political standing: My father was openly anticommunist while her father was an outstanding party member. Luckily, the meeting went on smoothly since they found out that they have been students at the same lyceum, which gave them a feeling of being classmates and shared their memories about professors and such. No political subjects were touched.

Mother Has Cancer

The year 1957 was probably one of the most evil of my life. It started badly and ended dreadfully. In February, we have finished our first semester exams and had a short vacation. We decided to go to Predeal, a ski resort in the Bucegi Mountain. Before leaving, my mother told me that she will go to see a doctor for something that she felt in her breast. I had an uneasy feeling about leaving her, but we have planned this vacation in advance, and there was nothing to let me expect something bad.

We took the train to Predeal and settled down. I checked in at a hotel, and Mona went to her villa, where we spent the rest of the day. In the evening, the phone rang. It was my mother telling me that the doctor told her that she has a tumor and has to see a surgeon. I put the phone down and felt that the world is crushing around me. Mona tried to inject some hope, but it was useless. Our vacation was finished, and not only that, in retrospect, I know that this was the time when all it mattered to me was my mother's illness. And that included Mona.

The next morning, we were on the train going back to Bucharest. I was looking out the window and had a premonition. I knew that I was going to lose my mother. A long struggle was in store for me, trying to save my mother's life. Indeed, she had breast cancer, and it was quite advanced. In this nightmare, Mrs. Niculescu was helpful introducing us to the best specialists. My mother went bravely through radiation and then surgery. She was in the hospital recovering after surgery when we celebrated her fiftieth birthday. I bought fifty tulips and took the flowers to the hospital, where I was spending all my free time.

By June, disaster struck. My mother developed bone metastasis. They were extremely painful, and I knew we were losing the fight. As a last hope, or most likely a delusion, I decided to try to send her to France, where we thought medicine was more advanced than in Romania and where people from the higher-ups would go for treatment. I started the paperwork collecting medical advice. Of major help were my neighbors, Mr. and Mrs. Bălănescu. He was quite high in the Communist Party hierarchy, being the chief editor of an important magazine. They were friendly with me, I was giving penicillin shots to their two sons, particularly the elder one, who was treated for rheumatism and needed prophylactic penicillin.

In the meantime, I was finishing my medical school. The last hurdle was called the state exam, a sort of exit examination covering, internal medicine, ob-gyn, pediatrics, and, scientific socialism. I don't know how I managed to pass these examinations, considering my state of mind. Eventually, I did and even ended up among the first three of my class. By the time I took my last exam, I came home, and my mother was waiting for me. She handed me a letter that she wrote for this occasion and that I keep to this day. She wrote this letter five months before her death as she was struggling with cancer spreading through her body. This remained her will:

"Burşi my treasure, I know I will not be able to put out a word therefore I resort to this paper and let it talk. This month there are 18 years since I took you to school for the first time. I can see like today a scrawny little kiddy, with black shorts and white collar with a blue ribbon. I knew then that I go hand in hand with a future scientist, I felt it then and I feel it now. Burşi my desire is and should be also your watchword in life: don't be an ordinary man, become someone the whole world should talk about. You have everything you need for this so go ahead! Head up! Do not be scared by difficulties because we know how to fight and to overcome difficulties. I give you my blessing as your mother in the new stage in which you enter today in the same month in which for the first time you stepped on the road of the book. Do not forget that we are the people of the book and of learning. Good luck and happiness! Mom. September 16, 1957." Sidonia saved this letter and brought it from Romania, and when I read it, I see my mother giving me the letter, and I still feel the pain of losing her so early, when life was just beginning for me, and she could have at last enjoyed the reward for her long and difficult struggle to take care of me and bring me up.

Fig. 7. Adine and Maurice, Summer of 1957.

The passport and visa for France for my mother were issued quite promptly. Concurrently, my mother started chemotherapy. By that time, chemotherapy for solid tumors was just at its beginning. One of my professors of internal medicine at the Colentina Hospital was a certain Dr. Dulce. He was a hematology specialist, and cancer of the blood was already treated with chemotherapy. He advised me how to manage and obtain the compounds. The first injections worked well. The bone pain subsided, and by the time when she was ready to leave for France, my mother was upbeat and confident. A few days before leaving, my father came to say good-bye. Their meeting was between the two of them, and when it ended, both seemed pleased. I still wonder what was said, but nobody thought then that within three years, neither one will be part of this world.

At the beginning of November, Mona and I took my mother to the North Railway Station and installed her in a sleeping car that would take her straight to Strasbourg. She waived, we waived, nobody cried, the train took off, and that was it, the last moments when I saw my mother. In Strasbourg, she stayed at her cousin Colette and was given in the care of a doctor that was interested in cancer therapy. He tried several new compounds, but he was not used to chemotherapy and blamed it for the rapid evolution of the cancer. The reality was that the cancer my mother had was one of the most aggressive. Professor Crăciun, my teacher of pathology who saw the microscopic slides had already told me so. The cancer spread like a wild fire through my mother's frail body, and the end came after less than three months in France.

For me, this loss was and remained very painful. Although it was not unexpected, I have put a lot of struggle and hopes in fighting this awful disease. And now everything was gone. I had some afterthoughts about the decision to send her away, knowing that this may be useless. In retrospect, I am glad I did it at least for one reason. Her grave is in Strasbourg and not in Romania. I went to Strasbourg many times since I left Romania. I have the feeling that she is at home there. When as it is customary, I put a little stone on her tomb, I always have a special feeling that is hard to describe. It is pain, but also the feeling of telling her "here I am, Mom, and will never forget you. I'll love you as long as I live."

First Year of Medicine

After graduating from the medical school, the government has allowed a one-year internship to be carried out in Bucharest. I choose to do a six months rotation in a children hospital and another six months rotation in internal medicine. The children hospital that I choose was the pediatric section of the Hospital No. 9 Gheorghe Marinescu. There I became friendly with an attending physician, Dr. Viorica Voiculescu. She was an energetic and bright pediatrician, an elegant and beautiful lady with the walk of a queen, willing to share her medical experience with the younger colleagues and also socializing with us. She was the wife of Prof. Vlad Voiculescu, one of the best neurology experts in the country.

We were asked to do night rounds, and I still remember my first night shift. I had a case of a five-year-old boy that was in a coma because of tuberculosis meningitis. Although he was a hopeless case, I tried to keep him alive at least through the night of my shift. This kept me busy the whole night. Further night shifts were more difficult. There were serious cases to monitor, and some were losing the battle for survival. We were now real doctors although we were under the guidance of an attending physician, and this was real medicine with life and death, daily and nightly issues.

After six months, I moved to the internal medicine section of the Bucur Hospital, a small hospital not far from my home. There I worked under the supervision of Dr. Eugen Mateş, a big man with red hair, very friendly, and a good physician. Here I was not required to do nightly shifts, and I was dealing mostly with chronic cases. I learned there a lot of practical medicine that helped me later on.

During this year, I took the opportunity to go and work at the Microbiology Institute. I was assigned to the group that was in the process of developing tissue culture, a technology that was just a few years of age in the world. Leading this group were Drs. Ion Aderca (Hans) and Marius Ianconescu. They accepted me willingly, and I learned a lot on the technology of tissue culture. The trypsinization procedure that I learned there, which was used to prepare cultures of cells, I applied years later to the chromosome analysis of solid tumors. Both Hans and Marius were outstanding scientists. I was very much interested in this new technology; the capacity to grow cells in the test tube was fascinating and seemed to open endless possibilities. This fascination with looking at living cells growing in a test tube stayed with me for the rest of my active life. I had an original contribution to their work doing some special staining on the cells they were growing, and Hans and Marius appreciated my contribution and gave me credit on a paper published in 1959 about the procedure they have developed.

With time, Hans and Marius became my friends, and they stayed by me with some exceptions, in good and bad times. Hans was married to Geta Danielescu, a colleague in the Microbiology Institute and an expert on interferon. They had a child, Andrei, who later on moved to Canada. Marius, who was younger, was married to Hilda and had two children, a boy and a girl. Later on, Hans divorced, remarried, and immigrated to Israel and farther to the United States. Marius migrated to Israel, where I visited him in 1990. This was soon after Hilda died of a heart attack. He was mourning Hilda and was depressed. They were both chain smokers, and his apartment where we stayed in Rishon-Lezion, a suburb of Tel-Aviv, felt like a smokehouse.

Father's Troubles

My father ran into political troubles a few months after my mother's death. This is what happened as related by Petre Pandrea in his book, *Memoirs of a Valach Mandarin* page 245. "On May 9, 1958 Alfons Nachtigal, the prince of Bucharest lawyers and my friend the Lord, was removed from the bar association because in doctors lawsuit he claimed that it is a miscarriage of justice that was easy to repair as it has been repaired the lawsuit of poisonous doctors staged by L. Beria in the (Soviet) Union." Several doctors, most of them forensic pathologists, including the director of the Forensic Medical Institute, were in jail and put on trial accused of receiving bribes. My father was referring to the trial mounted by Beria, Stalin's henchman, against several doctors accused of attempting to poison Stalin and other leaders of the Communist Party of the Soviet Union. Most, if not all these physicians, happened to be Jews, and the whole affair was presented as another conspiracy of the Zionist imperialist cabal. After Stalin's death, the trial was dismissed. Beria was put on trial, condemned, and executed by his party comrades.

In the defense of the Romanian doctors, my father was just giving an example of a staged trial that at the end proved for what it was—a fake. The leaders of the Interior and Justice Ministries didn't appreciate this comparison and punished him severely by disbarring him, thus leaving him without any income. According to comments that I heard at that time, they considered putting him in a concentration camp. Only his stage in the fascist concentration camp during the war seemed to have saved him for what would have been a death sentence.

However, removing him from his daily activity to which he was so dedicated and successful, had severe psychological consequences and probably expedited his physical demise. On top of all, he was left without any income, and he had to appeal to Willy, his brother in Mexico, to provide money for his daily expenses. As far as I was concerned, after all what happened with my mother's illness and death, that was not good news. I had to limit myself and my grandmother to my salary that I was receiving from the hospital as an intern.

A Warning?

Summer of 1958 came, but for me there was all work and no vacation. Mona set off with her parents to the Black Sea Mamaia resort, and I went several weekends to see her. I used to take a night train that would arrive there in the morning. Her parents were, as usual, kind with me, and invited me to share lunch with them at the restaurant of the fancy Rex Hotel, where they were staying. The hotel was open to the upper echelon of the Communist Party. At the restaurant, I recognized one of the daughters of the supreme leader of Communist Party, Gheorghiu-Dej, with her husband, Mr. Grigoriu, who was a pop singer.

At one of my visits, as we were having lunch in the hotel's restaurant, Professor Niculescu started giving me a talk. This was quite odd; he almost never talked to me during my many visits to their home. The essence of his talk was that since I was not a member of the Communist Party, and on top of that I was also a Jew, I had no future in Romania. I should add that this was the time when a massive emigration of Jews from Romania to Israel was ongoing in conjunction with the removal of Jews from all positions of any significance in the party and throughout the administration and the industry.

I still remember vividly this scene because it was so unusual and unexpected. First, to have my future father-in-law talking to me on a personal matter, and second, the contrast between the surroundings, the restaurant filled with all these higher-ups party members, and the subject of the talk. For me it was like saying, "Man, don't you see you don't belong here?" Still at the time, all this talk was irrelevant for me; my commitment to Mona was forever. This was a time when after my mother's illness, I was returning to her; she was all I had left. I would not have conceived life without her.

Eye Surgery

At the end of the six months stage at the Bucur Hospital, Mona and I decided to take a short vacation and to go hiking in the mountains. It was a gorgeous September day when we joined another couple, Jean, and a colleague of her, Ana. We decided to go to the Ciucaş Mountains that have not very high peaks, around six thousand feet, but are very nice and easy to hike. As we left Bucharest by train, I remember having a terrible headache, a migraine that lasted for a couple of days. However, it finally went away, and the four of us had a wonderful time in the mountains. Back in Bucharest, I still had a few days of work at the hospital, and then I was supposed to go to the Argeș County to take my job assigned by the government.

It was a day at the beginning of September, when Mona and I were together at my apartment. It was a sunny afternoon as we were happily sitting together when suddenly I became aware that a dark curtain covers my right eye. The next day, we went to see an ophthalmologist, Dr. Regenbogen. He was a younger doctor that had something unusual in those days in Romania, a private office at his home. We have seen him a few months before for Mona had some eye problems. He examined and told me that I have a detachment of the retina and advised me to come the following day to the Colțea Hospital, where he was working, to be seen by the best specialist for this condition, Dr. Eliza Climescu.

As we left, Mona got worried and asked me to come and sleep at her home so that next morning, her mother could take me to the hospital. I accepted her invitation and spent a bad night in Albert's room, trying to remember all the conditions that could have triggered the retina detachment among which cancer of the eye (melanoma) was one of them. One has to remember that this was going on just a few months after my mother has died of cancer.

The next morning, Mrs. Niculescu was ready to take me to the hospital. Drs. Climescu and Regenbogen were there, examined my eye, and decided that it was indeed a retinal detachment of unknown origin that required immediate hospitalization and surgery. In those days, the treatment of these cases consisted of surgery followed by total immobilization for several months. I was told that the rate of success for the surgery was about 30 percent, meaning that I had just a chance of three to recover my sight. I was admitted to the hospital, and they put a huge gauze wrap around my head like a turban that covered completely my eyes. I had to carry this turban for two months as I was supposed to stay in bed with the head lying on the right side. I was not supposed to move in bed and, under no circumstances, to leave the bed.

After several days, I had surgery. I was taken to the operating room where, without anesthesia, Drs. Climescu and Regenbogen started putting points of thermocauther (diathermy) on the back side of my eye, in the area corresponding to where the detachment occurred. It was like burning flesh without any anesthesia. The pain inflicted by this surgery was unbearable, and I don't know how I did not faint. Mona was there by my side, and I am still grateful to her for this. After this torture called surgery was over I was taken to my bed. The pain in the eye became worst until the attending doctor gave me a shot of a painkiller, and the pain subsided.

During the following two months Mona came almost daily to visit me. I cannot tell how much this meant to me. Only my mother would have cared so much for me, lying in bed, with the head wrapped like a mummy, unwashed, with a beard like that of Fidel Castro itching badly. There was no way to wash my face. I cannot express in words my gratitude to her, for what she did for me during those awful days. If it would be only for what she did during those days, I am forever grateful to her; she was my angel.

After two months, they removed the cover, examined my eye, and decided that the surgery was a success. However, Dr. Climescu advised me to be extremely careful in everything I do, sort of handle my head like a soft egg: no physical efforts, no weight lifting, no swimming, no tennis playing, briefly a total handicap. Since the cause of what happened wasn't known, I think they were afraid that it can happen again and involve also the other eye, leaving me totally blind.

In fact, that's how the state medical commission advised on my case, and they were not a charitable organization. Since I was still employed by the Bucur Hospital when this disease happened, I would benefit from the social assistance provided by the state. The medical board reviewed my case and decided that I am a total handicap and should receive a pension of 250 lei per month. I was supposed to be reviewed periodically, which I did, and this turned out to be a simple formality. My eye was not getting better and will never do for the rest of my life. I guess this very modest sum was related to my salary and my age. For the following months, the money proved to be enough to cover my rent and a daily meal.

After I went home, Professor Niculescu came to visit me. I was quite impressed, and I still don't know how to interpret this visit. I am saying that because, after my discharge from the hospital, I went to see Dr. Regenbogen at his home office. After he examined my eye and decided that everything looks good, he asked if he can tell me something outside the medical matter, which, of course, I agreed. He told me that Mrs. Niculescu has visited him and asked him to advise me to go to Vienna, Austria, to seek medical treatment. For him, who knew my relationship with Mona, it came as a surprise as it was for me. It is possible that a medical visit to Vienna may have been beneficial for my eye condition, but going alone there would have been foolish, and she didn't say anything about having Mona accompany me to Vienna. In those days, most people that managed to leave Romania never returned home. Was this a kind invitation to leave Mona?

Quarrel with Father

After my eye surgery, my father used to come to visit me quite regularly at home. He was still living with Tuna, who was preparing to migrate to Israel. On one of such visits, he started telling me that I should apply for a passport to go to Israel. This was a time when many Jews were applying for such passports, and the government seemed inclined to let them leave Romania. There was an agreement between Israel and Romania, and Jews were purchased by Israel in exchange at the beginning for agriculture factories, and later for cash. I tried to tell him that I am very much attached to Mona, and such an action on my side would be out of question. Our discussion became quite intense and ended up in me telling him that I consider our relationship broken. He left, and I didn't see or talked to him for several months.

After this argument, our go-between was Florica, my father's faithful servant. She visited me several times and told me about the fights between him and Tuna and how unhappy he was. Finally, by springtime, after Tuna left, we resumed our relationship. In fact, he came and asked if he could move with me because he had to leave the apartment he was living in. I had a bitter taste and thoughts of my mother and her rough life, and I told him how inconvenient such a move would be.

Mama Mare Leaves

When my mother was in France, very ill, my grandmother took upon herself and went to the police to fill up the application form for a passport to go to France hoping of helping her daughter. She did that without telling me, or she told me, but I paid no attention to it. Getting a passport to go to a Western country in those days was reserved only for the higher-ups of the Communist Party. To my surprise, by spring of 1959, she received her passport. Obviously, the government was happy to get rid of an eighty-plus-year-old lady that cannot contribute to the building of the communist society but keeps consuming and, moreover, is of French origin, which she can always claim and raise a fuss about it.

I had a very hard time deciding what to do. Mama Mare was for me like a mother; the bondage between us was very strong. One day, she asked me why I don't marry Mona. I was very surprised because this subject was never discussed between us. It is likely that she thought that she was old and ill, and was concerned that I will end up soon having no one around me unless I get married, and start having a family. Unfortunately, under the circumstances, this was not possible; I was disabled, without a future and had no income.

My financial situation with my very small state-provided aid of 250 lei per month as income was dire. This represented about one third of a regular salary of a resident. The only hope to get a better income was to leave Bucharest and go where the government has offered me a position in the Argeș County. That would have meant to leave Mama Mare alone at home in Bucharest, which was not possible because she started having crises of hypoglycemia (low blood sugar), for which she needed constant medical supervision. Besides I was classified as disabled following my physicians recommendation to avoid any physical effort. So I decided to let her go to France. I am still doubtful about this decision, but looking back, I don't think I had another choice. I am very glad her grave is in Strasbourg, close to that of my mother and easily accessible for me and my family.

After Mama Mare left, I was alone at home. Maria would still come and help out in exchange for using our attic room. To make ends meet from my very modest aid that I was receiving from the state, I used to go and eat lunch at the Lido Cafeteria. Lido was and still is, an elegant hotel downtown Bucharest. It had a cafeteria with good food but only tall tables so one had to eat standing up. I didn't mind it as long as the food was good, and I could afford it. At five lei a meal, I was still left with enough money to pay my rent and even have a little change.

By spring, Professor Niculescu gave me some work to do, and I got paid for it. I had to go to collect references for a book he was writing about herpes viruses. I was making files and giving them to his secretary. Then another book about rabies was in the works, and I was again hired to find the references. This work, which I liked, generated some income, and I learned a lot about herpes and rabies viruses. This income was a major relief for me, but it was not steady revenue.

A Life-changing Beach Vacation

The summer of 1959 came, and Mona was very busy preparing her state exam to graduate from the medical school. She didn't have time to spend with me and was locked up all day with a couple of her classmates. I decided to join a group of friends including Dan Stănescu, Luiza Creangă, a neighbor and friend of Dan, and a lady friend of Luiza, and take a vacation at the beach.

Dan Stănescu was a classmate and friend of Mona. During the Hungarian Revolution in 1956, some students expressed their sympathy for this revolution and even wanted to organize a public meeting. The informers took care to let the Securitate know about that, and a good number of the students ended up in jail. Dan was one of them. After he was let free, it took three years until he was allowed to resume his medical studies. In the meantime, he found a job as a nurse in a hospital. We became good friends, and we still are. He defected with his wife Bianca, and they ended up in Belgium, where he had a very successful career.

At the beach, the four of us were without our girlfriends (Dan and I), boyfriend (Luiza), and husband (unnamed lady). We rented two rooms in a suburb of the city of Constanța, the single important harbor in Romania at the Black Sea. The suburb was called Tataia (which means "grandfather" in Romanian) and was located between Constanța and the fancy sea resort of Mamaia. It consisted of modest homes, many of them with running water only outside the house. It had a nice beach along a high cliff. The beach was totally primitive; there was nothing built there. Tataia became my summer sea resort for many years to come.

Besides renting the rooms, our small group had also lunch cooked and served by the host, Mrs. Bondar. At this late luncheon, which occurred usually when we returned from the beach around 2:00 or 3:00 PM, we were joined by some other people that were renting rooms in neighboring homes. Some of these people would join us at the beach. One of them, Dr. Picky Grozea, was assistant professor of internal medicine at Colentina Hospital, one of the best-teaching hospitals in Bucharest. Another one, Mr. Sergiu Cunescu, was the director of the factory building buses in Bucharest. Sergiu was married to a movie artist, a beautiful woman who took a shower every day before our luncheon using an egg yolk to wash her hair. This made Dan complain that she was using our meals that we paid for. Actually, her hair was very beautiful she could easily qualify for a shampoo advertisement.

I met Ms. Luiza Creangă visiting Dan. She was an astounding beauty somewhat in the type of Elizabeth Taylor but more handsome. She was just stunning; men were turning their heads on the street and, when we were in Tataia, were looking over the fence to get a view of her. She was a quiet person, and by the time she joined us at our beach trip, her relationship with her boyfriend, Mr. Finţescu, was terminated. Luiza had a charming personality, but by then, I was totally committed to Mona. I mentioned Luiza not only for being a lovely company at the beach, but also for the encouragement and support that she gave me in resuming a normal life and getting a position. I never found out the details, but I think she talked about me with someone connected with the Ministry of Health, which was supposed to decide about my position. Connections were important in those days as they are now.

We had a pleasant time at the beach, and we went at least once at restaurants in Mamaia. Dan was a witty guy, and the two "girls" were wonderful companions. After all the hardship I went through, the illness and death of my mother, and my disease and handicap, I returned to Bucharest with confidence that I can return to a normal life. For me this vacation was a real boost for my morale. I am grateful to Luiza for giving me a new confidence to return to a normal life, without the permanent fear that the eye trouble will return, and also for her support to have my position awarded by the Ministry of Health renewed.

End of Romance

It was the fall of 1959, when Mona decided to have a party at her home. It was to celebrate her graduation from the medical school and, in a way, her reentry into the social life she missed during the preparation for her final exams. It was a long time since she didn't have a party, and I am sure she missed this. Unlike me, she enjoyed attending parties. She asked me to attend, which I did. As I got there, a rather large crowd was already in place, munching on the good things that were offered. Mona was floating among her guests like a fairy. As I was sitting by myself in a corner, Mona came to me followed by a tall man, looking older than his age. She introduced him as Mr. Sebastian Costinescu. We exchanged the usual greetings, and then he moved on. Mr. Costinescu started his teaching career at the Military Technical Academy, where he was employed as an officer and assistant professor. He moved his teaching career at the Polytechnic Institute of

Bucharest, where, in 1959, he was promoted associate professor. He was also a researcher at the Romanian Academy.

At that time, I felt very much out of place. I was a poor, unemployed guy living on a meager monthly stipend, with no expectations or connections, with a father who was removed from his profession as an outcast of the communist system. What did I have in common with Mona's guests, some of them children of members of the Romanian Academy, a quality that in those days assured an income far above a regular salary, and benefits matched only by the high-ranking members of the Communist Party? How did I match with guys like Mr. Costinescu, who was already associate professor and probably had other titles as well?

When Mona introduced me to Mr. Costinescu, I felt that in my relationship with Mona, I was the past and he was the future. The dices were played, and the game was over. Mr. Costinescu had all the assets required by the world of Mona and her family: a successful academic career, a future that was promising to add more titles, a desire to move up on the ladder that was important for the Niculescu family. I had none of those.

Looking back in time, I wonder why Mona felt obliged to introduce Mr. Costinescu to me. Did she know then that he was her future husband? If so, what was she expecting from me, my blessings? Wanted to impress upon me how much better he was, sort of an excuse for the change? Was it a revenge for something wrong that she thought I did? I am not a suspicious guy, on the contrary, but it was not by chance that of all the guests, she picked him to introduce. I will probably never know what happened, but I felt sorry for her. She must have gone through some very tough time to put up that play.

This may have been the final straw that made me decide that I cannot and will not continue to live like that, without work, without income, a pauper in a poor society. After all, I had a good profession that I wanted to practice. Under the circumstances, the summer beach vacation had multiple effects. My physical activity at the beach proved that my eye has healed well enough to sustain normal movements without detaching again, and my sight was again as good as before. Also, it connected me with people that lived and enjoyed life without depending on benefits bestowed by the Communist Party. Therefore, I felt like it was time to start taking some risk and try to return to a normal life.

The medical state commission that was assessing me every three months was ready to extend my retirement forever. However, I decided to go to the Ministry of Health, and to ask to be sent as a physician where I choose when

I graduated from the medical school, somewhere in the Arges County. My demand was granted, and I took the train and went to the town of Pitești, the capital of the Arges County.

I had a relative living in Pitești. She was Bica Aladjem, a cousin of my father, the daughter of Peter Nachtigal, a brother of my grandfather Jacques Nachtigal. Bica was married to Dan Aladjem, a good-looking Sephardic Jew. They lived in a rather large old house on the main street. Like in every medium-sized provincial city, in Pitești, everyone knew everyone either personally or through gossips. So it was not a problem for Bica and Dan to have an appointment with Dr. Ștefănescu, the head of the Argeș County Health Department.

When Dan Aladjem and I went to the appointment, we were well received by Dr. Emil Ștefănescu. He looked favorably at my request for a position in the Arges County and assigned me to a position of residency in the pediatric section of the county hospital in the Călinești Village. At the end of our interview, I told Dr. Ștefănescu that I was engaged, that my fiancée was a fresh graduate of the medical school, and I would like very much to have her join me in the Argeș County. As I mentioned that she was the daughter of Prof. Florin Niculescu, Dr. Ștefănescu became enthusiastic. The prospect of having in his territory the daughter of such an influential person was obviously very attractive. All the gates were open for Mona in the Argeș County.

It was October 1959, and I had to be at my new job by November 10. As soon as I returned home, I went to talk to Mona about this new opening in our lives. She was not home, and I ended up chatting with her sister, Tina. As we were in her bedroom, Professor Niculescu asked me to come to his office. To me, this was totally unexpected. During all these years that I visited the Niculescu family, he has never approached me. Now with a determined and somewhat angry voice, he delivered a short speech telling me that Mona and I should separate now, that "you should follow your way and let her follow her way." In other words, "leave her alone." And this was the end of our talk, or at least what he saw as his talk. There were no explanations, no discussion; it was an order. I went back to Tina and told her what happened. Tina had no comment, she just kept looking at me with her very large dark eyes, and I think there was some silent compassion there. I left the Niculescu apartment, where I spent so many happy days like in a nightmare.

Soon thereafter, I met Mona and told her about the possibility to go together to the Arges County. I count this as the first real proposal to get married and make a family. Her answer was just tears and no words. Obviously, the decision of the Niculescu family to dump me was irreversible.

Within the following months, I had more proof, if it was necessary, that the Niculescu family wanted me gone. It was January 1960, when I called Mona and she asked me to accompany her at her office, which was in a village, not far from Bucharest, where she practiced family medicine. I accompanied her there, and it looked like we were on the brink of renewing our relationship.

After a few days, I got a call from my friend Marius Ianconescu, who asked me to come at his home. I went, and there was Mrs. Niculescu, who started a friendly talk, telling me that my life will go on without Mona, that one loves when young but that all goes away, etc., a nice discourse that in summary said, "Leave us alone." Later on, I found out from Marius that Mrs. Niculescu has asked him to go and talk to Mona, and convince her that my future is only outside Romania, and she will destroy it by keeping me in the country. They were indeed covering it all.

Looking back in time, with more life experience now than I had then, I tried to understand what was it that made Mona's parents openly pushing me out. By the time all these happened, I was inclined to think that they thought I was a hopeless failure. Who would want to marry their daughter to a guy who will be, for the rest of his life, disabled and living on a meager pension? After being a medical student with a bright future, I have become a crippled young man.

On the other hand, after talking to Mona, it seems that her parents' mind-set was more related to a belief that I have applied for passport to migrate to Israel. This sounds strange since after my release from the hospital, I was not in the physical condition to start such a process. After all, the medical state commission has decided that I was a lifelong handicapped on the verge of becoming blind. What would a disabled guy like me do in Israel? Be admitted in some nursing home?

It is possible that Mona's parents used this reason to justify their decision to remove an undesirable fiancé from the family. My present gut feeling is that the whole process started with my father's troubles. The warning talk that I got in the summer of 1958, a few months after my father was disbarred, from Professor Niculescu was just that, a very honest warning, and I was foolish not to pay attention to it. He really meant what he said; he really thought that under the political conditions in Romania, I have no chance to succeed, and it turned out that he was absolutely right. In spite of my work and dedication in Romania, my professional achievement will be established only in the United States. One fact that supports this explanation is that the Niculescu family has never challenged me about the passport application story. Why not? Maybe they were not sure and didn't want to risk an embarrassing negative answer.

By the time this happened, I had to pursue the order and to follow my way in life. I decided above all to be truthful to myself and my beliefs, and to stick to what I think is important in life: integrity, good work, and treating other people as you would like to be treated yourself. I tried to follow these principles, and now that I am at the end of the road, I look back, and I am definitely not ashamed of what I have accomplished under the difficult circumstances that I had to overcome. Could I have done better? There is always room for improvement, but let's try to be real. In the end, it appears the old man has given me a good advice. Notwithstanding that in the process, he has inflicted a longtime and painful wound.

Soon after we separated, Mona married Mr. Sebastian Costinescu. A distinguished engineer, Mr. Costinescu became professor at the Bucharest Polytechnique School. As Albert, his brother-in-law, told me years later, he refused to leave Romania although he was offered in France a university professorship. Nonetheless, I feel sorry for Mona Niculescu having to live in that part of the world. The truth is that Mona does not belong to that world and never did, and I will never understand how her parents didn't realize that, or, after all, maybe it was her decision to stay and fight. In any case, it was enough to look at her and to recognize that Mona belongs to a different world. My recollection of her as I saw her at the May 1 manifestation, before knowing who she was, stays with me like an old family picture. She looked such a stranger! And in spite of everything, she remained a stranger for this part of the world.

What I find almost funny was what happened the following summer. I went for my beach vacation to Tataia together with my friends Marius Ianconescu and Hans Aderca. They found out that their director, Niculescu was in Mamaia, at the Rex hotel and decided to visit him. They asked me to join them which I did. When we got there we found out that Prof. Niculescu was at the beach with his wife and the recently married couple, Mr. and Mrs. Costinescu. Mona was happy to meet me and we went swimming and we behaved like old friends. Several days later Marius told me that the Niculescu family has asked him to notify me that I should not come back. Mr.

Costinescu has been angry because of me. It seemed that they were afraid of me like of a ghost!

Unexpectedly, my love for Mona, which has ended so painfully for me, has paved the way and set up the grounds for what was to be my destiny, my lifelong unconditional love and bonding with Sidonia. From the very beginning, when I fell in love with Sidonia, I knew that I have been there before, and I told her so. However, my love for Sidonia was to be a total bonding between our souls, a sense of total belonging, that can be experienced only once in a lifetime.

Final Thoughts

The years I spent in the medical school were obviously peculiar to say the least. Beyond my medical education, some very important events have occurred that influenced the rest of my life. First and foremost, I lost my mother, who died prematurely, the victim of a terrible disease—breast cancer. In addition, I lost my maternal grandmother, who was, for me, like a second mother. I have met what could have been "the very special one" of my life, and I lost her. I went through the misery of a major health problem that almost left me handicapped. I watched my father, the best lawyer in the country, become unemployed and poor. Altogether, I had some of the saddest time of my life when I lost my mother and some of the gladdest time when I was with Mona.

I enjoyed immensely the medical school. I am convinced that I received at the Bucharest School of Medicine, one of the best medical education that one could have in those days. I had some wonderful teachers, and I am grateful to all and each one of them. In 1984, I went and took the ECFMG exam in the United States and succeeded from the first attempt, in spite of the fact that I went totally unprepared, and there were twenty-seven years from my medical school graduation. I give credit for this success to all those professors that have done such an excellent job.

Those were the years when I saw and felt the communist regime taking over all aspects of life. I had to deal with it in the medical school. It decided on my career; it destroyed my father and probably also my engagement to the girl I loved and I was planning to spend my life with. It was for me a lesson to be learned, and I was in the process of doing it. This was the first time, when not being a member of the Communist Party, prevented me for occupying the position that, through my track record in the medical school,

I was entitled to. It will not be the last one. Looking back, I can probably safely say, that it was then when our ways split.

I find it a supreme irony of my destiny that the man who hurt me so much has been in fact one of my most important benefactors. When Florin Niculescu told me that I should "follow my own way in life," I was badly hurt because he meant to break up my engagement to Mona. By the same token, this has pushed me to follow my way, to achieve what I could by my own and, eventually, to leave Romania and start a new and far happier life for me and my family in America.

Florin Niculescu not only marked my future road in life, but he also actually contributed to its fulfillment. The visit of Joe Melnick, one of the most renowned world virologist who came in 1963 to Romania to visit the Microbiology Institute, has opened for me the gates of America and decided my fate. My connection with Melnick was my passport to America and to the world of science. Without it, I might as well have counted the days to my retirement from the Institute of Microbiology, a total unknown for the scientific community. Above all, I am forever grateful to Florin Niculescu for opening the pathway of my destiny to meet and marry Sidonia, a gift from heaven, my soul mate, the love of my life and beyond, that healed the wound that he has inflicted and brought all the happiness that I have lost and more, much more.

By the end of 1959, with my family reduced to my father and with Mona a fresh wound in my heart, I was ready to tackle the challenges of the medical profession. I was leaving Bucharest with the feeling of excitement that one must have before a military battle. I was committed to win the next battle for the memory of my mother, who told me how convinced she has always been in my ability to do very well in my profession. I wasn't going to disappoint her.

CHAPTER 4

The Hospital
1959-1961

Călinești Hospital

By November 10, 1959, I arrived at Călinești County Hospital. Călinești is a village located about seventy miles north of Bucharest and about ten miles south of Pitești on the two-lane highway, Pitești-Bucharest. This tree-lined, good quality highway was built by the Germans in preparation for the war against the Soviet Union to be used to move their armor and supplies. The village is located in the Argeș River Valley and spreads over a hilly area, rich in orchards with plum trees and vineyards. The closest town is Topoloveni, about five miles south of Călinești.

The Călinești Hospital was one of the fifty county hospitals that were built in the countryside by King Carol I at the beginning of the twentieth century. In 1960, Călinești Hospital had five sections that were located in separate buildings. The central building hosted the administration, the sections of surgery and ob-gyn, and also the laboratory and radiology. The sections of internal medicine, infectious diseases, and pediatrics were each in a separate building. The medical staff included two ob-gyn specialists, two surgeons, two internal medicine specialists, one infectious disease specialist, and one pediatrician. After I arrived, another resident joined the internal medicine service. This was a young lady, Dr. Lidia Chervasie, who was also from Bucharest.

Google. The hospital Călinești is located in the village of Călinești, Argeș County, at a distance of 18 km. from Pitești. In the years 1906-1908 the Rural Hospital Călinești, which worked with 25 beds, a single-unit general medicine—and a doctor until 1944. In 1985 the new pavilion of the hospital, a modern construction with a high degree of comfort came into service. In 1988 the Călinești Hospital was a health institution with ample possibilities for investigation and treatment of various diseases, sitting at the disposal of the inhabitants of the South-Eastern part of the Arges County.

I was replacing Dr. Cighir, a pediatrics resident who had just finished his residency and was leaving to take a specialist position in a city. The pediatrics section had thirty beds and one attending physician, Dr. Ileana Dobrescu. She was a tall woman; she was unmarried and lived several miles from the hospital with her parents. She was coming to work riding her old bicycle on the highway. She welcomed me and seemed glad to have me there. Being alone, I assumed it would have been difficult to handle the burden of so many patients. Besides, she had to be there day in and day out no matter what; the other physicians from different sections of the hospital would have had a hard time replacing her.

The first night, I slept at the hospital; but the next day I moved into a rented room in a house on the same street where the hospital was, less than half a mile down the road. The home was near the highway. My hosts were a family of peasants. The man, called Matache, was working at the railway station loading timber. His wife, Marioara, was taking care of the household, cooking and running the family; she was the boss, no questions asked. Their son and daughter-in-law worked in the fields and took care of their animals: horses, cows, pigs, chickens, etc. They lived in a separate house but in the same courtyard.

The room I rented was rather small; it had a bed and a table. Since winter was closing in fast, they had a woodstove built in the room. It was small but very efficient. The house had no running water, and the toilet, which was somewhere in the backyard, was primitive. I soon learned that there were lots of fleas; they were jumping around and biting wherever they could reach first, which was the lower part of the legs, just under the pants cuff. Over the time spent there, I had to use lots of DDT to keep them somewhat under control.

I was well received at the hospital by Dr. Dumitrache, the director of the hospital and a specialist in internal medicine. Dr. Popescu was the chief of internal medicine. Both were living in the village or not far from it. The ob-gyn doctors, Dr. Berceanu and Dr. Geantă, were both from Pitești and were commuting daily. Dr. Berceanu was commuting by car. Owning a car in those days was uncommon. In surgery, the chief was Dr. Dumitrescu, who had a reputation for being an excellent surgeon and a very religious person. He was assisted by Dr. Bea (Beatrice) Voinescu, a young woman who lived in Călinești with her husband, who belonged to a prominent family from the village.

I immediately befriended Dr. Mircea Răiciulescu, the infectious disease specialist. Like me, Mircea was new there and was also from Bucharest. He had family, a wife and a son, in Bucharest and was a weekend commuter. We got along well from the beginning. We liked each other very much, and for the entire time I was at that hospital, he was my best friend. I don't know why, but I trusted him, and I think this was mutual. We shared many views, and this was probably decisive for our friendship. With time, I met his family, his wife, who was working in Bucharest for the national radio, and his sister, a nice-looking brunette who visited Mircea in Călinești. I spent one New Year's Eve at my father's home with his family. He loved the company of my father, and I think this was the last New Year celebration when my father was still in good health.

Soon after I started working at the Hospital, Dr. Mircea Botez joined the Surgery Department. He was somewhat older than me, lived in Pitești, and commuted on a motorcycle. We got along very well. We shared a feeling of trust and the same desire to preserve our personality under any circumstance and environment. He had a motorcycle with a sidecar. I would squeeze into it, and I would ride with him to visit other physicians in the county. We enjoyed each other's company in the hospital when we were on call or on the road riding the motorcycle.

The daily routine began with the morning rounds of patients. Dr. Dobrescu and I did this together, and the two of us discussed each case and decided on tests and treatment. For me it was an excellent opportunity to apply what I had learned and to learn more from each patient. This was also the time of the day when we would examine new patients and admit new sick children to the hospital.

At noon, I had lunch at the hospital with some of my colleagues. It was a small group, and the atmosphere was friendly. Mrs. Babin, the hospital cook, was making sure we were well fed. After lunch, I would go home and relax, have a nap or read something. At 5:00 PM, I would go back to the hospital to do the evening rounds. I would again see the patients, most of the time by myself. Many weekdays I would spend the rest of the evening in the hospital, either being on call, or keeping my friends, Mircea Răiciulescu or Mircea Botez, company when they were on call. We would have dinner together, chat, and listen to some music.

At the hospital, quite often it would be my turn to be on call for the night shift, the weekend, or some holiday. Sometimes the other physicians would ask me to replace them for the night shifts or the weekends since they had families and I didn't. These calls were paid for on top of my salary, so it was a way to make some money, and I would almost always accept. My salary as a resident was not great, and this brought some significant additional income. Coming after years of very low income, I appreciated the possibility of having enough income to be able to save for the first time in my life. I was just applying a lesson I had learned.

When I was on call, I was covering all of the hospital sections. I was the boss. I was responsible for all the patients that were in the hospital, and I was supposed to examine all the patients that walked in, or were brought to the hospital by the ambulance. There were all kinds of emergency cases, from women getting ready to deliver, to sick children having difficulty breathing, or adults with acute appendicitis requiring emergency surgery.

One night, I recall a man who was in a knife fight was brought to the hospital with a deep cut on his right arm. I had to use whatever surgery training I had to sew his arm so that he could use it again, hopefully not for another fight. Some of these cases, especially the surgical cases, were directed to the Pitești Municipal Hospital using the ambulance that belonged to our hospital. When I was on call, I was in charge of answering the phone calls requesting ambulance transportation. For some cases, I would decide to send the ambulance and, after examination, to refer the patient to the hospital in Pitești.

The hospital had a special room for the physician on call where I could rest and sometimes even catch a few hours of sleep. In a hall, there was a television set available to all the patients who could walk. Many of those evenings, I would be seated there along with the patients watching the programs. I think the patients felt better knowing there was a doctor at hand, as they knew who I was. I was quickly learning what responsibility means when you have to take care of a lot of sick people.

An important person at the hospital was Comrade Ionescu. He was the driver of the ambulance that belonged to the hospital. At the direction of the physician in charge, he would go and pick up the emergency cases throughout the county that was served by the hospital. Together we did quite a number of trips to Bucharest, with sick children who required specialized medical care. I guess he was profiting from those trips.

On one of those trips, we had to take a demented young man to the psychiatry hospital in Bucharest. The man was agitated, and we had no means to constrain him. We just locked him in the space behind the cabin. On the way to Bucharest, the ambulance was stopped by the police for a routine check. The man became violently agitated against the policeman, and we had a hard time trying to explain to the policeman what was going on.

Comrade Ionescu was also the local Communist Party secretary. In the hierarchy of the Communist Party, the secretary had the decisive role in running the local organization and in decision making. I think Comrade Ionescu was a typical example of the millions of party members who would get the red card to improve their financial standing within the system. All of the talk about communist ideology was just that—talk. However, these individuals, like Comrade Ionescu, were probably aware that their status was due to the party and were probably grateful for that. Of course, being grateful doesn't mean being faithful. Several times Comrade Ionescu offered to make me a Communist Party member. It would have been a simple formality since he was the party secretary and the political power in Călinești, but I refused politely. I didn't like the system, and to become an active supporter of it for the sake of some potential advantages, I found to be beyond my values. This decision proved to be fateful for me. Deciding not to join the Communist Party meant that I was giving up my chances of rising on the professional scale with the help of the red membership card.

Years after I left Călinești, as I was walking with my family near our home in Bucharest, a car that was coming down the same street stopped, and the driver, Comrade Ionescu, came out to greet me. He proudly told me that he was now driving some high-ranking officers of the Securitate in Bucharest! Quite a promotion! No doubt the little red card helped.

Friends

The first months, which included the winter holidays, in Călinești were hard for me; it was really like moving to a different world. For the first time in my life, I was alone. I had no one to talk to as I used to, no one to tell how strange and new many things were. The break with Mona was fresh and very difficult to handle. I was used to sharing everything with her, and now there was nobody to share with. We had common friends; now what was I going to do? Who would continue being a friend and who would not?

Slowly, things started to be sorted out; I was moving out of the fog into clear air. I started tightening my friendship with people who, until then, were just colleagues or acquaintances. Some, like Mira and Vlad Pauker, managed to have relations with both Mona and me. They went to Mona's wedding and told me how she managed to make it through it. Others, like Norbert and Dana Schlomiuck, had little understanding for Mona for our break up, and over the years, they maintained this point of view. For me, it was difficult to listen to their accusations since I liked to think that this decision was imposed upon her by her parents. I had to admit that the evidence was not in her favor, but I knew that this was not the case. In reality, I felt sorry for her, and I knew how hard it was for her too. In the long run, my view was, and still is, that life's destiny rewards and punishes each individual for what they do. Each of us pays the price for our decisions, and there is nothing we can do about this. Each of us follows our own path in life, which, many times, seems to be drawn by something and not by our own will.

Actually, Dana and Norbert were eager to see me dating one of their neighbors, Tanți, and succeeded for a while to get me involved with her. Tanți was a very quiet, beautiful girl. Tanți was from Timișoara, a city on the west side of the country. She was trained as an educator and was getting ready to graduate and find a job, preferably in Bucharest. In those days, one couldn't move to Bucharest unless they had a job there, or married someone who was living there. She was my first date after I broke up with Mona, and for me, it was something very unusual. After being so close to Mona for about four years, I almost had no idea how one starts dating someone. Anyway, our dating began well, and I was trying my best to please her.

Soon after we started dating, Tanți went to work for several weeks in a children's summer camp near Brașov, a city close to the Carpathian Mountains. On a weekend I took a night train and went to visit her. By morning, I made it to the camp, and she seemed to enjoy my visit. The camp administration allowed her to spend the day with me, so we walked around and had a nice day together.

When she returned to Bucharest, we went vacationing for a week at the Black Sea. We rented a room in Tataia at the Popa family and went to the beach there. For dinner, we went to restaurants in Mamaia with which Tataia was connected by a trolley bus. Although there was some friendship developing between us, our relationship was not what I was hoping for; there was no real warmth and sharing.

After we returned to Bucharest, one evening while I was visiting her, she told me that she would like to discontinue our relationship; as they say in Romanian, "She gave me the night slippers." The bottom line was that Tanți was interested in a marriage that would give her the right to live in Bucharest and to be able to bring her mother from Timișoara to Bucharest. As a commuter without a prospect to return to Bucharest with a stable job anytime soon, I was not the right man. From my side, compared to Mona, she was far too quiet and introverted, and I had doubts that our relationship would survive. All in all, it was an easy breakup. I had no regrets, and obviously, she was not my soul mate.

Not long after that, Dana and Norbert left the country and migrated to Canada. They now live in Montreal, and I visited them a few years ago. They both had a wonderful career as university professors, and we enjoyed every second we spent together recalling the years with our shared memories. They kept in touch with Tanți, who, after a childless and failed marriage in Romania, moved to Switzerland and lives there alone.

This was the end of my first post-Mona date, and I survived painlessly. The lesson that I learned was that, after four years of Mona, it was very difficult for me to adjust to another female companion. As soon as I would meet one, it was always like searching for Mona number two. I was conditioned to her voice, her emotional and intellectual response, her judgment. Now I was facing totally distinct personalities, none of them like the one I knew or expected. This stereotype followed me for years, and I think what turned me around was meeting Sidonia, but this is another story that happened later in my life.

In the meantime, I developed my relationship with friends and their families in Bucharest. I was now frequently invited to the homes of the Aderca or the Ianconescu family on Saturday evenings, when they would have get-togethers with other friends. This was something new for me because when I was with Mona, we had rarely been invited to parties, particularly those given by families. Most of the time, I was the youngest one among those who were invited; and being a bachelor, I would almost always bring a female friend with me who would somewhat brighten the mood.

This was a different position for me, and I have to say I enjoyed playing this game.

Through the Ianconescu family, I met the Barta family, a couple of film directors. Dona Barta was a petite blonde and a nice lady. She and her husband, Gabi, had a daughter, Theresa. They invited me to their gatherings where I met people related mostly to the film industry that was developing in Romania. Our friendship continued after I returned to Bucharest. Unfortunately, Dona developed breast cancer at a young age. She survived almost twenty years without complications, but then developed brain metastasis and died soon after surgery.

Another circle of friends was centered on Dr. Viorica Voiculescu. She was a pediatrician who was on staff at the Gheorghe Marinescu Hospital, where I did my internship. She kept a close relationship with a classmate of mine, Nina Scriban. We got together at Dr. Voiculescu's home or my apartment, with other young physicians, and we listened to music or, just talked and shared our life experience. Dr. Voiculescu managed to obtain the book, *Dr. Zhivago*, written by a Soviet writer Boris Pasternak and translated into French. The author received the Nobel Prize for literature, but the book was considered illegal by the communist authorities. Dr. Voiculescu shared this and other books with me. Our meetings were a breath of fresh air in those days, proving that there were still islands of free-thinking people around me.

This was a time when I would visit my father and Dora, his new wife. My father had moved to Dora's apartment and was trying to make ends meet by selling what he still owned, and getting his monthly financial support from Uncle Willy in Mexico. My salary was not enough to allow me to support him, and I doubt that he would have accepted such an offer. He was still hoping that the communist regime would provide him with the pension that he was entitled to, but this was not to be. Anyway, having some hope was better than having none. He was also working on a book, but I never got to see the manuscript. Very likely, it was not finished by the time he died. Nevertheless, he seemed more relaxed and happier with his life than he had been during his years with Tuna as a wife.

Our rapport was warmer than it had ever been. The shadow of Tuna was no longer between us, and that helped. Unfortunately, he had his first heart attack on Christmas night, after having a pleasant and somewhat heavy dinner at Oscar's home. On closer questioning, it turned out that he had had angina for at least a couple of years, which he tried to ignore. In those days, there were no significant treatments available for this disease, and his fate was unfortunately irreversible. After several months of bed rest, a routine treatment for heart attacks in those days, his chest pain resumed in a ferocious way. As I was not there, neither he nor Dora were telling me everything that was going on.

Life in Călinești

Over the winter of 1959-1960, I became used to my new life. I was spending the week at Călinești, but on Saturday, I would take the train and spend the weekend in Bucharest. The hospital and my home in Călinești were about two miles from the railway station. To reach my home from the railway station, I would walk a trail through the fields. I became used to this walk, even when I was coming back from Bucharest by night, which was most of the time. The trains that stopped in Călinești were almost all of the slow-going variety because they were meant to stop in many small stations along the track. Most of the time, when leaving Bucharest, I would take a late evening train and take a nap, like everyone else in the car, until it was close to Călinești. The trip would take about three hours, and with the walk from the station, I would be home around midnight.

After a few months, when I had saved enough money from my salary, I could afford to go to the Consign Store in Bucharest and buy a British-made Pye radio with shortwave bands. At the store, I was told that the radio was sold by a foreign diplomat who had left the country. I took that radio to my room in Călinești, and it changed my life. It became my connection to the world. I had news from all over the world, I had music, and it was a life channel in the isolation of the countryside. Like me, the diplomat had been another lonely soul.

It was usually either Friday afternoon or Saturday around noon when I would go back to Bucharest. At those times, the atmosphere in the train was lively. It was not unusual that someone would pull out a bottle of plum brandy and pass it around. Plum brandy, called *țuica* (pronounced "tsooeka"), is the national alcoholic beverage in Romania, and the region where Călinești was located had plenty of plum orchards. Most families in the area would make their own plum brandy, and there was an endless range from weak to very strong, depending on the concentration of alcohol. In the beginning, my sanitation rules were very much at odd with this practice; but after a while, I became used to it, and in fact, the only outcome was that I would arrive home quite tired. There was no way to refuse the drink. That would have been a major offense, and everybody would have been shocked. From the North railway Station, I would ride a tram that would take me close to my apartment.

This culture of drinking was part of the lesson that I learned in those years spent in the rural environment. In my teen age or college student years, I rarely drank alcoholic beverages. At home in Călinești with the Matache family, when I would be at home in the evening after dinner, Mr. Matache would invite me to his room, and his wife would bring a decanter of wine from their own production and pour it into glasses. We would start chatting and drinking one glass after another. Sometimes, instead of wine, we would have the țuica (plum brandy). When the drink was finished, I would go to my room, and Mr. Matache would have his well-deserved sleep. The next morning, he would go back to the railway station to continue the heavy work of loading lumber onto cars that, in those days, usually went to the Soviet Union as part of the war reparations.

The talk with Mr. Matache was interesting, just finding out what he was thinking in respect to his life experience. For instance, Mr. Matache was so impressed by the German army, which, during WWII, went through Călinești, that he was thinking that only this army could free Romania from the Soviet occupation. The truth is that the German armor that I saw as a child during the war in Bucharest was very impressive. The cars and trucks seemed superior in quality in many respects to that of the Allies. Still, Mr. Matache was ignoring the defeat that the Red Army had inflicted to the Germans.

Some days in the summer, after the evening round at the hospital, when I would be at home, Mrs. Matache would invite me to join them for dinner. They would eat outside in the courtyard, sitting on very low stools around a large round, low table. The food usually consisted of pieces of pork meat that since January had been saved in big glass jars immersed in fat. She would take these pieces of meat and just drop them into a saucepan to be heated. The meat had already been cooked before being preserved.

Besides that, she would make a large *mămăliga* which is the Romanian equivalent of polenta, consisting of boiled corn meal, which actually resembled southern grits. The way Mrs. Matache boiled it resulted in something shaped like large round bread that could be sliced with a string. Everybody around the table would take pieces of meat and a slice of mămăliga. Sometimes she would add some eggs to the saucepan with the meat. The meal was very nourishing, and no one was worried about calories or cholesterol.

Pig slaughter was a big event in the Călineşti Village, almost a celebration. It took place at the beginning of January, and it happened throughout the village almost on the same day or at least during the same week. Almost every household would slaughter its pig by this time of the year. In Romania, January is usually the coldest month of the year, and temperatures during the day can easily drop to minus many degrees.

The event started in the morning when the pig was slaughtered and butchered. Mrs. Matache would then proceed with the cooking. The skin and organs would be cooked right away, the skin fried into pieces shaped like a ring and eaten immediately. The organs, such as kidney and liver, were used to prepare a soup. A few guests were invited to share the good meal, the fried skin, and the soup. The meal was accompanied by boiled ţuica, drunk while hot in small glasses. On the freezing days of January, this combination of food, accompanied by some boiled ţuica, can generate a lot of heat and good mood.

Most of the meat was deep fried and immediately stored in big glass jars, making sure all the pieces were well covered with the melted fat, which was poured over the meat. This would be the family's source of meat for the rest of the year. In other parts of the country, particularly in Transylvania, people would also make their own cold cuts and sausages, but the Matache family was not into that.

This pig slaughter celebration is part of a way of life that has likely gone on for thousands of years. That part of the world that became Romania only in the nineteenth century, has survived all the vicissitudes of history and nature because it had this kind of self-sufficient household economy. There was always, or almost always, enough food to assure survival and reproduction, and the pig was part of it. An animal that would eat almost anything, reproduce itself easily and abundantly, and finally provide enough meat and fat to cover the needs of a family for about a year was an essential part of this way of life.

The Romanian population had been overwhelmingly rural until the twentieth century. Then under forced industrialization, in conjunction with the destruction of the rural civilization implemented by the communist regime, the population has become predominantly urban. The negative consequences of this striking change are felt as I write these lines, and the search for a balanced society may go on for a long time. The fact is that the

Romanian peasant society was not interested in changing its historical way of life; it was self-sufficient and regarded any intrusion on its territory as an aggression by alien forces.

It is not by chance that in the province of Moldova at the beginning of the twentieth century, many towns were predominantly Jewish. The Romanian population didn't wish and was not interested in moving to the urban realm. They didn't need asphalt roads since their horse-driven wagons would work very well on dirt roads as they did for centuries. They didn't need running water; the wells were good enough to provide whatever water was necessary. The spiritual needs were covered by the local priest who had the total monopoly over it, and a midwife was enough to take care of the health problems. Like many similar communities around the world, this population survived and was happy with its way of life perpetuated over centuries. Any outside encroachment, peaceful or not, was a threat to its survival. The slaughter of the pig was an important part of the life cycle.

The only personal relation I had in the Călinești Village was with Mioara. She was a nice-looking young woman with a round pretty face working as an educator at the village preschool. She visited me at the hospital, and we met in Bucharest on a weekend. After a walk downtown, she accepted my invitation and visited my apartment. For a village girl to do all that, coming to the city and even going into a man's apartment was unexpected. I was indeed impressed how she trusted me and probably liked me, but in those days, I was still recovering from my separation from Mona and looking for Mona number two. Mioara's chances of winning me over were very slim. This brief romance ended soon in a horrible way. Coming back to Călinești after a weekend, Mrs. Matache told me that Mioara had died from electrocution at her home while ironing clothes. Although our friendship was very short, this event left me extremely saddened and fearful. Was I being followed by a hurtful destiny?

In Charge of Pediatrics

Sometime in 1960, Dr. Dobrescu, the head of the pediatrics section, went to Bucharest for more training, and I was left alone in charge of pediatrics. This lasted until I left the Călinești Hospital for good in December 1961. This was quite a challenge, for we had many patients, and some of them were in serious condition. During this time, I had my rewards in seeing children who came to the hospital in bad shape recover. Unfortunately, I also had cases where the outcome was not as good.

Compared with what is now available in the practice of medicine, we had rather primitive means of fighting diseases. The hospital had a modest laboratory that would perform just basic analysis, and in radiology, a physician would examine the lungs and heart. Sometimes I wonder what my medical students would be able to do under those circumstances. Still we managed to take care of many of those sick children. In my work, I was helped by several nurses, two of them of remarkable quality. The head nurse was Mrs. Maria Teodorescu, and she was assisted by Mrs. Mioara Popa. Both of them got along very well and were extremely reliable. I recall them as being excellent helpers in my daily and nightly care of sick children.

I have never asked a parent for any form of compensation. Although this would have been illegal, it was practiced all the time by my fellow physicians. For me it was not necessary. I was happy with whatever money I was making from my salary and the additional bonuses for extra hours of supplementary weekend shifts. Nevertheless, almost always, the parents would bring some modest gift from their own production, usually eggs, chicken, or a gallon of wine. They were used to doing it. I assume they felt that I would be more careful with their children if they did. They had very little cash since very few of them were state employees. Their only potential source of money was if they managed to sell some of their produce on the farmers' market in the nearest town, and this was not easily done.

One of the most bizarre events happened when I treated the child of the local police chief. The child, who was two or three years old, was brought to the hospital badly dehydrated with a severe case of infection. I treated him like an intensive care case, and in a few days, he recovered. This was not unusual; sick children can quickly go either way. The child was accompanied by his mother, the policeman's wife, and my chief nurse told me who she was. When the child was getting close to being discharged, his mother came to me and discreetly offered me a nice sum of money, about 15 percent of my monthly salary. I refused, not only on principle, but also thinking that her husband could show up next and take me to jail for taking bribes, which was punishable by years in jail. I thought the case was closed, but this was not to be.

The following day, the policeman showed up in my office with the money in hand, insisting that I should take it, that I deserved it, etc. I managed to resist his offer, although he insisted strongly. In a way, I was pleased that these people showed their satisfaction with what I was doing there; it gave me a feeling of confidence and of mission accomplished. Unfortunately, I had a few cases of children who died, and I must say that each loss of a child troubled me very seriously. For several days, I was followed by thoughts of what happened, and that made me very unhappy. I was always wondering if I did everything right.

The Bogați Village Experience

By the end of 1960, the government decided to take inventory of the public health situation in different populations throughout the country. I was appointed as a member of a commission that was tasked to survey the health of the general population, including children in the village of Bogați. In Romanian, *Bogați* means "the rich ones," and indeed this village seemed to match its name. The place where we were lodged must have belonged to a wealthy family before the communist regime, because it had a pool, something that in Romania was almost unheard of. Now the home belonged to the people, and very likely, the owners had been chased out or sent to some concentration camp.

The medical dispensary was in a building that I was told was built before WWII with money from the Rockefeller Foundation. It was a nice building with plenty of room for consulting patients. The problem with this place was that the village was located twenty or thirty miles from the main highway and railway station. The village was spread out over hills, and was reached only through a dirt road full of potholes. There was only a bus going there from the railway station. It was a bumpy ride going there and coming back. On this bus, most passengers were oilmen who were working in the oil fields that were recently developed in the area.

The mud after rain or snow was pretty deep. I remember once, the bus dropped me close to the train station. As I was hurrying to the station to catch the coming train, I went through a patch of deep mud. One of my galoshes became trapped in the mud, and being in a hurry to get to the train, I didn't bother to rescue it. It was already dark, and this fishing expedition would have had little chance of success.

In the Bogați village, the priest and the local physician, a woman, played the role of hosts for this commission that I was part off. For them, it was a happy event to have such guests for so long. There were parties almost every evening, many times with poker games lasting late into the night. The priest's home was fitting for the Bogați village; it was large and very hospitable. Dr. Răiciulescu was also part of the commission, so we were together in this adventure, which made me feel much better.

We started our work in January since the winter months were most appropriate for having the peasant population of the village available for this health checkup. It was pretty cold this time of the year; I recall sleeping one night in a village home that was without heat. Outside, there must have been a deep freeze, something like minus twenty degrees Celsius. The windows were covered with thick ice. I was in bed, and the only source of heat was an electric heater near my bed. The rest of the house was frozen. It was almost funny! At that time, I was only twenty-seven years of age; and fortunately, the whole action lasted only three months, so by the spring of 1961, I was back in Călinești.

Admission to Oncology Institute

Soon after my return to Călinești in the spring of 1961, I found out that there were trainee position openings at the Oncology Institute in Bucharest. One of the positions perfectly suited my interests. It was in the division of pathology and was focused on using a new technology for those days—tissue culture. Under the direction of Hans Aderca and Marius Ianconescu, I had already gained some experience in growing cells in culture at the Microbiology Institute, and it was a new area that was developing in the world, and that attracted me very much. In fact, I ended up doing tissue culture for the rest of my active life. The recent progress on the use of stem cells and its application for treatment of different disorders is based entirely on the tissue culture technique that was developed in those years.

For me, it was time to decide which way to go. I was reaching the last year of a residency in pediatrics, and after completing three years, I could have taken the Romanian equivalent of the board examination and become a specialist in pediatrics. This is what my predecessor in the Călinești Hospital had done. As a pediatrician specialist, he could have stayed in Călinești but chose to go to a rather large city and practice there. That meant that I would be a pediatrician for life, and the question was, did I want that? The answer for me was quite clear, and it was negative.

There were at least two important reasons for that. One, I had major difficulties coping with the night shifts. Losing a night of sleep was very hard on me, and it would take two or even three nights to recover. Pediatrics involves a lot of night activity since children tend to get sick mostly during the night. The other reason was that, emotionally, I was not coping well with losing cases. It is inevitable in medicine not to save every patient, and that happens also with sick children. Each case of a dead child left me with some emotional trace, and I felt that with time, this could influence my personality in a negative way. Possibly, the death of my sister has sensitized me to this outcome.

On the other hand, pathology seemed to me the best part of medicine since, at the end, this is where the precise diagnostic lies; it is the supreme court of medical practice. On top of that, to do research in oncology and to directly fight the enemy that mercilessly killed my mother was a dream come true; it was almost like a mission that I could not and should not refuse. Moreover, the tissue culture experience that I had at the Microbiology Institute made this area extremely attractive; to watch living cells grow right in front of your eyes and to be able to study them was, for me, the realm of a new world.

So I went to talk to the director of the Oncology Institute, Dr. Octav Costăchel. Costăchel received me in his office and had me seated in front of him, quite close to him, separated by a small desk. With a head resembling a fox, with dark hair, possibly dyed, with brushed eyebrows, his inquisitive dark eyes looked at me with interest. He asked me a few questions about my experience in tissue culture and seemed interested in me, but was reserved. He told me that I would have to pass a competitive examination because there was only one position open, and there may be more candidates.

To prepare for this exam and brush up my pathology, I went to see Dr. Harry Ioachim, who had been assistant professor in the Department of Pathology. He was the husband of a medical school classmate of mine, Noemi Rosenfeld. Dr. Ioachim was a staff pathologist at the Panduri Urology Hospital. He received me kindly and showed me some microscopic slides that helped me brush up on my pathology.

I assume that he lost his position as assistant professor when he applied for a passport to leave the country. Soon thereafter, Dr. Ioachim and Noemi left Romania for the United States. In New York, Ioachim became a well-known pathologist and professor at the Lennox Hospital affiliated with Columbia University. I met Dr. Ioachim in Romania in 1996, at a meeting for expatriated scientists organized in the city of Brasov. By then we were professors of pathology, he in New York and I in Columbia, South Carolina. We were quite well known in our field of expertise, he in blood disorders and I in atherosclerosis. This was the take-home lesson for those who were willing to learn. The two of us who, for one reason or another, were kept in the lower ranks in Romania were rightly graded by our value in the American society. And people still wonder why some countries remain in the second or third tier while others continue to lead the world.

The admission examination for the trainee position at the Oncology Institute consisted of a written test of pathology in which I was asked to describe the differences between two major classes of malignant tumors according to their origin. It was a broad and interesting subject, and the test was given by Prof. Emil Crăciun, who had been my professor of pathology in the medical school. I wrote a good assay on this subject; I felt that I had passed the examination and that I would be hired.

My Father's End

In May 1958, the last trial in which my father was the defending attorney was that of several physicians, including the director of the Forensic Medical Institute, who were accused of receiving bribes. In their defense, my father accused the interior ministry of copycatting the famous physicians' trial in the Soviet Union set up by Stalin. Comrade Drăghici, the minister of internal affairs, didn't appreciate being compared to the infamous Beria, Stalin's henchman, and my father was disbarred without the right to have a pension, although he was almost sixty-five. Apparently, he was fortunate not to be sent to some concentration camp like many others. However, his financial situation deteriorated quickly. He had no savings. He had to start selling his books and other valuable possessions, and he appealed for help to his brother, Willy, in Mexico, who started sending him a $100 per month allowance.

During this period, his relationship with Tuna became strained. She had applied for a passport and visa to migrate to Israel, while my father refused to do so. His explanation was that at his age, being a lawyer and not knowing the language, he would have nothing to do over there. Also, having been a part of so many political trials, he knew too much about the communist regime to be allowed to leave the country. If he would have written a book about all that he had witnessed in the communist justice, it would have sounded, most likely, like another *Gulag Archipelago*.

By contrast, Tuna was no longer involved in politics; she was intensively learning Hebrew and was about thirteen years younger than my father. They were asked to divorce in order for her to get a passport, and as far as my father was concerned, I think he was grateful for that. So their marriage ended in divorce. Tuna left the country and went to Israel where, I was told, she got, to my account, at least her fourth husband; not bad for a woman who looked like a tramp and was one!

My father stayed behind and married Mrs. Dora Gheorghiu, a lady that he met while defending her former husband who was accused of being a spy for UK or USA. He moved to her apartment, and I used to visit them every weekend when I would go to Bucharest from my job as a resident at the Călinești Hospital. Those were the years when our rapport became quite good. I felt sorry for him, sorry to see his downfall from being the master of the bar and becoming unemployed and poor, waiting for his allowance to come from his brother, Willy, in Mexico.

In the winter of 1960, he developed a bad case of heart disease. After having a nice family Christmas dinner at Uncle Oscar's house, he had his first heart attack. The following months, the disease progressed, and the angina attacks became more frequent and very painful. In those days, there were not many ways to treat this disease. By June, the health of my father took a turn for the worst. He had a heart attack and was taken to the Colțea Hospital while I was at Călinești. When I came for the weekend, I went to see him in the hospital. On the evening of June 17, while in the hospital, he had a massive heart attack; and by the next morning, he had expired with me trying desperately all night to revive him. Strangely, by morning, he opened his eyes, looked at me, and smiled. I will never know if that meant anything; I would like to believe that it was like saying "I am glad you are here." After less than an hour, he passed away. It was June 18, Sidonia's birthday.

The burial took place at the Giurgiu Cemetery in Bucharest, and in spite of the shortness of time, which is usual for Jewish burials, a large crowd came. Some friends gave me a strong antidepressant. The effect of the drug was stunning and terrible. I was there at the burial of my father feeling like I was watching a movie with which I had nothing to do, looking at all those people who were obviously emotional and not being able to react in any way. I have never taken an antidepressant again.

The chief rabbi of Romania, Dr. Moses Rosen, performed the service and spoke about my father. Dr. Rosen was a political appointee, like everybody in the communist regime occupying an important position. He spoke highly of my father who had been an important defense attorney for the Zionist leaders who were put on trial and tortured by the communist regime.

> Wikipedia. Moses Rosen (July 23, 1912-May 6, 1994) was Chief Rabbi (Rav Kolel) of Romanian Jewry between 1948-1994 and president of the Federation of Jewish Communities of Romania between 1964-1994. He led the community in his country through the entire Communist era in Romania and continued in that role after the restoration of the democracy by the Romanian Revolution of 1989. Since 1957 was deputy from an electoral section of Bucharest in the Romanian parliament (the Great National Assembly) during the Communist regime and after 1989 in the democratic parliament. The entering of Romania in the war against the Soviet Union, as ally of Nazi Germany, brought more hardships to the Jewish population. Rosen had to hide himself in order to avoid a very probable deportation to Transnistria as suspected "left wing" or "Bolshevik Jewish activist."

The following days and weeks, I realized that I was now alone. There was nobody left of my family. It is true I had some very good friends, but my mother, Mama Mare, and now my father, were all gone. Between 1958 and 1961, I lost all three; moreover, and not the least, I also lost Mona. This time I was indeed alone, all by myself. I went back to Călineşti and took care of my sick children. Judging from the amount of eggs, chicken, and wine that was accumulating at Mrs. Matache's house, I was very much appreciated. I would never have asked any of the parents for anything, but the parents felt obliged to bring something—eggs, chicken, wine, things they had around their household—as a token expression of their gratitude for my taking good care of their children. I remember one woman telling me that she brought a goat to my house. I asked her to take it back immediately. What was I supposed to do with a goat? And for her that was certainly something important. However, these were all signs that people appreciated what I was doing for their children.

After my father's death, I received a phone call at the hospital that I had been accepted at the Oncology Institute, and I was to begin work on December 1. My departure came at a time when my loneliness was balanced by the friendship that was surrounding me at the Călineşti Hospital from my good friends, Răiciulescu and Botez. I was leaving this small community just when we were bonding better than ever. It was like abandoning them, but I had no choice. Continuing to stay at Călineşti would have meant, for me, becoming a pediatrician for the rest of my life, something that I had no desire for whatsoever. It was also the end of commuting, which was not something that I was going to miss.

More than anything, I was strongly attracted by the idea that I would get the training necessary to improve my medical education and, above all, to be able to do research. Since I had entered the medical school and participated in the student research group of the Anatomy Department, I felt the attraction of exploring new domains. I am, by nature, a curious guy, and I always wanted to find out what there is farther down the road. The time spent with Hans Aderca and Marius Ianconescu at the Institute of Microbiology has reinforced this urge. I have seen what it means to enter into new field and the satisfaction that comes with it. On top of that, I regarded cancer as a personal enemy that had killed my mother and brought havoc into my life. I felt obligated to do something about it.

Wrapping Up

This was a period of my life in which I learned a lot, among other things, that one should never despair and give up because the way of one's destiny is unknown. Although life in Călinești was rough and rather primitive compared with what I was used to, in this rather short interval, many changes happened with me. I entered this stage in my life classified as disabled for life. I had lost my mother, my grandmother, my father, and Mona. I entered an unfamiliar realm, and no one could tell me what to do to be successful. When this stage in my life reached an end, I was full of confidence in myself and in my destiny. I knew I could survive under difficult life conditions; I knew that, professionally, I could do well and do what I always wanted—to be a doctor. In brief, I had proven to myself that I was able to follow my way in life and do it successfully. What is more, I learned to live alone, without family and without a comrade with whom I could share everything. And this lesson served me well over the following years until I met Sidonia.

I also learned that one should try to understand others no matter how different they may be, because if you treat others with respect and honesty, most of the time, they will treat you the same. I learned the value of friends and friendship. The friendship of Mircea Răiciulescu and Mircea Botez will stay with me for the rest of my life. For the years that I spent in Călinești, they were my surrogate family. I have very good memories of these friends, and I am grateful for their friendship and company. I regret that after I left Călinești and returned to Bucharest, neither one would maintain our association. In a way, I felt like someone who had escaped from a jail or a concentration camp and those left behind felt that I no longer belonged to their world.

More than anything else, this was the time of my life when I learned what it means to be responsible, not only for myself, but also for other people. I learned what it means to make decisions that could be lifesaving. In spite of, or maybe because of, the rather tough life conditions to which I had to adjust, this time of my life was an important contribution to the development of my personality, of my character. It was like moving out of an ivory tower into the real world where mud and fleas are a common encounter.

This was also a time when I really practiced medicine. I was among sick children and adults, day in and day out. I saved lives, and I lost lives. I learned how these people look at you and expect you to save their lives or the lives of their loved ones, and to return them to health and their family. I learned to admire the good physicians and to despise the bad ones. Later in life, during the many years when I taught medical students, I kept all this experience alive and tried to pass it on to them. I would be gratified if I knew that I succeeded even a little.

When my father and I became older, he reaching his old age and I starting my adult age, I overcame my anger and developed a kind of fondness for him. However, this was not the love that I had for my mother, not the total devotion that I had for her. In a way, I felt sorry for him. It is true that during the first years of my life, he did a lot to provide his family with a good life, and that he helped me financially to complete my studies. Could he have done more? Probably yes. It would have been easier for my mother, and I would have been happier for that. The truth is that in spite of all the gossips about him making lots of money, he was always complaining that he had none. Between his mistress and Tuna, it seemed there was not much left. The fact is that when he was disbarred, he became poor overnight. It seemed that he had no savings, none.

It is also true that he had been very successful in his profession, and he became one of the best lawyers in the country. Petre Pandrea, in his autobiographical book, *The Memories of the Valach Mandarin* (Albatros Publishing House, Bucharest 2000), calls him "the most famous lawyer of the Capital in the period 1949-1956" (page 97), "the prince of Bucharest lawyers," and "the diamond of the Bucharest lawyers crown" (page137). But was this all it was? Following his affair with Tuna, he lost his family and risked his life, for what? He exposed his children to poverty, lost a beautiful and exceptional wife, and ended up in his old age seeking affection from mistresses who were probably more interested in his money than in him. Then he had this ambitious tramp abandoning him and taking with her a fortune bought with his money. All these things happened because he got involved with a woman interested only in climbing the social ladder, and using him to reach this goal. It is not up to me to judge what he did to my mother and to his children, but in the end, it was a lesson to be learned, which I did.

I spent those years practicing medicine in the countryside, where the government had sent me. I graduated from medical school with an honors diploma, and my record as a medical student would normally have qualified me for a position in an academic teaching and/or research institution. Only Communist Party members from our class, and a few others that had personal connections with party higher-ups, were hired in those positions. The best and the brightest graduates were all sent to some rural positions where they will waste at least three precious years.

I managed to get a position in research at the Oncology Institute only because at that moment, the communist leadership was starting a political détente. In the long run, this proved to be only an intermission, after which the communist system will return with a vengeance to the same discriminatory policy based on party membership and political connections. This emphasizes again that the political system had a tremendous influence on my life, and I was not alone. My struggle to improve and rise professionally in spite of the communist regime has just begun.

Chapter 5

The Oncology Institute 1961-1966

Learning about Cancer

By the time I joined the Oncology Institute in December 1961, the institute was expanding, both in the clinical and the research sections. I was part of a group of young physicians who were hired to fill up training positions in surgery, chemotherapy, radiology, and pathology, all related to oncology.

Romania was entering a stage that lasted almost a decade, in which there was a détente that was apparent, both inside the country and also in foreign policy. The major change in the political orientation of the Romanian Communist Party leadership was aimed to free itself from the total servitude toward the Soviet Union, and to develop a more nationalistic policy. This implied an opening to the West, until now something impossible under the strict obedience of Romania to the Soviet Union. In this attempt of communist Romania to free itself from the Kremlin patronage, the party needed at least some sympathy from the people.

During these years, surviving political detainees, after many years of detention and torture, were released from jail. This opening to the West was seen on the music scene where Western singers were invited, and also in the movies. Sidonia and I went to concerts given by Petula Clark, Lionel Hampton, and even the great Louis Armstrong. Western newspapers, mostly of leftist orientation, could be purchased freely, and radio stations such as Voice of America or Radio Free Europe could be listened without being jammed.

As a result of this new turn in government policy, the quality of research and clinical care in the Oncology Institute increased significantly. This more liberal attitude was reflected in the new policy of hiring, which did not involve questions about Communist Party affiliation, or so-called social origin. Although neither my friend and colleague Ștefan Mironescu, nor I, were Communist Party members, or could claim a healthy social origin, we were hired in this national health research institute. Obviously, all that mattered was the professional quality, something that until now was very unusual to say the least. Along with the two of us, a bright young immunologist, Nicolaia Foca, and new trainees in chemotherapy (Mogoș, Silvia Goga), radiology (Constantin Șandru), and surgery (Șaptefrați) were hired. The Oncology Institute already had a few outstanding scientists, such as Prof. Alexandru Caratzali and Dr. Petre Tăutu. Among the clinicians, there were several excellent radiologists (Bunescu, Dragon), and surgeons (Trestioreanu, Mudric, Suciu), and the best cytopathologist in the country and most likely in the world, Dr. Victor Ionescu. None of them were party members, and there were a few that very likely had some thick files at the Securitate. Under those circumstances, the addition of the new trainees was bringing some young blood and adding a new feature to the institute.

When I joined the Oncology Institute, I was assigned to the pathology section, division of experimental pathology, the tissue culture laboratory. The head of the pathology section was an elderly lady, Dr. Iliescu, who, I soon learned, was the protégée of a politically well-connected person, Prof. Vasile Mârza. The head of the experimental pathology was Dr. Ioan Pop, and the head of the tissue culture laboratory was Dr. Lidia Fadei. Dr. Fadei was a middle-aged woman enthusiastic for her research on experimental tumors. She had a strong Russian accent, and most likely, she was of Russian origin. I rapidly learned the routine of the laboratory. My previous experience in the field of tissue culture at the Microbiology Institute was very valuable, probably superior to what was going on in Dr. Fadei's lab.

The head of the genetics laboratory, Dr. Alexandru Caratzali, was a human geneticist, the first of his kind in Romania. He is rightly considered the founder of medical genetics in that country. Dr. Caratzali was a pediatrician who was trained in France before WWII. His major interest was genetic disorders, and he studied under the guidance of the famous Professor Turpin in Paris. By the time I entered medical school, he was professor of biology. The communist government enforced the Soviet Union policy of presenting the classical genetics, started by Mendel and Morgan, as "imperialist pseudoscience," and the Soviet so-called scientists, Michiurin and Lysenko, as the true geneticists. This was done not only to establish the Soviet supremacy over the satellite countries, which Romania was, but also because these scientists were claiming that the environment could change the heredity, a convenient tool for a society in which individuals who were not genetically endowed could pretend to be the leaders of the society.

After Stalin's death in 1953, the science policy of the leadership of the Soviet Union and that of the Romanian Communist Party changed by 180 degrees. Classical genetics was reinstated, and Dr. Caratzali was allowed to pursue his studies of hereditary disorders. By the time I started visiting him, his laboratory was developing the newest techniques for genetic analysis of human beings. By the time I joined the Oncology Institute, the Caratzali-Pricăjan team was studying the chromosomes of the leukocytes, the white blood cells. Mrs. Sidonia Pricăjan was playing a major role in this development; she was really the hands-on person who was developing these new techniques. By 1964, Sidonia would become my wife. Her story is so important for my life that it filled up a separate chapter.

For the first time, scientists all over the world could directly examine the chromosomes of human beings and find out if they were abnormal and what these anomalies were. This is what was going on in Dr. Caratzali's laboratory, where, for the first time, I saw human chromosomes under the microscope. I fell in love with them; I developed a real passion for studying chromosomes that lasted until I came to United States, almost twenty years later. In the process, I became an expert in chromosome studies, particularly as related to cancer. As soon as I entered the Oncology Institute, I started learning about the role of genetic changes in cancer. Soon it became clear to me that the cancer cell was the result of profound genetic changes that happened in a particular cell, and its development was the result of more genetic changes. This concept, which was emerging in those days, is still the basis of cancer research.

My immediate goal was to be able to study the chromosomes of cancer cells from solid tumors, an area which was studied very little then. There was nobody in Romania doing work in this area. I started looking first at the cancer cells grown in tissue culture, and soon I moved into the area of experimental tumors, tumors that were grown in laboratory animals. For that, I had to develop techniques that would allow me to study the chromosomes of cancer cells. In those days, there were few established procedures to do that, most of them derived from techniques used to study plant chromosomes. This was an area of research which was new, not only in Romania, but all over the world. While I was in her laboratory, Dr. Fadei allowed me to pursue my interest. For me, this was a period of what I could call an epiphany. Not only was I doing new and exciting things, but also in the institute library, I had access to all the scientific literature of the world. These were the years when I was learning about cancer, why and how it arises, how it develops and advances and, in particular, about the importance of changes in the genetic material in these processes.

When I follow the medical literature today and learn about the new findings related to changes in the genes that cause cancer cells to develop and grow, I recall the concepts that were developed about that time when scientists were able, for the first time, to look at the chromosomes of cancer cells and find out how altered they were. When I look back on those times, I realize that the basic concepts were already developing, and the progress in technology that took place over the years revealed facts to support and better understand those concepts.

It is encouraging to see that some of these findings about changes in the chromosomes find their way into the treatment of different types of cancer. Finding out the detailed mechanisms and factors involved in cancer allows for the development of new drugs. All these efforts may contribute to the fight against this terrible disease. However, I think there is a need for fresh ideas that should provide the background for significant progress in cancer treatment to make it a curable disease.

Within one and a half years after I joined the Oncology Institute, a new wing was added to the old building. This new wing contained large spaces for research laboratory and also new scientific equipment. This was a time when we had everything we needed for our research: chemicals, hardware, etc. If we needed something for our research to be bought from abroad, we simply had to put in the order and wait for the product to come. The library had a large number of subscriptions to the most important medical journals of the world, and we were allowed to ask for reprints. The institute paid for all the mail. During those years, I accumulated several thousand scientific papers.

When the new wing of the building was ready, Dr. Costăchel, the director of the institute, decided to move me out of Dr. Fadei's lab into the new laboratory that I was to share with my friend and colleague Ștefan Mironescu. We shared the largest laboratory and the most modern equipment, among other things, a Zeiss microscope with which we could make movies of living cells. This was sold by the Opton Company, which was a branch of the Zeiss Company that had fled East Germany and moved to Oberkochen in West Germany.

In this new laboratory, I continued my work on chromosomes while Dr. Costăchel was trying to find and hire a senior scientist to lead our group. Dr. Gancevici, from the Cantacuzino Institute, expressed some interest in moving to the Oncology Institute. He had training in cell biology techniques in a famous institute in Denmark. He brought some laboratory equipment and was coming sporadically to visit us. We started some work with him, but he was undecided between our institute and the Cantacuzino Institute. This ambiguity upset my friend Ştefan, who was anxious to see things moving and moving fast. So one day, he decided to kick Dr. Gancevici out of our laboratory. Without much delay, Ştefan ordered our technician, Mr. Grigoraş, to pack everything from the lab that belonged to Dr. Gancevici, put it on a truck, and send it back to the Cantacuzino Institute. This action didn't please our director, Dr. Costăchel, who was hoping to hire Dr. Gancevici. He called both of us to his office, and Ştefan had a lot of explaining to do, which he did. I will never know what happened, but in the end, Dr. Costăchel left us alone, and the two of us continued to work independently in the large laboratory.

After a while, Dr. Costăchel assigned me a trainee, Max Pop. Max joined my laboratory fresh out of college. He had the equivalent of a master's degree in biology, which gave him a broad view of biology but no hands-on experience in the laboratory. As expected, he had to start from scratch, which he did. He learned the microscopy fast and spent his days at the microscope, looking and drawing chromosomes of cancer cells. Max was having a sort of double life, being a scholar during the day and spending the evenings, probably late into the night, with friends at the luxurious Athénée Palace Hotel restaurant. To stay alert during the day, Max used to bring a thermos filled with Turkish coffee, which he drank throughout the day, and that kept him awake. To my surprise, Max evolved into a successful scientist. He joined the National Institute of Health in Bethesda, Maryland, first as a trainee supported by a fellowship, and then he became a staff member. Some years ago, he invited me to his laboratory to present a seminar, and we managed to publish a good paper together.

Although we worked on separate projects, Ştefan and I frequently talked about our work and ourselves. We had been classmates in the lyceum and then again in medical school. Ştefan and I have decided that we had to recover the years when we were sent by the government to the countryside instead of getting the training and doing the research we were interested in. As medical students, we were both very active in the scientific research groups affiliated with the Department of Anatomy, and it would have been normal to be retained by this department after graduation. What happened was that after graduation, only the Communist Party members were hired by the medical school, although they had no research activity, and most of them had, at best, passing grades acquired under suspicious conditions.

Ștefan and I reached the consensus, that if we wanted to become competitive on the international level in our fields, our workday should be at least twelve hours long, and not the eight-hour schedule from 8:00 AM to 4:00 PM. Therefore, we would have lunch at an excellent cafeteria not far from the institute, and then continue to work until 8:00 PM or 9:00 PM. This cafeteria was located in one of the most luxurious neighborhood of Bucharest. Homes were mostly villas built before WWII by wealthy people, each with a flower garden. In the entire neighborhood there were no commercial sites and no high-rise condominiums. Now the communists had taken over, and the villas were occupied by high-ranking party members. Throughout the neighborhood, there were also a few embassies. People who used the cafeteria were mostly high-ranking party members and their employees. Food was outstanding, and prices were reasonable. It so happened that this cafeteria was within walking distance from our institute, just right for a nice walk to stretch from the laboratory work and back for a good digestion. This was to be my schedule until the birth of our son, Noël, in 1965, when I decided to go home earlier for his evening bath.

Joe Melnick, My American Gate

An event that had tremendous consequences for me occurred in the summer of 1963. By then, I was starting a collaborative research project with Hans Aderca, my mentor in tissue culture at the Microbiology Institute. This research was about a virus called SV40, that had recently been found in monkeys used for the production of the polio vaccine. The SV40 virus, which had contaminated batches of polio vaccine, proved to be able to induce tumors in animals such as hamsters. It was called an oncogenic virus. Hans provided the virus, and I injected it into hamsters. As expected, after several months, the hamsters developed malignant tumors, and my laboratory studied the chromosomes of these cancer cells.

> Wikipedia. Joseph Louis Melnick (October 9, 1914-January 7, 2001) was an American epidemiologist who performed breakthrough research on the spread of polio, with The New York Times calling him "a founder of modern virology."

One day, I received a call from Hans, telling me that the famous American scientist Joe Melnick, and his wife, Dr. Matilda Benyesh-Melnick, were visiting the Institute of Microbiology. He asked if I would like to come and meet them. The Melnick couple came to visit the Microbiology Institute in Bucharest because they knew Florin Niculescu from the papers he had published before WWII while at the Pasteur Institute in Paris. While visiting the Microbiology Institute, Joe Melnick met Hans Aderca and Marius Ianconescu, and I think he was impressed about their work. Melnick was told about our collaborative work on SV40 virus; Melnick's department was one of the world leaders in the area of SV40 virus research. The Melnicks apparently wanted to know what I was doing with the SV40 virus, so they decided to call me to join the discussion. For me, the opportunity to talk to such a famous scientist was a sign from heaven. It came totally out of the blue, and I wouldn't have missed it for anything.

So I almost flew to the Microbiology Institute, and was introduced to the Melnick couple who were nice and friendly. Sometime during our chat, Melnick asked me if I would be interested in doing some work in his department. What a question! It was like having someone ask you if you wanted to go to heaven. There was only one answer. Looking back in time, it is very likely that this meeting was the most important event in my professional life; it was a crossroad that has changed the course of my life. Did I appreciate this at that time? Frankly speaking, I did not. I was proud to meet such a famous scientist, and to have him interested in my work; it was a good sign that I was on the right path. But then did I see further? No. I couldn't be happier at the Oncology Institute, and I was still very busy with the research I was doing; my main project was to finish the study of a tumor that was growing in hamsters and showed very peculiar features. As far as leaving Romania at that time, the thought just didn't occur to me.

Miracle on the Mountain

During the weekends, I would frequently go hiking in the mountains. The National Tourist Office run a train that left in the morning from the

North Central station going to Prahova Valley and returning that evening or the following day. Within two hours, one could be close to some nice hiking trails and all that for very little money. I took advantage of those opportunities and made frequent trips, many times with friends like Hans Aderca and Marius Ianconescu. I looked at those trips as a way to be more productive in my research, and I think it worked.

On a weekend in June 1963, Hans Aderca and I decided to go to the Bucegi Mountains and hike up a glacier valley called the Snow Gap. This was one of the very few places in these mountains where the ice sticks around through summer. The very steep valley was beneath some peaks called Miller's Teeth. We started hiking, and from the beginning, I knew we were in for a very tough job. The climbing was almost straight up, and we had no equipment for that. However, we managed to reach almost the end of the valley, when we were faced with a huge wall of rock. We couldn't find the passage under it, and there was no way to climb it. We had to return by the same valley. We started to descend, and this was even more difficult than climbing. There were instances when we had to drop our backpacks because there was no room for us to stand up. Finally, we got close to the end where the glacier was squeezed between two huge abrupt walls of rock.

Fig. 1. The Snow Gap is the area of ice below the sharp peaks called the Miller's Teeth.

We starting to cross the glacier, and as I was the first one walking, I slipped on the ice and fell on my back. I found out later that the metallic teeth on my boots were blunt and, instead of holding onto the ice, were sliding on it. As I was sliding down on the glacier, Hans realizing what had happened, threw himself on the glacier, and I managed to grab him. We continued sliding down together, and after a few seconds, he told me to let him go. At that moment, I realized I was doomed, and I lost consciousness.

I don't know how long this blackout lasted. When I regained consciousness, I was standing up in the bright sun at the bottom of the glacier against the rocky wall. I was on the trail near the right wall of rock that was bordering the glacier ravine. My first thought was, *This must be heaven, and here I am*, but I saw Hans rushing toward me. As soon as Hans reached me, which was almost immediately, I realized that, no, I was not in paradise. I was still on this earth. Hans told me that after I released him, I started rolling down on the ice like a ball until I hit the wall of rock at the bottom of the glacier.

When I checked my backpack, I figured out what happened. In my backpack, I had an aluminum box with food, including tomatoes. The box and the tomatoes were squashed. I must have hit the wall of rock with my back and the backpack with its content took the hit. I believe that some miraculous force had saved my life. If I had hit the wall of rock with any other part of my body, it would have been a deadly blow. We walked back to the railway station. On the train back to Bucharest, we met several friends, and everything seemed all right.

When I arrived home, I started feeling pain in my back. I couldn't sleep, and I was having nightmares. The image of me sliding down the ice was coming back again and again. The close encounter with death was not leaving me. Later in the summer, when I went to the beach, I had a very hard time walking down the steep cliff bordering the beach; I almost couldn't do it. Just looking down paralyzed me. It took great effort to walk down; the steps caused me to recall my fall on the glacier. The pain in the back lasted several months, and I still feel it when the weather changes.

Good Times

My work in the laboratory was going well as I was finishing my paper on the chromosomes of some peculiar experimental tumor. Dr. Costăchel, the director of the institute, seemed to be quite happy with what I was doing. In addition to my research, I was helping him introduce to the Romanian medical community the concept that genetics is crucial in understanding the origin and progression of cancer, a concept that, during the years of Soviet domination, was rejected. Consequently, I was receiving bonus payments almost every trimester, which made life quite comfortable. Beginning of 1964, Sidonia moved to my apartment, and now we started having luncheon together at the same cafeteria. By June 1964, we got married, and we were a happy couple that enjoyed the sympathy of our colleagues.

Around this time, Dr. Caratzali left the Institute of Oncology, very likely as a result of one of his frequent fierce fights with Dr. Costăchel. At that time, Dr. Costăchel asked me to take over his laboratory. I moved there and became the head of the genetics laboratory. Besides Sidonia and my trainee, Max, the group included two more biologists, Liliana Cârnu and Agripina Matache, and a laboratory technician, Mrs. Popa. This allowed me to expand my research projects significantly. This was the beginning of working with Sidonia, who, by then, was my wife. We loved being together in the laboratory, actually everywhere, and all the time.

My First International Meeting

It was the beginning of May 1965 when an important international meeting on melanoma was taking place in Sofia, Bulgaria. Dr. Costăchel, the director of the Oncology Institute, decided to attend this meeting and to present a paper. He embarked a few of his collaborators, including Sidonia and me, on a bus and took us to the meeting. Sofia was just a day of driving away from Bucharest. In Sofia, we visited some beautiful churches with onionlike golden towers.

Fig. 2. Sidonia is resting after visiting the Sipca Monastery.

Fig. 3. Sidonia is walking through the park of the Sipca Monastery.

Fig. 4. Sidonia is taking a brief break during the trip and is chatting with a colleague, Mrs. Mimi Nedelea.

Fig. 5. Sidonia visited the Alexander Nevski Cathedral in Sofia.

At the meeting, Costăchel asked me to present his paper. It was my first international presentation, and it was supposed to be given in English. I was a little concerned because the content of the paper was not exactly in my field and, in attendance, were several well-known American experts in the field of melanoma, which was the topic of the presentation. The presentation went very well, and Dr. Costăchel was happy, and so were we.

On the way back home, the bus took us on a highway going south of the Balkan Mountains through the famous plain of roses. The landscape was wild and beautiful. Going north and crossing the mountains through a pass, we stopped and visited some old monasteries and churches with gold-covered, onion-shaped towers. Being together on this first international trip was, for Sidonia and me, an outstanding experience; we were happy and enjoyed every moment of it.

Leaving the Oncology Institute

Sometime in 1965, I sent a manuscript containing the results of my studies on chromosomes of an unusual experimental tumor for publication to the *Journal of the National Cancer Institute*. This was a very prestigious scientific journal, and to my knowledge, until then, nobody from Romania had ever published a paper in it. Being what I considered to be an important paper, I didn't want to share the credit with a manager who had no idea what was going on. If I had shared the manuscript with Dr. Costăchel, chances were that it would never have gotten out. He had a difficult way of thinking; he wanted badly to contribute to the work that had been done, but his ideas were out of whack with the content of the paper. I had nothing against adding the boss to papers containing my work. I have papers coauthored with Joe Melnick and Fred Rapp, since I thought that, by their administration, they made this work possible. They never changed a word in the paper.

My options were either single-author paper or no paper. I saw this paper as the launching of my career as a tumor geneticist, and I knew I would have to pay the price, and that retaliation would be severe. How severe? Anything was possible, and I was prepared for the worst, making sure that there was an exit door available. The only mistake I made, and I still regret it, is that I did not try to take Sidonia with me. I paid severely for this blunder; we ended up being separated at work for eleven years, and she was submitted for more than a year to an unpleasant situation. That was a very high price to pay for this mistake. In my life, I would classify this as my second major mistake, the first one being my return to Romania from Houston, Texas.

Although I didn't spread the news, as soon as the journal came to the institute library, word had reached the institute, and the director, Dr. Costăchel, was informed. He called me to his office and had a very open talk with me. He told me that what I did was unacceptable, but he was willing to keep me if "I would accept being his slave." If I would accept his "slave" proposal, he would be very generous with me. Anything was on the table, salary, a new apartment, just name it.

I asked him for several days to consider his offer, to which he agreed. As we were talking, my mind was already made up. I knew I could not remain at the Oncology Institute; my time there had expired. To continue to stay there was to sacrifice my career. I would have been required to do whatever Dr. Costăchel dreamt of, which was usually far-fetched scientific ideas that went nowhere. With people close to him, he would have brainstorming meetings lasting late into the night and ending with pseudoscientific projects. I didn't see any future in staying there and becoming his slave.

So I called Dr. Aderca and told him that I was ready to move to the Microbiology Institute. He was being the intermediary between me and the director of the institute, Prof. Florin Niculescu, the father of my former fiancée, Mona. The answer came soon; I was hired. I found it interesting that the same person, Florin Niculescu, who, several years before, told me that my way in life was different from that of his daughter, was willing to bring me into his institute and even to promote me to scientific investigator rank 3, which was about as high as I could go at that stage in my career. This confirmed my belief that he had a high appreciation for me professionally but, for some obscure reasons, preferred to have his daughter married to someone else. Therefore, he was probably hiring me because he was interested in strengthening the quality of research done at his institute.

After I left the Oncology Institute, there were more defections. Ştefan Mironescu and Nicolaia Suciu-Foca were among the first ones to leave the institute. With Nicolaia, I continued to collaborate, and we managed to publish several papers in prestigious medical journals such as *Cancer Research* and others. Over the following years, a good number of the best clinicians and scientists such as Petre Tăutu defected. I can think of several excellent radiologists such as Drs. Bunescu, Dragon, Spiridon, Şandru, all leaving the institute and the country. Everyone realized that the working environment in the institute was deteriorating rapidly, and there was no hope of getting better. Instead, all indications were to expect the worst, and they proved to be right.

Thoughts

The five years that I spent at the Oncology Institute were of tremendous importance for me. This was the time when I entered the world of scientific research. I started by being a trainee, and I left the Oncology Institute as a recognized expert in chromosomes and cancer. I should emphasize that, for reasons that probably had to do with its survival, the communist leadership decided to change their Stalinist way of ruling Romania and to adopt a more relaxed policy. I took full advantage of this change, and what I accomplished was the result of them letting me do what I wanted to do. Unfortunately, this change was just an intermission, and within a few years, the communist leadership, now under Ceauşescu, reverted to a Romanian version of the old Stalinist policy.

Leaving the Oncology Institute seemed to have been a blessing for my career. Max Pop, who, after I left, occupied my position as head of the genetics laboratory did not produce anything scientifically significant during the years he was the slave that Costăchel wished to have. Moreover, the institute underwent many defections as mentioned before, particularly of the best and the most qualified clinicians and scientists. If I had decided to stay, I would most likely have gone into obscurity and would have become one of those disillusioned and frustrated scientists that filled up the positions while waiting for their retirement. My destiny took me in a totally opposite direction, and I followed what it offered, moving like a blind man being led by a powerful hand on a mysterious trail.

Speaking of destiny, I have to add that the jewel of the crown for these years is when I met, fell in love, and married Sidonia, my trustful and loving companion for life, my soul mate forever. Moreover, with the birth of our son, my wish for having a family was fulfilled. I was blessed to live through three miracles, one that saved my life, and the others my wife's and my son's life. This powerful hand of destiny has been very generous with me.

During those years, there were several people that I would never forget and to whom I would always be grateful. Dr. Alexandru Caratzali was the first person to show me the chromosomes that I fell in love with and kept me busy for the next twenty years. Prof. Florin Niculescu, my ex-future father-in-law, told me to follow my way in life and then hired me at his institute. Through him I met Prof. Joe Melnick, and the rest is history, my history. Joe Melnick, who brought me to the United States, will remain forever in my thoughts. He opened for me the door, not only to outstanding research, but to the United States with all of what that meant for me and my family. When I think that only a few years before I was a resident in a county hospital and before that incapacitated, I consider that I was well on my way to fulfilling my mother's last wishes.

Chapter 6

Sidonia

When allowed to flow freely, love overcomes all obstacles.
—Brian L. Weiss, MD

Meeting Sidonia

Sidonia is the most important chapter in my life. We have been together for fifty years, and we shared happiness and difficult times. We managed to build a family and to start a new life in a new world. We loved each other more than words can say. We trusted each other, and we shared everything that was worth sharing. Most of all, we longed to be together. As I am writing this story, my heart is hurting badly because Sidonia is no longer by my side, with her sweet smile and serene and gracious presence. Still I can say that her soul is with me and will continue to be as long as I live and maybe beyond. I have no doubt that we were soul mates that destiny brought us together, and we recognized that and decided to spend this life together. We did it, and on balance, we had far more happiness than sorrow.

My first encounter with Sidonia occurred when I was hired at the Oncology Institute in Bucharest. An important member of the institute was Dr. Caratzali, my professor and examiner at the admission to the medical school. He was the head of the laboratory of genetics and is considered to be the founder of medical genetics in Romania. I paid him a courtesy visit and Dr. Caratzali received me kindly and introduced me to his assistant, Mrs. Sidonia Pricăjan. When he introduced me, he didn't spare accolades, claiming that I was a bright medical student. I doubt that Sidonia was really impressed about my previous accomplishments as a medical student, but years later, she admitted that she liked me as a person. I have to say that I noticed how she was moving around the laboratory in a smooth and quiet way. Drinking the Turkish coffee that Dr. Caratzali mastered to prepare, none of us could foresee the future to find out that only three years later, she would become Mrs. Sidonia Nachtigal. Isn't that another example of how destiny works, leading us like blind people along a pathway that can reach unforeseen sites? At that time, I was only concerned about my performance in the Oncology Institute, and I didn't know or actually care if I would see Mrs. Pricăjan again. As far as she was concerned, it seems likely that she counted me among the many visitors Dr. Caratzali was receiving daily in his laboratory.

After joining the Oncology Institute on December 1961, I started visiting Dr. Caratzali's laboratory, because the study of chromosomes in cancer became my top interest. The professor would treat me with his excellent Turkish coffee that he insisted on preparing himself. Our talk was mainly about our work; he would share some of their new results and ideas, and I would tell him about my progress, or lack of it, with my studies.

By the time I started visiting my old professor on a more or less regular basis, Mrs. Pricăjan had been in his laboratory for several months, and was already his associate. She was always around, listening to our talk while continuing her activity. Sometimes there would be only the two of us, and then we shared our laboratory experience. Often she would help me out when my store of colchicine, a chemical that I was using in large amounts for my chromosome tumor analysis, would run out.

With time, the communication between us extended outside the laboratory talk. I learned that Sidonia had a nickname Țuțu (pronounced tsoo-tsoo), was married, and had a daughter, Carmen, whom I met when she was brought to the laboratory by her mom. From our talk, I got the impression that the Pricăjan family life was not a happy one, but Sidonia was quite reserved on this topic, and I was not interested on it. For the whole year 1962, she was Mrs. Pricăjan; and I was Dr. Nachtigal.

From Colleague to Friend

It was Christmas Eve 1962, a year since I joined the Oncology Institute, when visiting Dr. Caratzali laboratory, I learned that Sidonia had developed an infection. She was recommended treatment with antibiotics, and I volunteered to give her a shot of streptomycin as prescribed by her physician. As a medical student and even as an intern, I used to give shots of antibiotics to neighbors and thus make some money.

In the evening, I got my syringe ready and took off for the Pricăjan residence. Being Christmas Eve, on my way, I stopped at the farmer's market and bought a flower bouquet. I was expecting to visit a family that is celebrating Christmas Eve in the traditional Romanian way, with decorated fir tree and a special dinner. I got on a tramway that dropped me close to where she lived. Like me and many other families in Bucharest, she was living in a shared apartment. I rang the doorbell and Sidonia opened the door. Somewhat embarrassed she told me that her husband and daughter had left town to share the holidays with his family. There was nothing of the Christmas celebration I was expecting. Sidonia was left behind, sick and alone. I understood now why she wouldn't tell me she looked sick at the lab.

I was impressed by what I saw. It was distressing to witness such a sad situation. I gave Sidonia the shot and then, I did something that came to me unexpectedly. I felt that I have to do something to ease the gloom surrounding us, and I kissed her. It was not a passionate love kiss, it was more like a good night kiss, or like a parent kissing a child after some bad tasting medicine. She seemed to me like an abandoned child. She was alone, forsaken by her husband and her child, this special evening when every family gets together to celebrate what they consider to be one of the most joyous moment. It was like I was giving her a cheer on kiss, trying to tell her "Don't be sorry, there will be a sunny day for you." Did I know then that this kiss will lead to the love of my lifetime? No. Did I know what this kiss meant to Sidonia? No. It seemed to be such an innocent kiss! Still, looking back I can safely say that this was for both of us, the beginning of our life long, unconditional, total love, that will change and dominate our lives.

Following that I did something that I have never thought before: I invited her to visit me. By then Sidonia was probably stunned. She was supposed to get an antibiotic injection and what she got? A kiss followed by an invitation to visit the man that kissed her. True, it was not a passionate, love kiss, with hugging and embrace, yet it was a sweet kiss, totally unexpected, coming from a guy that has never even tried to touch her, never tried to flirt with her. Moreover, this guy had a reputation of a womanizer. What this all meant? Sidonia's answer was "I will come on a sunny day" which could have meant a polite way of saying "no," but also a promise to come. It will take weeks for Sidonia to decide what to do. By now she treated me with a delicious sour cherry liqueur that she has made. I left and went home thinking what I saw and realizing what she has never told me before: that her marriage was on the rocks, probably a useless piece of paper.

The following day, I left town to spend the holidays and New Year in the Bucegi Mountains, in an elegant hotel called Cota 1400 (it was at this elevation, 1,400 meters, about 4,200 feet) with a group of people that included some nice young ladies from the Oncology Institute. However, from the hotel, I called Sidonia and asked how she was doing. She was my patient, and on top of that, the thought that this fine and gentle woman was left to spend the holidays alone bothered me.

It may have been January or February when a sunny day came, and with it Sidonia. I just don't remember when this happened. By then I never thought that this would be one of the most important day in my life, and likely, neither did Sidonia. She was not the first woman coming to visit me. Over the years, quite a few women came to visit my place. Some were married, some were not. Some were interested in having sex, some were not. From the very first time when Sidonia came I knew she is going to be different. She didn't seemed interested in an affair, particularly with a guy like me that, in those days in the Oncology Institute, had a reputation of a philanderer.

I was thirty years old, unmarried, no steady girlfriend, not bad looking, able to carry on a conversation, a physician, and a rising star in the institute, overall a potential husband for several young colleagues that were reaching the age of becoming housewives. Even Dr. Costăchel, the director of the institute, used to tease me, calling me "philanderer." Gossips were abundant, and when I was seen in the hallways talking to one of those young ladies, gossip would start about me dating this woman.

Sidonia was aware of those gossips and my reputation, but after spending about ten years in Bucharest she knew only her husband's friends and their wives and she couldn't trust them. She needed an honest, reliable friend and I suppose that during this year of working together in the lab she concluded that I was a reliable and honest person that she can trust. When she came, she shared with me her life story, her family problems, and her anxiety. It looked like she just wanted to get out of her troubled family life and have an open chat with a friend. I was her only trustful friend.

Childhood and Youth

Sidonia was born on June 18, 1929, in Alba-Iulia, a historical town, but her family moved to Cluj when she was just three years old. She always considered Cluj-Napoca the town of her formative years; this is where she went from elementary school to college. This is how Sidonia describes her attendance at the Elementary School No. 7 in Cluj-Napoca between 1936 and 1940: "When I was 7 years old I started school and I remember perfectly my first day there. I recall a huge building with long hallways very tall ceilings and lots of people, parents and kids and myself keeping closely my Mom's hand and sticking to her. I was scared and I cried when she left, leaving me in class with my future colleagues and the teacher. My teacher for 4 years was Elena Şenchea, a very sweet person, beautiful, with completely white hair. I was impressed about that and since then I loved young persons with white hair; now I like it also in older persons. For me the white hair gives a note of distinction to the person. I loved my teacher during those 4 years. At the beginning, I didn't like school too much; I had a hard time adjusting to my new life style program and obligations. I missed home, my friends from home, and definitely my freedom. I clearly remember my Mom coming daily with Mimi to pick me up from school, and how happy I was to join them. When I saw them, I always started to run toward them and hugged Mimi. Sometimes she asked me to give her my backpack to carry it for me, which I did with pleasure. She was proud to look as a school girl. We always met close to my school, in a very nice little park surrounding an old, I think 11th century, protestant church, with the statue of King Matei Corvin. He was a Romanian from Transylvania who became king in Hungary. The Romanians from Transylvania, whose king he was, were very proud of him, even though he served the Hungarian interests. There it was the little park we liked, with flowers, benches, and a lot of kids playing around. One could buy some candies, ice cream, cookies, and many more, from street vendors. During winter we always got roasted chestnuts which we loved, we were crazy about. Mom always treated us with something, just to cheer us up. Often we put the chestnuts in our muffles to warm our hands. Winter or summer, I loved our 'stops' at the 'Big Horse' as we called the park, because the king was riding a horse.

"In every class we had the picture of our king, Carol II, or later Mihai I, plus maps of our country, Europe, or the World. We started and finished every day of school with a prayer-Our Father. The classes were of 50 minutes followed by a 10 minutes break. In class, the girls and boys set in separate benches, two by two, in the first row the shorter ones (which I was), and in the last one, the tallest. Each had her or his place which we kept for all the year. We wear the uniform of the school, and the girls had the hair braided or kept with a hair band. The boys had to cut short their hair. Mid-morning we had a longer break to have the snack we brought from home. We couldn't find or buy anything at the school. In the backyard we relaxed, stretched and played during the breaks.

"In those years, I had two very close friends: Georgeta Dicu and Ovidiu Blaga. Never in my life I had a lot of friends; a few but I was extremely close to them, they were as family for me. Ovidiu Blaga lived close to us, so in the morning we met midway, and went to school together. In the afternoon often we did our homework together. We had homework every day, sometimes lots, at all levels of school. He was very good in Math which I really wasn't. After we finished our homework I liked to play with his toys: cars, airplanes, trains (he had an electric one), and to build homes and bridges. Going to his home, I liked to use the elevator (we didn't have one) even though I was scared not to get stuck between floors. I remember his mother as a nice sweet person and kind to me. She always gave us a snack. When we started high school we lost contact. High schools were separated for girls and boys, and we were not encouraged to have friends of the opposite sex. Rarely did I meet him in the city or a park, and usually we didn't talk too much so I lost totally his trace.

"It was completely different with Georgeta Dicu—we called her Puşa. We became close friends soon after we started school, then in high school we were again colleagues and we even sat in the same bench. Mean time I got taller and stopped growing. Later we met in Bucharest and it happened that our kids went at the same school of Music (Alina and her son). So more or less, we were in contact all the time, and we remained very close friends, until our emigration separated us and we lost contact. I feel as I have to try to find her again, but since we left our country I never went back, but I hope one day the future will bring us together again. She was the one who called me from the beginning Sidi, the way my grandma was called. We were a funny pair in elementary school because of the difference in height. We spent a lot of time together at school and weekends. Her Mom always gave her a big snack considering Puşa is too skinny. Puşa couldn't eat it so she wanted to share it with me to please her Mom, like she ate all of it. I ended by taking just a little from mine and had a lot from hers."

The only boyfriend that Sidonia mentioned was a medical student called Ionel, whom she dated when she was in high school in Cluj. Apparently, things went well between them until trouble started with religion. It happened that Ionel was Catholic whereas Sidonia was Orthodox. Sidonia would accompany Ionel to his Catholic Church, but every time she would go into her Orthodox Church, he would refuse to enter the church, pretending to smoke a cigarette outside. At some point, their discussion turned to a possible marriage, and Ionel wanted to make sure that children would all be baptized Catholic. Sidonia, being a good Orthodox Christian but also a peace lover, offered to split, making half of them Catholic, and half Orthodox. This was unacceptable for Ionel, and they broke up, but not before he cursed her to marry a medical doctor of different faith. And to my good luck, the curse worked!

Sidonia had good memories of the time when she attended the Cluj University. She would frequently go to the Opera House and get seats in the gallery by bribing the ushers. She would go with a group of students, and after some significant aria, they would vociferously hail the singers. The Opera Theater in Cluj was one of the best in Romania and had several outstanding singers. Another event that she enjoyed was the soccer games. Cluj University has been, for years, a very good soccer team, most players being students or alumni. The team played many years in the first national league. Sidonia was telling how she would attend their games and, with her colleagues, loudly support the university team.

Marriage

While a student at the Cluj University, Sidonia met Mr. Artemiu Pricăjan. He was a student in geology and seemed to have been an outgoing person, which she was not. Possibly, she found this attractive. After graduation, Mr. Pricăjan got a good position in Bucharest. They got married in Cluj, and the young couple moved to Bucharest, where they had a private Christian Orthodox wedding. I found it rather funny that their godfather, the supervisor of Mr. Pricăjan, was a Jew. Maybe he was christened, but in those days, there were many Jews, particularly those that had high-ranking positions in the government, that took Romanian names and tried to hide their ethnic origin.

Soon thereafter, the Pricăjan couple had their first child, Carmen. Adjusting to life in Bucharest, a large city compared to Cluj-Napoca, Mr. Pricăjan became socially active, being involved with friends and party goers.

In the meantime, Sidonia was confined at home, taking care of their child and the household.

As a geologist, Mr. Pricăjan was often traveling throughout the country. When Carmen was not in school, Sidonia and Carmen accompanied him. One of these trips took them to the Danube Delta, one of the most diverse regions of Romania and Europe. They were lodged in a home, and their hosts were, like most people there, fishermen. As long as they lived there, Sidonia ate the meals together with her hosts, and they were all based on fish. For dinner, they had fish soup and fish meat. The lady host cooked this every day; the small fish was used to make the soup, and the big fish was boiled in the broth and eaten separately. According to Sidonia, every evening after dinner, the woman asked her husband what he wanted to eat the following day, and his answer was invariably "fish soup."

One funny story is how her host served her caviar. The fishermen were fishing for sturgeon from the Danube, taking out the precious caviar, and preparing it for export. When leaving work, they were searched to make sure they were not taking out this valuable item. One day, the fisherman managed to take some caviar to bring to Sidonia; but to smuggle it, he had to wrap it in newspaper. Sidonia didn't mind and ate a respectable amount of the newspaper wrapped caviar. Her life in the Danube Delta was certainly rustic, and she learned a lot about this rather remarkable community.

Mr. Pricăjan, who was less pleased with the fish diet, was eating at the local restaurant. From her story, it was obvious that between she and her husband, there was not a close relationship; it sounded as though each of them followed a separate life. They didn't even share their meals.

It seems likely that with time, and the Bucharest environment offering more entertainment opportunities than the university town of Cluj, the presumed initial bondage of the Pricăjan couple dissipated. According to Sidonia, her husband had the habit of patronizing women, with unpleasant medical consequences for both of them. And the rest is the sad history of a family self-destruction.

Sidonia had been intending to divorce for some time. She had Carmen soon after she got married, and I assume that, for some time, while taking care of her child, she was hoping that her marriage would improve and survive. She was not taking decisions lightly, and she was a cautious person, trying to hang on to the present and hoping for the future. However, over the years, she understood that her husband was hopeless, their lives were drifting away, and she had to find a way out of the quagmire.

The first step in this separation was to find a job to gain financial independence. Sidonia family was in Cluj-Napoca and unable to give her any support, and in Bucharest, she knew only her husband's friends, and they were not her friends. Mr. Pricăjan didn't think she would be able to get a job. He seemed satisfied having a wife who would do the cooking, the laundry, and the babysitting, and let him do whatever pleased him. He treated her more like the nanny of their child than like his wife. This is hard to comprehend since she had a college degree from the University of Cluj, the same one he graduated from. In Romania in those days, women, especially if they had a college degree, would take jobs since for a family, one salary would not be enough for a decent standard of living. According to Sidonia, in 1961, when she was hired at the Oncology Institute, Mr. Pricăjan was caught totally by surprise. Actually, when she told him that she had been hired, he fainted, not a joyful sign. For Sidonia, this was the beginning of her way to independence.

From Friendship to Love

Sidonia's visits had an unforeseen effect on me. Soon after Sidonia started visiting me I knew that she was fond of me. I became totally charmed by her. By that time, I was cynical and blasé. It had been four years since I was dumped by the Niculescu family, years in which I tried to find an alternate for Mona, and all my attempts had failed. I was always looking for Mona number two, and she was not to be found. I was convinced that I had no chance of finding someone I could love. However, here was this lovely woman sharing with me her anxiety and her troubles, but also bringing her warm personality, fondness, and gentleness, a sense of tranquility and serenity that was catching. She trusted me as a friend with whom she could talk about her life, but it turned out that she was fond of me. This innocent Christmas Eve kiss followed by our meetings, has told this abandoned woman living in a family that didn't care for her, that there is love, that she can be loved, that she will be loved. I suspect that she liked me before but when I kissed her she became fond of me. Still she was uncertain about me. Did I love her? What was she for me? Was this another affair? Her misgivings will last for several months. Knowing all the gossips about me, she must have wondered how far to go in our relationship.

For me Sidonia was a surprise and an enlightening encounter. I was facing the most beautiful soul I have ever met and soon I recognized that.

It was her fondness for me that made me realize what a loving, affectionate soul was behind those beautiful, shining dark eyes. In what was probably my first love note addressed to Sidonia, I wrote: "You are my dear, very dear. It's just love and even a blasé as I cannot be deceived. Yes, and yet here I love you. Yes, you. Just like that, you entered my soul, don't know how, don't know when, and I feel you there, warm and dear, with all of you, with your eyes, with your walk, look, hair and your perfume, with everything that belongs to you and it's yours. That's it. Good night. I love you."

After one of Sidonia's visits which occurred in the afternoon, when she ate some oranges, I wrote to her: "I came back home late. I found the scent of orange and with it you, your image always present. You are my very dear, and I cannot help to say and repeat this. I tell you now as I said before, that I cannot help saying it, that I think it would be a shame not to tell you, not to say that I always think of you, as you are always present in my mind, in my life, that I am happy that you exist, that more or less, I belong to you. My soul is full of you with warmth and tenderness, with as much honey as it would properly be for a greedy bee like you."

In another short note I said, "I miss you, I really miss you. I always feel your absence, something always draws me to you, and I'd like always to see you, to kiss you, to take you in my arms, to caress you. You do not know how it is, but that's it. I'd like to spend a lot of time together with you, to talk a lot, I always feel I have to tell you a lot of things and then I look at the phone. And so. I always think how many things could be done together with you, and then my mind leads me far away. I love you, and above the little troubles and the rest, I am sometimes happy to feel it. I kiss you all over, all, with thousands of kisses, and I caress you all over, over, endlessly far and all. I."

By April 1963, I wrote to Sidonia: "I love you as I loved only once in my life. You came; you entered in my long years of loneliness. You brought warmth and light, tenderness and love. In the rays of your sun I thought my life starts anew. I live in your shadow, in your perfume, waiting for you, adoring you." Those were not empty words; they were my true feelings about her and they tried to tell her what she brought into my life. This was about two months since she started visiting me. By then I was already unreservedly in love with her.

My feelings for Sidonia were expressed in my letter of July 1963: "Adored Creature, I do not know what place I have in your mind, soul, and your life. But I know that to me you are the woman that I love, who by a gesture, a word, a look, a smile, can give me happiness or sadness. You are the woman ever present in my mind and soul, in my thoughts, in my days and nights. You are the creature along with whom, in my mind, I live every moment of my life with all its joys and sorrows. I tell you all these things not to fill an ordinary letter or a declaration of love written in a style more or less flourished, but from the desire to let you know who you are and what you are to me, what you signify in my life and thoughts. I do not write these lines with the intent to force you to answer me, to ask you to answer me. With one single word of yours, with a single expressed wish of yours, I will choke with my own hands this rare and precious flower, ray of light of my life. I would have never thought that I would be able to have again such feelings for a woman. Willingly, or most likely unwillingly, you made bloom this wonderful flower on dry and burned soil, a strong love, sincere and wholesome. Willingly, or most likely unwillingly by you, I belong body and soul to you, with what I have good and bad in me, my thoughts and my heart, they are all at your adorable feet, wishing to belong to you. Only once in my life I kissed the hands of a woman with such love and faithfulness. Only once in my life I was so happy and so unhappy because of a woman, and you know that, and if I would have to thank the hazard or destiny for bringing you in my life, I would have to thank also for healing a wound that seemed open forever."

    I have told Sidonia about my love for Mona, but I knew this time it was widely different. After collaborating on research, when our relationship has developed based on trust, it turned out I fell totally in love with her. Sidonia has become the love of my lifetime. When I look at a few pictures that I took of Sidonia visiting me, the most significant is the one in which she is sitting on a chair on my balcony. She is dressed in an almost formal dress as Mrs. Pricăjan was visiting Dr. N., but she rests her feet in some old sneakers of mine. Yes, she was coming for a formal visit, but like any woman who is coming home, she took of her shoes. Her soul was feeling at home, and she was relaxed and secure, aware of the love with which she was surrounded. Did she know then that, two years later, she would keep our baby on this balcony? Was this not our destiny she was following?

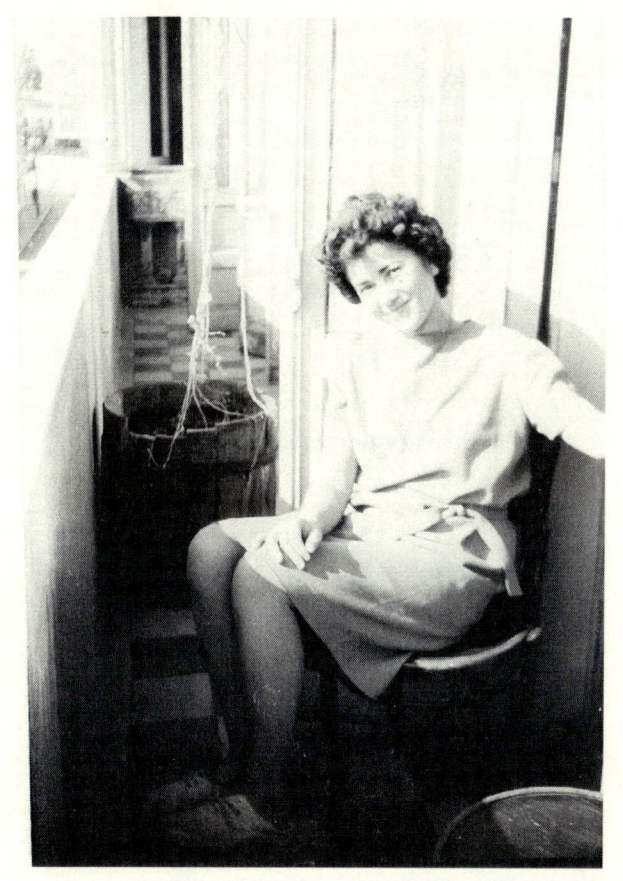

Fig. 1. Sidonia on the balcony of my apartment, summer 1963.

A Fateful Beach Vacation

By August 1963, I went vacationing at the Black Sea and rented a room at the Popa family in Tataia, the same home I used to go every summer since 1960. I was in the company of my friends, the Aderca, and Stănescu families. Before leaving Bucharest, I asked Sidonia to join me and I repeated my invitation through several letters. In the first letter that I wrote Sidonia from the beach, I told her: "Perhaps you do not even know what you mean to me. You do not know you're my oasis of happiness, serenity, delight, you do not know that you are the source of my life happy moments, and do not know that you can be the source of my unhappiness and sadness. You are their master and of the one who acknowledges it. You do not know what a phone from you means to me. You do not know what a caress of you means, do not know what joy is to take you in my arms, to kiss you more, than to caress you, forgetting of time, life, everything, and knowing one thing, that you're there, shining ray in my existence."

My last letter was a reply to Sidonia's letters that are no longer available. In my reply letter I told her "My happiness and my love, my passion and my gladness, my great happiness and unhappiness, my adored Țuțuca, right now I got your letters and in their passion, their endless kiss, their dizzying embrace, I understood the first letter signature "yours Țuțuca". God, you don't know how happy I was! My dear love, I think between us there is a misunderstanding. Can't you see that my great happiness is to be with you everywhere and if possible now at the beach? You adored silly, how can you ask (on the phone) if I want you to come? You must understand that what you are to me is immeasurable, you're everything that I have as fondness now, and as love, and the fact that you doubt this gives me displeasure. I do want only you, I recognize this is a lot, but there it is. I love you much, I am living with you in my mind, in my soul, in my view, every moment, I feel I am yours, I belong to you, and I am happy because I am yours, because I love you, because I dream of kissing your feet, kiss you all, bit by bit."

In these letters Sidonia has told me that she loved me. What was for me a sign from heaven, Sidonia signed one of these letters "yours Țuțu" (her nickname). I took it as she meant it, that she felt that she belongs to me. This was for me the supreme happiness. But she still teased me about "my affairs with other girls." And, to my vexation she even called and asked if I really wanted her to come. That was the result of all these gossips about me.

Finally, Sidonia came, and Mrs. Popa, my host, was delighted to meet her and told me, "This is the one." It didn't take long to make her choice and to tell me so. Actually, she didn't have to because the days that I spent with Sidonia were some of the most wonderful that I had had in a long time. From the very beginning, when I picked her up at the railway station in Constanța, we lived the life of a regular couple on vacation. For the first time, we went out in the open, all the way. We went to the beach together with the Aderca family. Geta Danielescu, the wife of Hans Aderca, liked Sidonia a lot, and she told me so. We took trips to Constanța, the main Romanian harbor on the Black Sea, to visit the tourist attractions of the city such as the Casino and the Roman mosaic. In the evenings, we went dining in restaurants in Mamaia; we never hid from anyone the fact that we were together.

Did we go unnoticed? Of course not. As soon as I got back to the institute, Ms. Constante, the assistant director, told me that she had seen me at the Constanța Railway Station with "a blonde!" To confuse Sidonia with a blonde was a stretch, but who knows? Simona Dumitrescu was another colleague from the institute who saw us, and she understood what was going on. A smart, petite young woman who looked almost like a doll, she liked me. After seeing us together in Constanța, her instinct told her very clearly that, for her, and for anyone else, I was taken, gone. Being a fair player and a nice character, she was one of those that later strongly advised Sidonia to marry me. In the meantime, back at the institute, the gossip engine was in full swing, and I was trying hard to stop it.

> Situated at the crossroads of several commercial routes, Constanța lies on the western coast of the Black Sea, 185 miles from the Bosporus Strait. An ancient metropolis and Romania's largest sea port, Constanța traces its history some 2,500 years. Originally called Tomis, legend has it that Jason landed here with the Argonauts after finding the Golden Fleece. Founded by Greek colonists from Miletos in the sixth century BC, Tomis was conquered by the Romans in 71 BC and renamed Constantiana by Roman Emperor Constantine the Great in honor of his sister. The name was shortened to Constanța during the Ottoman era. During the thirteenth century, Italy, especially Genovese merchants, dominated the Black Sea and Constanța flourished, only to decline two centuries later under Turkish rule. http://www.romaniatourism.com/Constanța.html#highlights

During those days, we never tried to pretend that we were not together. It was something new for both of us; until then, all we did was to meet in her laboratory in the institute, or in my apartment. Now as we spent all the time together, Sidonia proved to be a delightful companion, radiating a feeling of calm, serenity, and warm camaraderie, sharing the pleasure of the time at the beach or just being together. In those days we found out as we went to the beach, to visit local sites, or to a restaurant, that we were very fond of each other and happy to be together. It was a quiet happiness, a serene feeling brought on by the awareness that our personalities, being together, were a fulfilled, complete unit. A few years later, Sidonia rightfully defined this as "feeling at peace." In a letter she addressed to me in 1981, eighteen years later, she evokes these days at the beach, places we visited, people who saw us, etc. Those days remained forever imprinted in our memory.

Fig. 2. Sidonia at Tataia beach, gracefully holding her hat against the wind, and displaying her sweet, delicate smile that has charmed me forever. August 1963.

Fig. 3. An anxious Sidonia is returning to Bucharest after a conclusive vacation at Tataia beach. August 1963.

After the beach, we spent several days together at my apartment. We cooked and had dinner at my home. For us these were precious days; it was the first time when Sidonia came to my place and we behaved like a married couple. We had a taste of what our life would be if . . . . and we loved it. What really mattered was that we were happy to be together.

The day after I took Sidonia to the railway station to travel to Cluj, I wrote to her: "Since you left, I lived with your image up there in the car, and me down, looking at your legs, worshiping them, and intensely longing to always kiss them. It comes back to my mind, we, those last days, you standing there all the time, unspeakably sweet and precious, and I, happy by your presence, looking at you, and smiling to you and your presence there, close, very close. You are forever there in my mind, every second, every moment; I can look at life only through a prism in which you are present, giving a special shape and color, sharing your fragrance and sweetness, your kindness and serenity. I love you very much, a lot, and aside from our worries, you are all I have dear in this world. You filled my life and my soul, and I belong to you, only you. I know that I love you a lot, that I love you much, that you're my happiness, that I adore you, that I live with your image in me every moment, and that I wish intensely you to be happy, your life to be a luminous and smooth way, your face to be always bright and beautiful as it was at the beach, and during our last days together. I adore you and I'll wait for you." By now Sidonia knew that I, the philanderer, was not only her trustful friend by also her unconditional lover. How many times I told her in my letters that I belong only to her? There were no more questions about "other girls," or "catching me with someone." After all, she loved me and I loved her and this love was total.

Time has come now for us to decide which way we want to go in life. On my side there were no more questions to be raised; I belonged to her and only her. I told Sidonia repeatedly, all I wanted was to spend my life with her. It is true that I never mentioned the word "marriage," but was it necessary? Did she have any doubts that I belonged to her? I don't think so.

The difficult decision was upon Sidonia. She was considering divorcing for years. Although she loved children after she had Carmen, immediately after her marriage with Mr. Pricăjan, over the following eight years, she used everything available in those days in Romania to avoid having another child. To me this proved that quite soon in her marriage she knew that it's not going to work. In our marriage, as soon as she could, she had two children at an age when most women in Romania in those days, would avoid getting pregnant. She took a job not because she was bored, or to bring money in the household. Sidonia took this job because she thought that if she separates from Mr. Pricăjan she will need money to sustain herself. But by then she had no friend, no one to help and support her.

Now things were different. Sidonia had the option of resuming life with a man that loved her and whom she loved, or to continue living without love and without respect, taking care of her child. Sidonia's life has reached a crossroad that she never had to cross before and may never have again. She needed now the advice of her parents. She had to tell them about her marriage, about her relationship with me, everything, and so that they could reach a correct judgment. Her life, her fate was at stake. She had to choose her pathway.

Divorce

Beginning of September, Sidonia went to Cluj to visit her parents, to discuss her situation and intention to file for a divorce. I wrote to her, "Do not forget that you are expected and adored, and that I will embrace you wholeheartedly and with all my love. I can't wait for the moment when I can again kiss your feet and caress you much, all, all. You are my beautiful soul and so very much loved. You are my love, my only love, next to you, I feel happy, content, peaceful, true. Near you I find a climate I cannot meet elsewhere, and do not want anything else. I'll wait for you with loyalty and love, longing and impatience, with thousands of kisses and caresses, all my soul and me, everything. I belong to you and only you, and my wish is for you to be happy and contented. I wait for your hands to kiss, for your thighs to caress, for your eyes to watch and to kiss, lips, everything, everything. You're all, my only and precious lady, I adore."

From Cluj, she wrote me a letter that unfortunately I don't have. However, in my reply letter, which she kept, I said, "I cannot describe the feelings and thoughts that this letter produced. I love you more if this is possible, I adore you more, I feel you closer, and I was happy because I felt your light, relieved soul as a free bird that rises in a clear sunrise." Her parents have given her the green light for the divorce, and for our relationship, and this brought a much-needed relief from her predicament.

Not long after her trip to Cluj, Sidonia let her husband know that she intended to divorce him. For him this must have been quite a blow. The nanny of his daughter, his housemaid, the one he believed is unable to have and hold a job, was dropping him. This was a hit hard to take and he rallied his friends to help him and talk her out of this thought. Sidonia had to stand an onslaught from his friends to renounce her plan to divorce. Among those friends was Comrade Susan, a Communist Party activist in charge of supervising artists and taking full advantage of his position, cheating on his wife, Olga. Olga told Sidonia that she accepted this situation in exchange for the lifestyle that he was providing her, and advised Sidonia to do likewise. Comrade Susan tried to convince Sidonia to give up her intention to divorce, and one of his arguments was, "What do you have in common with a Jew?" Sidonia answered, "Jesus was also a Jew." I will always admire her for that answer, but the whole discussion was obviously pointing to me as the cause of the divorce.

Susan's question came obviously from a line of thought that Sidonia was leaving her marriage because of our relationship. How true was this? I venture to say that the truth lies somewhere in the middle. Sidonia was decided to divorce for years. She avoided having more children, she took a job, and she still pondered what to do, if and when to act. Then on Christmas Eve 1962, the destiny decided that she had waited and suffered enough and brought me into her life, first as a trustful friend and soon afterwards as her lover. By fall of 1963, after months of discussions, letters, encounters, time spent together, Sidonia knew that I belong only to her and that I want to spend my life with her. Sidonia knew that she has an honest friend to rely upon, and she knew that this friend loves her unconditionally. I believe that this gave her confidence to choose a different pathway in life. Through her own free will Sidonia choose the love pathway instead of continuing the undignified pathway that she was on.

A few years later Sidonia was rewarded for her boldness in front of this pressure coming from Mr. Pricăjan and his friends. Susan's son Marcel got married and Sidonia and I were invited at the reception that followed this marriage. Until then we had no contact with Susan. We were surprised by this invitation but decided to go. The reception was held at the fancy House of Scientists, a select club in a beautiful old aristocratic home downtown Bucharest. It was a large sit-down dinner and many of the old friends of Mr. Pricăjan were there. The Pricăjan family was not attending; presumably Mr. Pricăjan was told that we were invited.

We were welcomed and treated almost as special guests. Some of Mr. Pricăjan friends Sidonia knew from the days when she accompanied him at their parties, were friendly and chatted with us. It was one of the rare instances when the two of us danced. Sidonia never enjoyed dancing, but this time she relished showing those guys that she was the winner and they were the losers, it was her day in the sun, and I loved it, and I loved her! I was at her feet, adoring her boundlessly!

Even I had my share of that pressure. On a Sunday morning, I had the surprise visit at my apartment of Mr. Pricăjan, whom I had never met before. He acknowledged that he knew that I was Sidonia's friend. He asked me to convince her to give up on the intention of divorcing, arguing about Carmen's separation from her mother. Our talk turned out to be revealing. I was already aware that he knew about our relationship, and that we have been together at the beach. Besides admitting that, he didn't utter a word about it. That confirmed what I understood from my visit on Christmas Eve at their apartment that their marriage was defunct.

Since I befriended Sidonia, I had never noticed any love lost between her and Mr. Pricăjan. By the time Sidonia started visiting me, one evening, it was after 11:00 PM, and I was ready to go to bed, when the doorbell rang. I didn't expect anyone, but I went and opened the door. And there she was, dressed up in a black dress, a superb beauty, asking me, "Did I catch you with someone?" She was returning home from the opera theater, and decided to stop at my apartment. Until then, I have never seen her dressed up and she was a stunning woman. I said to myself, *what kind of man would let such a beautiful wife go alone by night? T*his has been one more instance that proved to me that Mr. Pricăjan was enjoying his life and let Sidonia have hers, as long as she accepted to stay married to him and be the nanny of their child. In his talk Mr. Pricăjan gave the impression that he was concerned that he will appear before his friends as a man who had been ditched by his wife, under circumstances that gave the appearance that she was leaving him for another man, and a Jew at that. After this talk, I knew that Sidonia has to get out of this marriage and the sooner the better.

The problem Sidonia had was that Carmen, her daughter, would not accept a separation from her father. Sidonia spent almost a year trying to find a solution to this problem. She loved Carmen very much, and separation from her daughter was the obstacle that she had enormous difficulty overcoming. Mr. Pricăjan made no secret that he was not going to let Carmen go with her mother. He told Sidonia, "If you leave, you lose the child." Obviously, he sounded confident he could control Carmen. This was his last argument to prevent Sidonia from asking for a divorce. By December 1963, Sidonia reached the decision to leave Mr. Pricăjan and to file for a divorce. I think this decision was made when it became clear to her that Carmen was on her father's side, and there was no hope of having the child with her after the divorce.

Separation and divorce in Bucharest, in those days, were not easy because of a terrible housing crisis. People were squeezed into existing apartments, the government had few buildings, and the population of the city had increased enormously due to peasants becoming factory workers. With help from our lab technician, Sidonia found a room to rent. It was not luxurious, but at least it was a place where she could sleep. Being December, beginning of winter, she had to buy wood to heat the room that had a wooden stove as the only source of heat.

For the Christmas holidays, we went to Bușteni. We rented a room and spent the days hiking and relaxing. Sidonia was trying to adjust to the new situation, being separated from her daughter. These were not happy days for her. By the time we returned to Bucharest, I asked Sidonia to move into my apartment. With some hesitation, she accepted. Her main concern was that she wanted to have Carmen visit her. Under the circumstances, my apartment would not be acceptable for Carmen to visit. This proved true. During the following years, Sidonia would meet Carmen only somewhere in town. The only time Carmen came to visit us was after the massive 1977 earthquake, when she was afraid to go back to her tenth-floor apartment.

To me, this only proved how right Sidonia was in her decision. I can imagine how we were portrayed by Carmen's father and his family and friends; most likely, I had my share of the blame for the divorce. She loved her father, and it would have been impossible for her to blame him for anything. After all, Carmen was a child who wouldn't understand what was going on. She grew up with her mother being treated the demeaning way she was, and was never told about her father's affairs. In this picture, her father appeared the innocent victim and her mother . . . And as far as I was concerned . . . In any case, if it is true, that I played a helpful role in this divorce, I'm glad I did. It turned out that in the long run it was a blessing for everyone concerned, including Carmen.

Fig. 4. Sidonia and I, vacationing in Bușteni. December 1963.

In June 1980, while we were forcefully separated, she being in Romania and me in the United States, Sidonia described thus her relationship with Carmen: "After 17 years, it turns out that this mother, of whom her family spoke about as they did, and told her all kind of things, is perhaps the only person with whom she can make out, communicate, and trust." It seems that Carmen was advised to avoid visiting her mother. This hateful mind-set intending to punish Sidonia by depriving her of her child, actually hurt Carmen who ended up feeling that she was growing up without a mother, when such a loving mother was available and would have been happy to be with her all the time. Hate is always a bad and blinding adviser.

After the divorce, Sidonia tried to recover, from Mr. Pricăjan furniture that was given to her by her parents when she got married. Mr. Pricăjan became violent, and she came back home badly bruised. Until Carmen's wedding in 1978, this was their last encounter. At the wedding, Mr. Pricăjan showed again how much he hated Sidonia. At the religious service where parents of the bride and the groom are standing in front of the priest, Sidonia was replaced by a girlfriend of Mr. Pricăjan. To complete the insult, at the sit-down dinner, Sidonia was placed with the guests. Mr. Pricăjan's girlfriend was seated by Carmen's side.

A few years later, Carmen and Alex, her husband, were admitted to the States because Sidonia was a permanent resident, and with our assistance became graduate students. By now the relationship between Sidonia and Carmen was that of mother-daughter, they loved each other. The woman that replaced Sidonia at the wedding came to Columbia hoping Carmen will take her in to live with her. Carmen refused and she ended up living alone in Columbia. Wasn't that the destiny, giving Sidonia a reward for the humiliation that she suffered at her daughter's wedding? I was indeed awed witnessing what happened.

Happy Marriage

At the beginning of 1964, after Sidonia moved to my apartment, my life changed forever. I knew that she was the one with whom I was happy to share my thoughts, my feelings, my life. By that time, I knew that it was time to have Sidonia with me for the rest of my life. My destiny has been kind; Sidonia was my gift from heaven that I will keep forever. My mind was made up, and I asked Sidonia once her divorce was final, to marry me. She agreed. We followed our pathways and decided to join our lives. I am convinced that our pathways were destined to cross, and our souls to be bonded forever like soul mates.

This was not a light decision. I had my share of opponents, and Sidonia had hers. One important argument that was put forward to her by some of her colleagues was that I was Jewish. Those were the years when the large Jewish community in Romania, counting well over half a million people, was leaving the country legally. They were sold by the communist regime to Israel for hard currency. The question Sidonia was asked by some of her colleagues was "What if he leaves you?" Sidonia went on and married me. She knew better. As she said years later, "we have a happy marriage." By the time she passed away our marriage lasted forty-nine years. I hope it will last forever.

By February 1964, the divorce was pronounced, and as expected, the judge gave Carmen into her father's care, and Sidonia was required to pay monthly child support. On June 27, 1963, we got married at the city hall of the sector where I was living. It was a bright, sunny day as Sidonia, her father, and I walked to the city hall. Sidonia was dressed in a white sleeveless dress. She was a beautiful bride. I was dressed for this event in attire that I inherited from my father. I had it adjusted by a tailor. Several of our colleagues from the institute, as well as Uncle Oscar, attended and brought us beautiful flowers. A public notary, Mr. Teodorescu, read us the law and asked the usual questions that are part of this ceremony, probably all over the world. We said "yes," signed in the register, and were pronounced husband and wife according to the law.

We exchanged our gold wedding rings, each engraved inside with our nicknames. Mine has "Țuțu" engraved, and Sidonia's has "Burși." In those days, one could legally buy gold jewelry, but they were horrendously expensive and were sold only under government control. Fortunately, I found a broken gold bracelet that had belonged to my grandmother Mama Mare. We took it to a jeweler, and it turned out that there was enough gold for our wedding rings. This was her wedding gift to us.

Fig. 5. We are married and happy. June 27, 1964.

That evening, we had a party at our apartment. Uncle Oscar; Aunt Jenny; my cousin Mariana and her husband, Paul; Ștefan and his girlfriend, Karin came, and we had a celebration till late in the night. I should say that Uncle Oscar and Aunt Jenny loved Sidonia from the moment I introduced her to them. During the following years they showed Sidonia all their love for her.

Their marriage and ours shared several important features. Our marriage was a simple and private event, the beginning of a complicated road that brought along many struggles and plenty of blessings.

Fig. 6. Sidonia and I enjoyed our wedding party. June 27, 1964.

For our honeymoon, we went to the Black Sea resort of Mangalia, where we rented a room in an apartment that, by chance, was close to the Perla Mării (Pearl of the Sea) Villa, where I used to stay with my mother and sister when I was a child. Uncle Oscar and his family were staying close to us, so we were together at the beach. Ștefan and his future wife, Karin, joined us for a few days but left to go to the mountains.

Fig. 7. Honeymoon in Mangalia. Sidonia is resting during our walk visiting the town of Mangalia. The tall minaret of the mosque is seen in the background.

Someone took a picture of us at the beach. We are holding tightly onto each other. We are like one body with two heads, and we belong to each other. Also our companion took a picture of us holding hands as we were lying on the beach. These pictures turned out to be the story of our lives from this time on to the end, and I hope even beyond.

Fig. 8. Honeymoon in Mangalia; Sidonia and I holding to each other on the beach. July 1964.

Fig. 9. Sidonia and I side by side on the beach in Mangalia. July 1964.

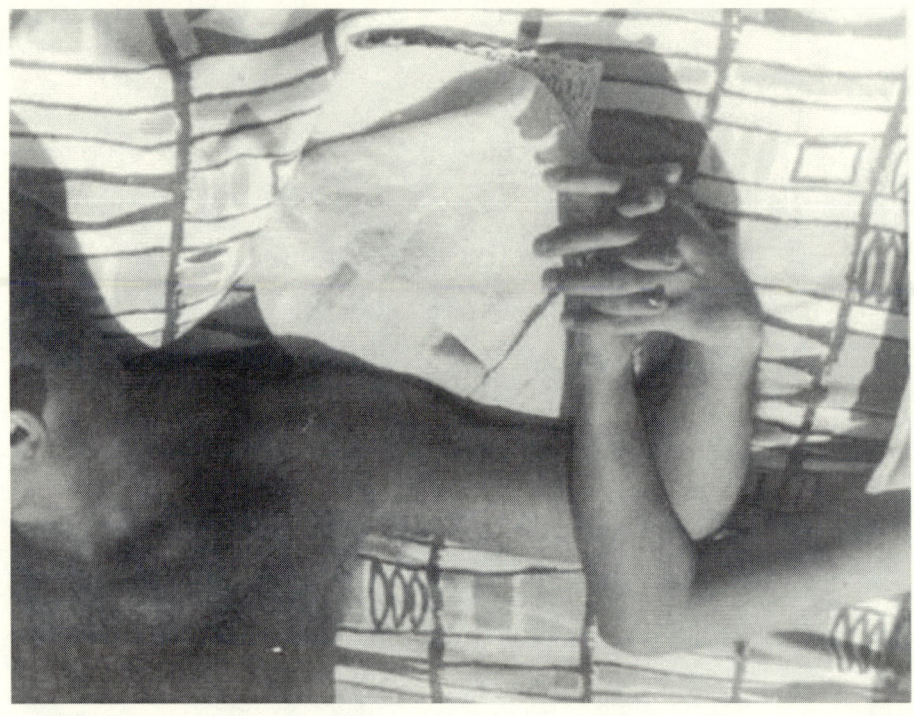

Fig. 10. Sidonia and I are holding hands on the beach in Mangalia. July 1964.

After the beach, we went hiking in the Bucegi Mountains. After hiking a whole day under heavy rain, we ended up renting a room at the Ialomicioara Monastery, a small monastery at the entrance of a rather large cave. The monks were extremely kind to us. The room was modest and had two separate bunk beds. We dried our things, we got a good sleep, and the following days, we hiked the beautiful trails nearby. This was our first hiking trip together, and we enjoyed it immensely. Sidonia was an excellent hiker and loved it. This was the beginning of many, probably several hundred, hiking trips that we took over the following forty years. Our last hiking trip was in 2008 in the mountains of North Carolina.

Fig. 11. An adoring husband looking at Sidonia. Predeal, January 1965.

Fig. 12. Sidonia, on a ski slope in the Bucegi Mountain resort of Predeal. January 1965.

For both of us, this was a new beginning. For me, this marriage was totally unexpected. When I went to the Oncology Institute, the only thing I had on my mind was my training and making progress in my research. Marriage was not on my horizon, and I was convinced that, after Mona, I would never find another love. With Sidonia, for about a year, we were just good colleagues, while I was having affairs with other women, and she was dealing with her family problems and considering a divorce. We were still Mrs. Pricăjan and Dr. N. It turned out that, as I encountered Sidonia outside the institute, I discovered her beautiful soul, her tenderness, and fondness that stuck to me and became my lifeline. The most important finding was that I was happy only when she was around. Now that we said the traditional "yes," I knew from the depth of my heart that my parents, particularly my mother, would have been happy for what I was doing. I knew I had by my side the woman who would be my friend and companion for the rest of my life, my love, my soul mate.

For Sidonia, starting again implied coming off a bitter struggle that left a deep wound. She was deprived caring for a child she loved very much, and it would take years to heal this wound. After a failed experience, I guess there is always the fear that it may happen again. She took this chance, and I have reasons to believe that she had no regrets about it.

With time, I learned some of the factors that played an important role in Sidonia's personality and life. Surrounding her, as she grew up, was a domineering father, a kind and loving mother, and a sister who was visibly handicapped. Her father was a fast-acting person, and he was not pleased that Sidonia was not. On the other hand, her mother was overprotective of her handicapped daughter, Mimi, and Sidonia was gently reprimanded every time there was a conflict between these two sisters, which, as everybody knows, are unavoidable.

Sidonia had a very strict upbringing. Obviously, she must have been a reserved girl, and her father must have made it very clear that he would not take kindly any deviation from a sober behavior. Moreover, every time she would go out to meet or visit other girls, her mother would ask her to take her sister, Mimi, with her. It is not unusual that youngsters would make fun of handicapped peers, and it is likely that must have happened with predictable effects on Sidonia. The only friends from her childhood were those from Vingard with whom, very likely, she would be allowed to interact without Mimi, who was probably kept home for protection.

Sidonia loved her family, and she was very close to her mother, but I believe she wanted to have a family of her own. She was still in high school when she discussed marriage with her boyfriend. She loved children, and I think she intended to have many. Probably she would have accepted a reasonably good husband and would have focused her love on her children. In her first marriage, she was ready to compromise in order to have her family, but she soon realized that her hopes were in vain. Her first attempt of having a family had failed and it took her years to get out of the sinking ship.

In our relationship, it took a while for Sidonia to believe that what I was telling her was the true expression of my feelings. By the time we started to meet outside the institute, she trusted me as a friend with whom she could talk about her life. When she started visiting me, she was fond of me, but knowing the gossips about me made her doubtful and cautious. Soon I fell in love with her and told her so. She was then faced with a major dilemma: Was this real? It was probably the first time in her life that she was told in unquestionable terms that she was loved, unconditionally loved. But this was coming from a man who had the reputation of a philanderer. How serious was this guy? How much did he mean what he was saying? These must have been questions raised in her mind, waiting for an answer. Obviously, when she accepted the invitation to visit me, she trusted me as a friend, but I doubt very much she has ever considered that I may become her lover or her husband. But now we were talking love, unconditional love.

Then Sidonia stored the letters in which I was telling her how much I loved her. On the yellow envelope in which I found them after she passed away, she wrote, "Letters from Burşi, to be kept." To bring those letters from Romania to the United States and to store them for so long, Sidonia must have considered them priceless. She never showed them to me or to anyone else. Together with my letters, she kept one of her brief notes that she used to give me. It says: "Precious and dear one, I arrived home at 6:45, Pupilica (Carmen's nickname) being invited to a birthday. I've changed. I made myself beautiful (??) and I went to the hairdresser down the corner. I think around 9 o'clock I'll be arriving back home very beautiful. I kiss you, I adore you and . . . . Ţuţu (Sidonia's nickname)." Keeping those notes Sidonia understood that between us it was not only friendship, it was love.

By the time Sidonia joined me at the beach, we knew we were in love, but Sidonia was not sure if I was committed to her. After all, she knew my reputation was that of a philanderer. The days spent together made us realize that between us, there was a deep, unconditional love. There were no more questions about "my affairs with other girls." I think that this was the time when both of us understood that our pathways were meant to be united for life. Although she wanted to divorce for quite some time, this may have been the incentive to go to talk about this critical step in her life with her parents.

After our vacation at the beach, I was unconditionally in love with her; I knew that Sidonia was the love of my life. As I was back to work, I wrote to her: "I adore you and I'm yours and only yours. You share me only with science and you know it is a very reasonable competitor. I adore you and only you, you're everything I love in this world, and when I think about you, I feel all what you mean to me. I kiss your feet, hands, kiss you all over, I embrace you strongly, I really, really miss you, I'll wait for you and wait every day, every night to pass, I adore you."

Sometime after we got married, I found out that the album of photos of my former girlfriends was missing, vanished. I didn't ask, but I knew that Sidonia found it and discarded it. Instead of being upset, I was happy. I understood that this was her quiet way of saying, "Here I am, and you are my man, and I am not going to share you with anyone in the past, present, or future." She knew of my previous love for Mona, and she was always baffled about the reason for our separation. For someone like Sidonia, who wrote, "I think that I had an extraordinary good fortune meeting you," this remained a mystery. I could not provide a good explanation.

But one thing was no mystery for Sidonia: I was her man and her man only. She never shared me with any other woman, and she knew without a shadow of a doubt that I was only her man. We belonged to each other for life and beyond, if there is something like that, and she knew that. If any woman would express something nice about me, Sidonia would tease me, and this was just her way of underscoring her absolute trust in me. For instance, when we were separated, Sidonia was telling me that our daughter's piano teacher has asked her to write me that "she is missing you, she would like to hear your gentle voice" and to ask me to write her. Sidonia's comment was: "Beware! When I'll meet you I'll shave your head!" Being quite bald, this didn't sound like a dangerous threat. I wonder if she was not actually pleased to hear other women complimenting me; after all, she knew very well that I was hers only.

Throughout our forty-nine years of marriage, Sidonia thought her only challenger for being my utmost love was our son, Noël. In a letter dated February 1981, Sidonia wrote: "I am in competition with Noël, on which one of the two you love more, and other questions of this kind. Impartially (I am saying) and honestly, I recommend you to tip the balance on me, because some Eves have already started to exercise at least some influence on your beloved son, and soon he will be grabbed by one, and then you will remain with nobody!"

A few months later, on Sidonia's birthday, this is what I wrote to her: "My adored, I cannot tell or describe exactly what it means for me to wish you Happy Birthday, how much I love these words, how deeply significant they are, when addressed to you, my dear and beloved. My adored and dearly Soul, nobody more than me, maybe not even your parents, wanted more to make you happy. As I learned, the way to happiness is not always easy, but my Love, for me there is no greater joy and reward more precious, than knowing that, at the end of the efforts and the sorrow I can make you happy, this is what I really want most. I want you to be happy, to enjoy every day, every moment, and then I'll be happy. Fate was generous with me, it has brought you in my way and united us for life, and I cannot tell you how grateful I am. My dear, very dear lady, I am completely at your feet that I love and kiss with untold, limitless love and longing. Forever, yours." If there was a competition, I don't think there was ever any doubt who the winner was.

Under the oppressive communist system, our bonding was not to be only a love story. After my defection in 1980, when Sidonia had to argue with the communist authorities to let her and our children leave Romania, her argument was, "This is my man, and the father of my children, and I have to be with him no matter where." Their attempts to pressure her to divorce me, telling her that as a good-looking woman she'll have no difficulty finding another husband, failed miserably.

A Dangerous Pregnancy

Soon after we were married, Sidonia developed some health problems and went to see a gynecologist, Dr. Ghiță Dumitrescu. He was an older ob-gyn specialist who had been a professor at the Bucharest Medical School but, for political reasons (he didn't like communists and made no secret of it), was fired and now had a small outpatient office. He treated her, and the result was that, within a few months, she became pregnant which was what we wished.

We went to see Dr. Fred Georgescu, who had been my instructor in ob-gyn, and I trusted him as an excellent physician. He assured us that everything was fine. Sidonia bloomed with the pregnancy. The prospect of having a child to take care of was, for Sidonia, a dream come true. As the pregnancy advanced, the baby started moving. We played a game where I would put my hand on Sidonia's belly and feel every time the baby would hit the abdominal wall, most likely with the feet, and we would say that he (or she, ultrasound was not yet available) is shaking hands with me.

Fig. 13. When Sidonia was pregnant we used to take rowing boat trips on the Herăstrău Lake in the north part of Bucharest.

It was a day in June, when Sidonia went home and I remained at the lab. Later in the afternoon, I went with Ştefan to swim in a lake not far from the institute. I went home around 6:00 PM. When I entered the bedroom, Sidonia was just coming out of the bathroom. She was pale and looked obviously scared. "What happened?" I asked. "Well, when I went to the bathroom, I was bleeding" she said. My ob-gyn training was good enough to tell me that, very likely, the bleeding was coming from a placenta previa, a placenta with a bad location in the uterus that manifests itself by bleeding in the last trimester of pregnancy. I also knew how dangerous this condition was, both for the fetus and the mother. The bleeding can start anytime, and within minutes, it can be so extensive it can kill mother and child. Since Sidonia had just started bleeding, I knew there was no time to wait.

We took a taxi and went straight to the Filantropia Hospital, where Dr. Fred Georgescu worked. The hospital was in the immediate vicinity of the Oncology Institute; actually, it shared the same grounds. The physician on call told us that Dr. Georgescu was out of town. He examined Sidonia, agreed on the diagnosis of placenta previa, and, as expected, decided to keep Sidonia under close supervision in the hospital. That evening I went back home alone and the home was empty. Without Sidonia, it was no longer home.

This was the beginning of more than two months of anxious waiting. Fred Georgescu came back from vacation and took over the supervision of Sidonia's case. His opinion was that, if she wanted the child, she had to stay in bed all the time. She couldn't even go to the bathroom; she tried a few times and every time the bleeding started. The strategy was to draw out the pregnancy as much as possible to allow the fetus to mature. This was critical for the future of the child. In those days, the technology of keeping premature babies alive and well was not as advanced as it is now; most of them would either die or survive but with severe disabilities.

The whole waiting period was really the story of Damocles's sword hanging over our heads. A bleeding could start at any moment, day or night, and could be life threatening for the mother and/or the child. For me it was a nightmare. I was at the hospital during the day, but at night, I would go home and never know what could happen. Moreover, some of my colleagues who were ob-gyn specialists were telling me that children born with this condition are always severely handicapped. Still, I knew how important it was for Sidonia to have this baby. She was not very young, and another pregnancy could have been doubtful. Sidonia wanted this baby, and she fought tooth and nail to have him or her. From June to the end of August, she stayed in bed all the time, not even using the bathroom. She saw what happened to another woman in her condition, how she lost her baby, and she did her best to save hers.

A Risky Delivery

August 30 began as a Sunday to Monday night shift. Dr. Ioanițiu, a friendly physician, was on call at the Filantropia Hospital, and I was at home getting ready for a quiet night sleep. Sidonia started bleeding sometime late in the evening. As soon as the bleeding started, Dr. Ioanițiu called Fred, who was at a Sunday evening party. He told her to try to slow down the bleeding and postpone surgery until the next day. Dr. Ioanițiu gave Sidonia a relaxing cocktail that was supposed to stop uterine contractions. This treatment worked, and the bleeding stopped. Dr. Ioanițiu monitored her closely through the night.

In the meantime, I was sleeping at home unaware of the drama that was developing. The next morning, I was at the hospital around 8:00 AM as usual. As soon as I entered Sidonia's room, I knew something was not right. Sidonia told me that Fred had already seen her and told her that she would go into surgery for a cesarean section that morning, as soon as he was through with his rounds. When she told me what happened, I became very anxious, but neither she nor I showed how we felt. I was fully aware of how critical the next hours would be. We had reached a fateful moment.

As Sidonia was taken to the operating room, I was told I was supposed to wait outside the room, in a hallway. I didn't know what was going on behind the closed door, but at some point, Dr. Ioanițiu came out from the operating room and asked me what blood type Sidonia was. I was so stunned I couldn't answer. I panicked; in my mind, transfusion meant loss of blood, lots of it, which does not happen in a regular cesarean section. They gave her the universal type O blood transfusion although I knew very well that like me she was type B.

After a while, a group came out from the operating room with the newborn baby. They entered a nearby room where there were big lights, and stood up around the table where they put the baby, a boy. The baby looked good, but was turning blue by the minute because he was not breathing. I will always remember the looks of those around the table, meaning, "It's lost." It was all for nothing.

Then Dr. Petrescu, the anesthesiologist, who had been my medical school classmate, said, "Alcohol." Someone fetched a bottle of alcohol and poured it over the baby's belly. Instantly, a miracle happened. The baby, who by now was dark blue, started protesting vigorously, breathing from the depth of his lungs and became pink right away. I will always remember that moment, the choice between life and death, happiness and sadness that miraculously came out so well. What a difference this moment made for our lives! When I look at Noël, with his PhD in applied mathematics from the Massachusetts Institute of Technology, I still see this blue baby and wonder about miracles.

I thought many times about this instance, and others, when there was a matter of life and death and some extraordinary intervention, chooses life instead of death. It happened to me several times, and I recognized them looking "in the rearview mirror." One event was my fall on the mountain glacier in the summer of 1963, then Sidonia's placenta previa and Noël's birth.

A few years later, I was driving home from the mountains with Sidonia, Noël, and Alina. We stopped at the border of a mountain river. It had rained, and the river was coming down very strong and high. I went with Noël, who was four or five years old, close to the river embankment, to look at the river. As soon as we got there, the ground under our feet fell into the river with us. The strong stream had burrowed deep under the river shore, which fell into the river under our weight. We were both in the water. I was above it, but Noël being much shorter was deep under water, and the stream was very strong and fast. I had an instant reflex and caught him as the water was pulling him away from me to his certain demise. I climbed out of the water with Noël in my arms. He was miraculously saved. These events in my life made me think of how our destiny takes turns, and we just have the feeling that we are in control. In spite of our efforts, what happens is many times beyond our control. We just follow our path.

After surgery, Sidonia was taken to the recovery room. I went to watch her, and as soon as she came out of anesthesia, I told her, "You have a beautiful baby boy." With her eyes still closed, she said softly, "I don't know if I will know how to handle him." The baby (Noël) was, by now, in the neonatal section in an incubator. He was quite big for a premature newborn, 2,750 grams (almost 6 pounds), but he couldn't maintain his body temperature. He was under special supervision considering that he was premature, born from a placenta previa pregnancy, and having a respiratory delay. Noël was born on a Monday, but Sidonia was allowed to see him only on Friday, just in case. Once Sidonia had him in her arms, she was happy, to say the least; it was her baby. She knew so well how to handle him that he grew up loving her boundlessly.

In a letter to Sidonia on August 30, 1981, sixteen years after these events, when we were separated after my defection, I told her, "I review and relive the hot days of the summer of 1965, when you fought with superb patience and will, with unspeakable courage for Noël's life. I watched you then and loved you. I was beside you as much as I could, although you were on the front line, and I was somewhere at the back, trying to help out as much as possible. I loved you much, very much then, and I love you now more, very much more. I admired you then, and I admire you even more now."

A Baby at Home

With Noël and Sidonia home, my daily schedule and my life changed. I would come home early and take care of the evening bath. Noël was a good baby but was getting up early morning and was crying a lot when hungry. The first pediatrician that we brought to check him was Professor Feldioreanu. A well-known pediatrician, he came, examined Noël, and told us that he was damaged by the placenta previa and delivery and required some daring treatment to possibly save him from being a handicapped child. We were in shock. Despair was setting up. I thought to seek a second opinion, and I called Dr. Viorica Voiculescu. She was an excellent pediatrician, and her husband, Dr. Vlad Voiculescu, was one of the best (probably the best) neurologist in the country. She came, examined Noël, ran a few tests, and reassured us that Noël was well. She also told us that she would talk to her husband and ask for his opinion. Her answer came back clear; there were no problems whatsoever, no need for any treatment. I cannot describe our joy, relief, and happiness. Again, this showed how a fateful moment in life can change the whole outcome. Dr. Voiculescu continued to consult Noël at regular intervals for the following months, and his development was just excellent.

When Noël was a couple of months old, we decided to have him circumcised. Early in our marriage, Sidonia and I agreed that we would keep our religion, she being Christian Orthodox and me Jewish. As far as the children were concerned, Sidonia proposed that they would be divided, one Jewish and the next one Christian. With Noël, we followed this understanding, and he had to be circumcised. For the ceremony, I found an old mohel, very likely the only one left in Romania. We decided to have a small celebration on this occasion and to invite some people.

To my surprise, two Jews refused to come: one was Uncle Oscar, and the other one was Hans Aderca. Both of them told me that they did not agree with this rite. On the other hand, Dr. Caratzali, Sidonia's boss, and my friend Ștefan Mironescu, both Christians, joined us. Actually, Ștefan assumed the role of the sandek, holding Noël during the circumcision. For both Sidonia and me, this was a unique event, neither one had been part of such a ceremony before. I have to admit I was not comfortable, but when I looked at Sidonia, how calm and serene she was, I felt that my love and admiration for her reached a peak. She was awesome!

The mohel did the cutting well and fast, but then he used, as a disinfectant and to stop the bleeding, gasoline and some brown fibers that were probably touchwood. We let him do it, but later on we were sorry because this combination didn't prove helpful for the healing process that had to take place. I still think that some sterile gauze would have done the job better.

> Wikipedia. The rite of circumcision (*brit milah*) is performed on the eighth day of a boy's life. The ritual usually takes place in the morning at the family's home. Circumcision is commanded in Genesis 17:10-14 as an outward sign of a man's participation in Israel's covenant with God, as well as a sign that the Jewish people will perpetuate through him.

Happiness and Love

Sidonia was happy and this is, very likely, an understatement. To have her baby and, on top of that, after all the ordeal that she went through during her last months of pregnancy, to have such a beautiful and healthy baby to take care of, was for Sidonia, the supreme happiness. Having to go through more than two months of staying in bed was a major effort, and she would boast now that she actually "hatched" this baby, that she was more than proud and happy to carry around. At the beginning, she had some problems breast feeding the hungry kid; but soon everything was working well, and Sidonia was beyond happiness. The baby was her gift straight from heaven. After all, I called him Noël because he was her Christmas gift. I thought that our romance has started on Christmas Eve and Noël pregnancy term would have been by the end of September.

Fig. 14. Sidonia with Noël, any mother prouder? 1965.

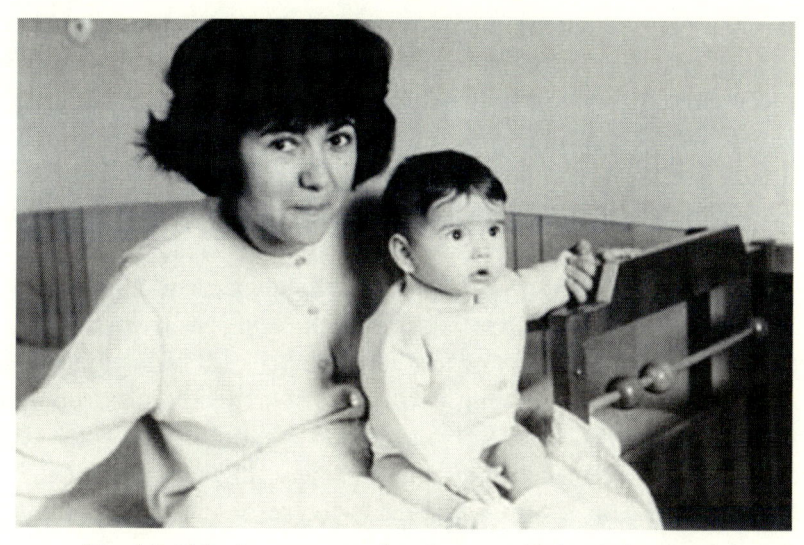

Fig. 15. Sidonia was more than happy with her baby. 1966.

By summer of 1966, when Noël was one year old we went to Tataia beach with him and stayed at Mrs. Popa home; in a way, this was the place where our love blossomed. What a difference these two years made in our lives! How much happiness our destiny brought us! We recognized it and were deeply grateful. It was a blessing!

Fig. 16. Sidonia and Noël on the Tataia beach. Summer 1966.

From the very beginning, being together was our happiness, our life. In 1966, when Noël was six months old, I had to go to the mountain resort of Sinaia to treat a stress-related fever. For the first time since we were living together we were separated. A few days after my departure, Sidonia wrote a letter addressed to me at poste restante in Sinaia. Since I didn't recover it, the letter was sent back to Sidonia, and she stored it to this day in the original envelope. These are a few lines from her letter that reached me forty-nine years after it was written: "My adored and loved dearly, I feel immensely comfortable with you, to know you are here, to see you working, reading, and last to taunt me a little, not too hard, and then it is sublime. It seems long since you have been missing from home and I really miss you and your beloved beautiful eyes, you all, your caress, warmth, and your embrace, the peace that I feel when I know you are here. In fact if I find it so hard now without you, you're to be blamed, you surrounded me with love and fondness, you've spoiled me, to be honest, I did not dislike it at all, on the contrary, and so now it's hard! Come quickly, I mean, time should pass quickly, to see you home with us, our baby and your girl, all three of us, we must be so, always and forever. I adore you, your little girl." Is there a better way to happiness than through unconditional love?

In a letter written on April 4, 1981, after Sidonia had the meeting with the communist authorities that signaled the start of the procedure for giving her permission to leave Romania, she said, "I see me flying away and reaching you. You do not know how much I want this, never in your lifetime till now, or from now on, someone ever wanted to be with you, beside you, more than I wish." I knew very well how much she desired to be together since I had absolutely the same yearning. In a letter that, by a strange coincidence, I addressed her the following day, I said, "Adorable, I dearly miss you. I guess I never loved you so much, and I think this separation will unite us so intensely, that I will not support any separation from you. In other words I'll keep you with me all the time." We could not stand being separated; we had to be close by. Our love was a bond that united us in an entity. Some call this being soul mates, and we definitely matched their definition.

In her last letter addressed to me from Romania, while she was at the beach, Sidonia wrote: "My love, I don't know how you have been able to do it, but, all the time at the beach, I had the feeling, sometimes the absurd certainty that you were with me. It occurred to me to hear something, or to see, and I will turn my head after you. My love, I really miss you, I cannot wait to see you, to kiss and embrace you, with all my love." She was right, my soul was with her all the time. When she arrived from Romania and I embraced her at the gate, at the Kennedy Airport, I felt her relief. We were together again, and she knew and I knew that, from now on, nothing could separate us, nothing. Our ordeal was over.

Sidonia's story will continue as long as my life story continues, hopefully longer than that. Our united hands will always stay united, so will our souls. In 2006, I gave Sidonia, for her birthday, the following statement of love. Each word is the expression of what I feel for her to the end of my life and hopefully beyond.

To you, I love

One day you will remember, our paths have crossed
And since we walked the road together
Together we shared the sweetness of happy days,
My happiness, my hope, my life lies in you
And my anxiety
You are the magical shadow that follows or precedes me
And never ceases to get into my heart
Without seeing you, I know you're there
From afar, I recognize your step and seek your hand
By a simple look, I understand you, you understand me
By a single smile, we become accomplices.
You're not my half, No! You're mine everything
And I could not live without you.
I'd like to repeat, simply, I love you
I love you endlessly

In her sympathy card, Dr. Greta Zimmerman, the dermatologist that cared for Sidonia, wrote: "Her picture in the obituary is beautiful and it is clear she was a very learned woman. You were lucky to have her, I am sure, but make no mistake—she was so very fortunate to have you." Indeed, we were fortunate to have each other; we were a blessed couple.

A Post Scriptum

The story of Sidonia is the story of our love. We loved each other more than anything else in this world. We were bonded together so tight that my only explanation is that we were indeed what others call, soul mates. We were fortunate that our pathways crossed, and we recognized that, and through our free will decided to unite our ways for the rest of our lives, hopefully even beyond. One can say that this was our destiny, and we just followed it. It's hard to prove or disprove such a possibility. My gut feeling tells me that there is a destiny, and there are miracles.

One fact comes across in our story: The first thing that we built in our relationship was trust. Trust is an absolute requirement for love; there cannot be love if there are hidden corners. Besides trust, there must be selflessness. I would always have been ready to give my life for Sidonia, and she sacrificed herself by going back to Romania and fighting from there for our freedom. And then, one has to follow what the US Marines say, "semper fidelis." Yes, one has to always help the other one, no matter how difficult the situation can be.

Our life was not a smooth sailing. We had to face difficult times, as we were living under the shadow of the Iron Curtain, the communist system. Our love gave us the strength to sail through these stormy waters and to accomplish what we wanted in our life. Our united pathway has followed a compassionate destiny. Together we built our family; together we broke away from the communist system and succeeded to bring our children to live in a free country. It was not an easy pathway, but that united us even stronger.

Chapter 7

The Ciugudean Family

I met Sidonia's family shortly before we got married. We planned our marriage, but before that, I had to be introduced to her family, who was living in the city of Cluj-Napoca. Around Easter, we took the plane to Cluj-Napoca, where I met Sidonia's father, Mr. Marius Ciugudean; her mother, Mrs. Valeria Ciugudean (Mutis); and her younger sister, Ms. Felicia Ciugudean (Mimi). The Ciugudean family gave me a warm reception. I felt that I was welcome in this family. Knowing from Sidonia that I like salads, they prepared what was considered in Transylvania a deli salad with something that looked and felt like steamed lettuce. I appreciated very much their effort to please me. It was an excellent start in our relationship, and it stayed this way all along.

With time, I learned the sad history of this family, a typical victim of the communist regime that punished them severely and condemned them to a life and an old age of poverty, having been guilty only of working hard and honestly. For me, it was sad to see this family that had known better times, trying to overcome the hard times that fell unjustly upon them. Since under the communist regime I had seen this happen before, I had the feeling of déjà vu all over again. To me it was obvious that the unfortunate events that were bestowed by the communist regime on her family had serious repercussions on Sidonia, not only for her professional career, but also on her character. I know from my own experience that poverty brings an inferiority complex that can last a very long time.

Marius Zeno Ciugudean

Marius Ciugudean, my father-in-law, was an elderly gentleman, born in Vingard, a village in Transylvania with half of the population Romanian and the other half German. His father, Nicolae, was the public notary of the village, a position of some importance in this rural community. The story is that Nicolae was originally from a village, Ciugud, only thirteen kilometers (approximately eight miles) from Vingard and was the son of a sheep owner. Sheep owners in this mountainous area had been there for thousands of years, and some were wealthy, owning a large number of sheep and sometimes mountains where they kept their flocks during the summer season.

According to Sidonia, Nicolae was married off by his parents to the daughter of another sheep owner, as was common in this area. The story goes that at the wedding, Nicolae did not appreciate the sheepish smell of the bride, fled the wedding and the village, and ended up in Vingard, where he settled down, became a public notary, and married Aurelia Maieru, a wealthy local girl. The wealth consisted of land that she owned and that she increased during her lifetime.

Sidonia remembered this grandfather whom she called "the old man," as a kind man who brought her candies in his pocket, and asked Sidonia to search for them. Sidonia was a bee for sweets, so the candies were more than welcome. He survived his wife, Aurelia, (from whom Sidonia got her middle name) by several years, and lived in a separate small home in the courtyard of the old house where now his son, Sabin, and his family lived.

Marius-Zeno Ciugudean had four siblings: Enea, Sabin, Ovidiu, and Elvira, the only girl. His parents were wealthy, with land as the main asset. The land belonged to his mother, Aurelia, who was from an old family in the village. Aurelia's maiden name was Maieru, but she was related to a family in Vingard called Turcu (the Turk), a name which may indicate their origin. Over the centuries, Transylvania was often invaded by the army of the Ottoman Empire, and it is possible that a Turkish soldier decided to stay in Vingard, call it home, and got married to a local girl. This is all speculation on my part, but the fact is that Marius Ciugudean, when he grew old, looked like an oriental, as can be seen in pictures taken when he was in Columbia, South Carolina.

Sidonia inherited these oriental features from her father. A few years ago, I had an exchange scientist from Japan visiting my laboratory. One day, I invited Dr. Ryoji Nagai for dinner at our house. We sat down for our meal, and suddenly, looking at Sidonia, he asked her if she was Japanese.

The negative answer didn't seem to satisfy him because, driving him back to the hotel he again asked me the same question. To him, she definitely looked Japanese. I should add, beautiful Japanese! Moreover, her blood type was B, which is rare in Europe and more common in Asia. Of course, this does not prove that she is of Asian origin, but the family name, her features, and the blood type seem to fit.

By the time I met Sidonia's family, Marius Ciugudean was retired and had a modest pension that was the only income for his family that included his wife and Mimi, his handicapped daughter. According to Sidonia, her father was a rather authoritarian head of the family. By nature, he was a fighter; and having two daughters didn't make him happy. Moreover, Sidonia was the kindest human being one can imagine. He respected his wife, consulted with her, and appreciated her opinions. After she had the second stroke that left her paralyzed on the left side of the body, he took care of her with unlimited devotion. After she passed away he lost interest in living.

When WWI started in 1914, Marius enrolled as a volunteer in the army. He probably could easily have been kept at home by his father, the public notary of their village, but Marius was itching for battle. He ended up in the Austro-Hungarian army and was sent to the front line in Serbia. There, he was made prisoner by the Serbs who were allied with the French. Together with many other prisoners, he had to walk to a seaport in Albania; from there, he was shipped to France. On his way, he survived typhus and hunger. In France, as a prisoner of war, Marius Ciugudean was sent to help with agriculture work in the vineyards of Bordeaux. At some point, the Romanian prisoners became organized in the Romanian Legion of France, and Marius enthusiastically enrolled in it. As a member of this army unit, Marius ended WWI on the defense line of Paris.

When the war ended, Marius was shipped home where he continued to be strongly patriotic, as he was until the end of his life. I think that, among his last words, was "Long live Romania." He was unhappy about having to leave Romania, and after he was with us in the States, at some point, Sidonia and I considered sending him back to Romania. However, by then, his health was deteriorating, and besides, we could not identify anyone there who would take good care of him.

After WWI, Marius Ciugudean studied law and became a judge in the city of Alba-Iulia. This is where he met Ms. Valeria Ignea, who was the daughter of a public notary, a position that is quite important in Romania. Apparently, Marius dated Ms. Ignea for five years, thus raising questions and gossips about their relationship in this small provincial town where both of them where important public figures. His explanation was that he wanted to have a stable financial situation, but that took a little longer than usual.

Fig. 1. Marius-Zeno Ciugudean.

This is what Sidonia thought about her father: "For a long time I misjudged my father, considering that he only takes good care of us for the material part of life. Later I learned from my own experience, that I was deadly wrong. He loved his family from the bottom of his heart, but didn't show it. But when one of us had a hard time, he always was there, opened his loving, warm heart, and was more than loving, caring, understanding, and only then showed all his love. He tried to find solutions and to fix the problems, offering with generosity his help. He loved us very much, but we got few hugs and kisses from him. All his love for us, and only for us, was closed deeply in his heart.

"My father was a very good observer of people, and could tell what kind of person is and what can you expect from him, for good or bad. And he was right. In Alba-Iulia where he got his first job as a judge at the court, he had lots of friends with whom he hunted and played cards. Even after he got married, he continued to do so. He also liked to play chess and I think he was a good player, but it was hard for him to find partners. After we moved to Cluj, he gave up hunting and cards and was devoted totally to his carrier as a prosecutor, which he liked very much, he did it with passion. He continued to hunt only occasionally in Vingard and never played cards again. In Cluj he had few friends most of them related to his job. He was blessed with an outstanding and an accurate memory. His memory was as a camcorder, he taped everything, and when he needed it, it was there. Mimi and Noël inherited him.

"Father was a person always with a book in his hands, lying in bed. There he studied the files for his cases; he was reading the newspaper and his law books. When he studied for his trials Mom always made us aware to keep quiet. He was very interested in History, Philosophy, Geography, and biographies of famous political and army leaders. He was interested very much in politics, listened to radio for worldwide news, read several newspapers. With family and friends politics was a favorite subject. He was never an active politician even though he was asked to join a political party he didn't do it, because being a prosecutor he had no right to be member of any party.

"As a judge and a prosecutor he was known as a very severe one and merciless for criminals of any kind. He was a person who used only his brain to judge people not at all his heart. Mom was at the opposite extreme.

"In 1933 my father was promoted and offered a position as a prosecutor in Cluj which he accepted. We moved to Cluj, one of the largest cities in Transylvania. It is a very nice city established hundreds of years ago, it has lots of history. It is the greatest university center in Transylvania, and is also a musical center with 2 operas, symphony orchestra, and 2 schools of music. My family lived basically most of our life in Cluj, where we had a period of prosperity and happiness before the communists took the power."

Mutis

Mrs. Valeria Ciugudean was the daughter of Mr. Valeriu Ignea and Mrs. Sidonia Ignea, born Hoban. She was a kind lady, who had survived a stroke that left her paralyzed on the left side. She was able to move around, but her left hand was totally paralyzed. Learning that I was a medical doctor made her happy, saying, "From now on I will have my own doctor." Mrs. Valeria Ciugudean was an educated lady, speaking fluently German. Actually, her nickname was Mutis, derived from the German *mutter* (mother). The Ignea family was originally from the Banat Province, which was, for many years, part of the Hapsburg Empire. Her parents died at a rather young age of heart disease, which seemed to have run in the family.

Fig. 2. Mrs. Valeria Ciugudean (Mutis).

Ms. Valeria Ignea had two younger brothers, Mircea and Titus that she took care of after their parents died. They lived in the Ciugudean household, and Sidonia was close to them. They were almost like her older brothers. Also attached to the Ciugudean family was Ms. Elena Hoban, who was a sister of Mrs. Ignea, and was part of the family while Sidonia grew up. It is noticeable that Marius Ciugudean accepted this enlarged family and supported them.

The first child of the Ciugudean couple was Sidonia, who was born on June 18, 1929, in Alba-Iulia. The next pregnancy of Mrs. Ciugudean ended badly. At term, there was a very large child, who could not be delivered by the natural way. In those years, cesarean operation was still a daring surgery. Marius had to choose between the life of this child and that of his wife, and he chose his wife. The child had to be sacrificed because it was endangering the life of the mother. This unfortunate event was followed by the birth of Felicia (Mimi) in 1932. By then, the Ciugudean family moved to Cluj-Napoca, where, later Marius gave up his position of public attorney and became a successful lawyer.

Mimi

Felicia Ciugudean, nicknamed Mimi, was about three years younger than Sidonia. Mimi had different illnesses during her early childhood, and grew up mentally handicapped. Her parents attributed this to encephalitis as a very young child, but in the family, there seemed to have been some who thought that she had some inborn defect. This is what Sidonia remembers about Mimi's sickness: "The first thing I clearly remember in Cluj is my Mom, in a large room with open windows, and a lot of mess, probably we just moved in, giving me directions to go to the Court (on the same street at about 4-5 minutes distance), and tell the person from the big door to find my father for me. He had to come home immediately, my sister being very sick. I remember as I left home looking back all the time to see my Mom at the gate, and I was scared being alone for the first time in the street. I had to cross a place which was the entrance to a car repair, and I was scared a car is going to come out and hit me. Then, I clearly remember entering the Court room which I remember as a huge one, large, very big, and at my left, far from me at a very high long table, I recognized after a while my father dressed in the black robe. Having a relieved feeling, I started to run toward him and shouted 'Daddy, Daddy come home Mimi is going to die.' I saw Daddy bent to his colleague and speaking shortly to him then coming toward me. He took me in his arms. My job was done, I felt happy and secure in his arms, I didn't care about anything else. Later, I learned that Mimi at that time was very sick, she got encephalitis which left her handicapped for the rest of her life.

Several times she struggled between life and death, and only a miracle saved her, but for the rest of her life she paid out for this medical extraordinary success. Mimi was very religious and loved to go to church and could take care of herself."

Sidonia describes thus her family religious activity: "My family from both sides was orthodox, as were about 85% of Romanians at that time. My Dad wasn't a religious person, very rare I saw him at the church, but he wanted his family to keep the religious traditions. My Mom was to the bottom of her soul religious, strongly believing in God, but she wasn't at all a practitioner. I definitely resemble her. Mimi all her life was a person who loved to go and to be in church. When they lived in Bucharest close to church, she attended the service every evening. When we were very young, every Sunday, my Mom went to church with us, and later, when she trusted me to go alone with Mimi, she just let us go together. Since I recall, for Easter the first trip was always to the church on Easter Sunday. I wore a lot of pink and red, and Mimi blue. Often we had the same pattern in different colors. Mimi loved that and I didn't mind."

Fig. 3. Mimi (front) and Sidonia (back) on a sleigh. Cluj, 1935.

After Mutis's death in May 1979, Tataie was reluctant to take care of Mimi, and her health declined rapidly, in parallel with the progression of

Parkinson's disease. By January 1980, she developed pneumonia and was admitted to a hospital where, after several days, she died. She was buried first in a cemetery in Bucharest, but in 1980, when Sidonia was preparing for her departure to the United States, she moved Mimi's remains to Alba-Iulia into the grave of her family, where Mutis is also resting.

Fig. 4. The tomb of the Ignea-Ciugudean family in the cemetery in Alba-Iulia.

Fig. 5. Mimi's remains (Felicia Ciugudean) were the last addition to this grave.

The Vingard Home

After having Sidonia in 1929 and Mimi in 1932, the Ciugudean couple decided to build their own home in Vingard. Until then, they used to go there and stay in what they called the old house, the house of Marius's parents, where his brother Sabin and his family now had permanent residence. I guess that, by then, Marius already had his vineyard started, one more reason to have a home in the village.

The home they built was quite modern, compared with what was common in those days in the Romanian countryside. It had running water, flushing toilets, and bathroom. After being abused by the communist owners for almost thirty years, during which no repairs were made, it still looked nice when I saw it in 1977. The home was surrounded by a large garden where the permanent housekeeper, Ms. Maria Boitoș, was growing vegetables and breeding chickens and ducks that enjoyed the creek at the rear of the garden. In the garden, a separate wine cellar was built, where the barrels with wine were kept. According to Sidonia, every year, her father was selling about a metric ton of wine to merchants in the near town of Sebes and possibly Alba-Iulia.

The Ciugudean family would shuttle from Cluj to Vingard with their Lincoln car driven by Sidonia's uncle Titus. The story of this car could stand as an advertisement for Lincoln cars. In 1941, when the war against the Soviet Union began, the car was commandeered by the Romanian Army. It went through the whole Russian military campaign, most likely up to Stalingrad, and at the end, it came back to Cluj still in working order. However, it was not returned to its owner, Mr. Marius Ciugudean.

Fig. 6. The home built by Sidonia's parents in Vingard.

Refugees and War

In 1940, Cluj and a large part of Transylvania were given to Hungary by Hitler and his allies. The Ciugudean family had to leave Cluj and take refuge to the city of Sibiu. They had to leave Cluj in a hurry because Marius Ciugudean had received death threats from the Hungarian individuals that he prosecuted as a public attorney. In Sibiu, Mr. Ciugudean practiced as a lawyer throughout WWII, and Sidonia attended school. They continued to spend time in Vingard, which remained part of Romania.

The story of Titus is even more remarkable than that of the Lincoln car. Titus, a younger brother of Mrs. Ciugudean, was an experienced mechanic. At the beginning of WWII, he was drafted. Being able to speak German and a good mechanic, he ended up as a driver in the German army and went all the way to Stalingrad. On the way, he was assigned a Russian prisoner to be his orderly. He treated the man well, and when the Red Army caught the German and Romanian military at Stalingrad in encirclement, they managed to get out together. Obviously, the help of the Russian orderly was crucial for getting Titus through the Russian blockade.

Titus walked his way back home over thousands of miles and, one evening, showed up at his family's door. Mutis, his sister, had lost track of him and considered him, like thousands of other Romanian military that went to Stalingrad and were caught in the encirclement, either dead or a prisoner. Every evening, Sidonia's mother asked her to pray for Titus's safe return because "God listens to children." Sidonia did it and it worked. Miracles do happen.

Communist Robbery

After WWII, the territory of Transylvania that was occupied by Hungary was returned to Romania, and the Ciugudean family moved back to Cluj, where they bought a home. A few years after Marius Ciugudean and his family returned to Cluj from their refuge in Sibiu, the communists took power and decided that there were too many lawyers in the country, and it was time to get rid of them, in particular, those that did not belong to the Communist Party. Marius Ciugudean was one of them.

Almost at the same time, the communist regime started expropriating land to create so-called agricultural cooperatives and state-owned farms. Again, Marius Ciugudean was a target; the communists took his vineyard and also the house that he had built in Vingard. The family had to flee Vingard in a hurry to avoid the violence of the new owners, the communist gang. So in a very short time, the Ciugudean family was left without any source of income. Marius Ciugudean was put out of his profession as a lawyer, and was robbed of his home and land. Almost overnight, the Ciugudean family became impoverished, a direct result of communist takeover.

By that time, Sidonia was enrolled as a student of the Cluj University, majoring in biology. Her father asked her to drop out of college and take a job, which she did. For one year, she was the breadwinner for her family, doing accounting work for a company selling hardware. By then, her father had found a job as a judicial counselor for an electricity company, and she could resume her college studies. She resented this break in her studies because, to her classmates who didn't know what was going on, it appeared that she had to repeat an academic year, which of course was not the case.

In the communist regime, the state of affairs of her father had long-term consequences on Sidonia. In the late seventies, when she was working at the Cantacuzino Institute, she was preparing to defend her dissertation to obtain her PhD, a doctoral degree. In order to be allowed to defend it, she needed the approval of the Communist Party committee. According to the rules established by Ceaușescu, any doctoral degree had to be approved by a special commission of the Communist Party under the direction of his wife, Elena Ceaușescu. This was intended to make sure that only party members, or people faithful to the dictatorial regime, could get doctoral degrees and, therefore, qualify for higher positions. The committee refused to give Sidonia permission to defend her dissertation because of her social origin. Her father had owned land, and therefore, she had a rotten social origin. This was happening thirty years after her parents' Vingard property was stolen by the communist regime, which, in the meantime, managed to destroy it.

The Other Ciugudeans

The siblings of Marius Ciugudean included Elvira, the only sister, and brothers Enea, Sabin, and Ovidiu. Married to Mr. Buda, Elvira lived and died in Alba-Iulia and had two sons, Marius and Didu (Ovid). Brother Enea lived in Ciumbrud, a village near Vingard and had two daughters, one married to a physician in the town of Câmpina, and another married to a postmaster. Brother Sabin was married to Miluța (Emilia). They lived in Vingard in the old house, were teachers at the village school, and had three daughters and a son, Titus.

Ovidiu was the youngest brother, was married to Victoria, and had two sons, Victor and Adrian, and a daughter, Cita, who died young because of an overdose of sleeping pills. Sabin and his children, except one daughter, and Ovidiu and his family have all moved to the United States. Victor is a retired oilman. His brother Adrian owned a cattle farm in Missouri. He passed away not long ago. As of this writing, Aunt Miluța celebrated her one hundredth birthday. She and her children live in the Los Angeles area.

When Aurelia Ciugudean, the mother of Marius Ciugudean, died, her will divided the land she owned into five equal size parts, one for each of her five children. This was very fair but created major problems that showed up years later. The five children, in a spirit of brotherly goodwill, divided the land according to everyone's preference. In the following years, they continued to exchange pieces of land according to their needs. Elvira had to sell her land to her brothers to cover expenses that her husband spent on liquor. In the process, Marius and Ovidiu ended up with land that they used to set up vineyards and build nice houses, whereas Sabin was more interested in growing corn and vegetables. They never bothered to obtain legal documents as to the ownership of the land and/or the exchanges that had taken place, and when it came to prove ownership, the inheritors had no legal papers to do it.

Sidonia in Vingard

There is no doubt that the years spent in Vingard were the golden years of Sidonia's youth. She enjoyed the freedom, the friendship, and the companionship that she had with the local youngsters of her age and her cousins. She would recount how she was in charge of feeding the fowl—chickens, turkeys, and ducks—and how these fowl recognized her when she went out to feed them. Also, she had her story about the dog, how he loved her, how he recognized her, and how he apologized for barking at her.

One of Sidonia's stories was how her father would ask her to get into the wine barrels in order to clean them. Her small size as a young child allowed her to fit into the barrels, but she didn't like it. She would carry a candle with her and clean the wall of the barrels before they would add the new wine. Another story she was telling was how she went with other kids to hunt for bird nests in the surrounding woods and got lost. They were recovered by a passing peasant with a horse-driven wagon who took them back home to the relief of their families. Those were the years when she developed a profound love of nature; later in life she enjoyed hiking in the mountains of Romania and America.

Sidonia was telling how her father was respected by the village peasants, and how he used to help them by giving free judicial advice. He seemed to have been generous with people that worked in his vineyard, so much so that when the communists took over and asked people to come out and accuse him of exploitation, none of them raised their hand.

In 1975, we decided to go for a camping trip in the Western Carpathian Mountains. On our way there, we took a detour through Vingard. We started our visit with Sidonia taking us to visit the old church. In the nearby cemetery were the graves of her ancestors who had contributed to the building of the church. We met the priest, a young man who complained about the lack of funds to maintain the church. The original intention was to keep our visit concealed, but soon, Sidonia was recognized by people of the village, and we were invited into several homes and treated with the traditional Romanian hospitality.

One important stop was at the home of Maria Boitoș, the woman who took care of Sidonia's home and garden. The meeting between the two of them was emotional. Sidonia went to meet friends she knew from the time she was playing with them. Also, Sidonia wanted us to see the water mill they used to obtain the wheat flour and the corn meal; to our astonishment, it was still working. For me it was a joy to see how she was received by these people and how they reminisced about the good times of their childhood.

Fig. 7. Sidonia meets Mrs. Maria Boitoș, the home keeper of the Ciugudean family in Vingard. Alina and Noël keep company. 1975.

By evening, we ended up at the house of Hans Pits's family, the man who took care of the Ciugudean vineyard. This house looked like a typical German village home with a large square yard surrounded by high walls, like a little fortress. We had a lavish dinner attended by the whole family and we slept in their special guest room. The reception that we got was beyond hospitality; it was a respectful welcome back, very likely set off by memories of better times.

Fig. 8. Sidonia visits the Pits family and holds the arm of Mr. Hans Pits, the man that managed her fathers' vineyard in Vingard. Alina is sticking to her Mom. 1975.

Uncle Ovidiu Visit

It was the fall of 1977 when Uncle Ovidiu came from the States to visit his family. Being between jobs, I took him together with Marius and two of their cousins, Ovidiu and Titus Maieru, for a tour of the old country, the places where they were born and lived. This took us through Transylvania, and it was a very nice trip. We visited villages where Ovidiu and the others shared history and souvenirs from their young age.

Under beautiful fall weather, with leaves changing colors, we reached Vingard, the village of the Ciugudean family. We went to visit what used to be Ovidiu's house, by now the office of the agricultural cooperative. It was just the season of wine making, and we watched the grapes being squashed in a big press. People from the cooperative were hospitable and offered us wine from their production, which actually was from Ovidiu's vineyard. The owner was now a visitor. We stopped and looked at Marius's house, which looked abandoned and ruined. We learned that the house has been used by the agricultural state enterprise to keep the sheep inside in wintertime. Obviously, this didn't help maintain the house and speaks volumes about how the communists have run the country.

Fig. 9. The Ciugudean family reunion in Alba-Iulia. From left to right: Alexandru Avramescu, Ovidiu Ciugudean, Ovidiu Maieru, Mimi Pălăgesiu, Ms. Pălăgesiu, Ovidiu Buda, Marius Ciugudean, Mircea Pălăgesiu, Titus Maieru.
The lady squatting is Mrs. Aurica Buda, the wife of Mr. Ovidiu Buda.

The story of the Ciugudean family is typical of that of thousands of Romanian families whose lives and well-being had been ruined by the communist regime. I should add that one of Marius Ciugudean's brothers, Ovidiu, in addition to having been robbed of his property, house, and vineyard in Vingard, spent two years in the concentration camp of forced labor, digging the Danube-Black Sea channel. Why? Because at one of the communist staged manifestations, he was asked to carry the portrait of a leader of the party, Ana Pauker. As he was resting during their walk using the portrait as an umbrella, he was asked by someone what was he doing. His answer was, "I am standing in the shadow of this tramp." As his statement was reported to Securitate by one of their innumerable informers, he was sent without a trial to spend two years in the labor camp, where the prisoners were building the Danube-Black Sea channel. According to some estimates, at least ten thousand prisoners died from illness and starvation in this camp. Is there any wonder why the Ciugudean family moved to the other side of the Iron Curtain?

CHAPTER 8

The Microbiology Institute 1966-1971

A Team

By June 1966, I left the Oncology Institute and started my work at the Microbiology Institute. I was assigned to the laboratory of Dr. Hans Aderca with whom I was already collaborating. He was running an excellent laboratory of tissue culture. A graduate student, Nina Şahnazarov, was a very active member of the lab. I started collaborating with her on a major research project, studying a newly discovered oncogenic virus, SV40. My studies on this virus had already started at the Oncology Institute, where I had obtained tumors by injecting this virus into young hamsters and I was looking at the chromosomes of the tumors. Soon, Nina and I had obtained cells in culture that were transformed after infection with this virus. These were normal cells that acquired abnormalities typically found in cancer cells.

Soon thereafter, two biology students, Luiz Hernan Graffe and Şerban Ionescu-Homoriceanu (Tony), joined us. The first to join us was Luiz. He was originally from Venezuela, probably a political dissident. I don't know how he found out about me and my research, but Luiz was in the lab almost daily. After a while, he got on board Tony, who was his classmate. These students would come and join us for work whenever they had time from their classes. During summer vacations, Luiz would go to Sweden to work and generate the income that he needed to live in Romania during the academic year. Once he brought me from Sweden a pair of clogs to wear in the lab and was very proud of me, looking like a Swedish scientist.

Our group, consisting of Nina, Luiz, Tony, and me, would have lunch in the lab. Luiz was the cook and also the provider of the food. Every day, he would prepare spaghetti with ground meat. From him I learned to cook spaghetti. The whole atmosphere was one of work with enthusiasm. These youngsters felt that they were part of something significant, and were proud of it. They were not paid, and the only way to compensate was to give them credit on papers that included work they had contributed to. In those years, we were by far the most active producers of scientific papers in the Microbiology Institute. The director of the institute, was constantly asking for more papers to fill the publication of the institute and we were obliging.

Sidonia Surgery and Move

It was the end of 1966, when Sidonia discovered that she had a lump in her breast. We went to see Dr. Trestioreanu, one of the best breast surgeons at the Oncology Institute, where Sidonia was still working. He advised immediate surgery to remove the tumor. Sidonia went into surgery, while I was waiting at the pathology lab, for the tumor to be examined while she was still in the operating room. Depending on the result, the surgeon will either close the wound, or go ahead, and do a total resection of the breast. For me, with the history of my mother dead because of breast cancer, this was an agonizing moment. Finally the tumor came, and was immediately processed in the pathology lab. Dr. Rodica Duțu, the best pathologist, looked at the slides while I was holding my breath and prayed. The result came, it was a benign tumor, not cancer. The surgeon was told he can close the wound, and Dr. Duțu called me to look at the slides. I was facing another miracle for us, we were again blessed.

The only follow up was, that the surgeon advised Sidonia to avoid the sun going to the beach. His personal experience was that, the beach and the sun promote the development of breast cancer, something that has never been scientifically proven. Nevertheless, we were not in the position to argue with Dr. Trestioreanu, therefore the following years, as we went vacationing at the beach, Sidonia will join us during the last days.

After my departure, Sidonia was not happy at the Oncology Institute, where she was asked to do work in which she was not interested. During this time Sidonia's relief was the joy of having her baby, Noël, who was developing as a beautiful and smart kid. We used to take him for a walk in the Carol Park, not far from our apartment. The park had a small lake, and we used to rent a rowing boat and float around.

Fig. 1. Sidonia and Noël during a walk in Carol park. May 1967.

Fig. 2. Sidonia and Noël in rowing boat on the Carol park lake. May 1967.

The summer of 1967, we went back to Tataia, rented a room at Mrs. Popa, and, enjoyed a quiet vacation at the beach. At the beginning I went only with Noël, and, I wrote to Sidonia who was left at home, following the surgeon advice: "Our adored and treasure, we just arrived and we miss you, and both of us invoke you. My soul, I miss you, and long for you now, as I missed you and longed for you, when loving you I came here alone, and I expected you to come. And you came then, as now, and I've been waiting for you then, as now, except that, now waiting for you are two, I and Noël. He always says and asks when you will come, and this happens "tomorrow", although I know that this "tomorrow" will be only a few days which will be an eternity. I adore you, and I love you very much, you are the little boys' treasure, and your boys want you always beside them. That's it, and you have to know that, I kiss you, I long and I'd like you to be here now, with the two of us, your boys. B and N".

Fig. 3. Sidonia and Noël at Tataia beach. July 1967.

The situation of Sidonia at the Oncology Institute becoming unpleasant, we started looking for a position for her elsewhere, and an offer came from Prof. Petre Raicu, head of the Department of Genetics at the Bucharest University. She was offered the position of assistant professor in the Department of Genetics of the University of Bucharest. By February 1968 Sidonia accepted this offer and soon she was very appreciated in the new position. Professor Raicu was politically well connected. He was what I would call a westernized communist. He had traveled to France several times, and was smart enough to appreciate were the golden eggs were. He tried by all means to imitate what he had seen in the West, and our lack of political affiliation didn't bother him. After hiring Sidonia, he proposed me to write a book on methods in cytogenetics. I accepted his proposal, and we signed the contract with the reputable press house of the Romanian Academy. When the book came out, it was a success; it sold out quickly. I didn't get any spare books, and I own only one copy.

Fig. 4. Sidonia in the Botanical Garden where the Department of Genetics was located. July 1968.

Visiting Soviet Union

By spring of 1968, I was offered by the Romanian Academy to travel to the Soviet Union as an exchange visiting scientist with the Academy of Medical Sciences of the USSR. For me this was a good opportunity to broaden our research project. Professor Melnick, who visited us shortly before, told me that there was a group in Moscow doing interesting work with SV40 virus. I was anxious to see what they were doing and, eventually, to obtain from them some scientific material we needed for our work. One of these scientists was Dr. Prigogina, whom I had already met at the Oncology Institute. Being forced to live behind the Iron Curtain under a similar totalitarian political system we shared some basic things. Words to spell this out were not necessary and could have been dangerous.

By May 1968, I was on a plane flying to Moscow. I was going to spend most of the two weeks in Moscow, but at the end, I would travel by night train to Leningrad (now Saint Petersburg) and spend three days there. In Moscow, I visited the Oncology Institute, where I met Dr. Prigogina and Dr. Deichman. These ladies were doing excellent research. We never spoke politics, but this was not necessary. We understood each other without words. At the Oncology Institute, I gave a talk about my work on SV40 virus and got some reagents, antibodies that were not commercially available that we needed for the completion of our work on SV40.

It was interesting to see the Soviet world; I had the feeling of entering a bear's den. This was happening only a month before the Red Army invaded Czechoslovakia. The Soviet Union, at that time, was recovering from the horrors of the Stalin regime that obviously had influenced every aspect of life, including science. Before Stalin's reign, Russia had an excellent school of genetics, which was wiped out with the complicity of Stalin's scientific stooges. I met one of their best geneticists, Dr. Dubinin, who was back from years spent in Siberia in some forsaken place because he represented what Lysenko was calling the "cosmopolite science." Dr. Dubinin was a world-famous geneticist who was quoted in classical books of genetics all over the world.

In Moscow, I had an interpreter assigned to me who helped me get around, and who made sure that I talked only to those that I was supposed to. He was kind, made arrangements to visit the Lenin mausoleum ahead of the long line waiting outside; and one evening, he took me to the famous Bolshoi Theatre to watch a concert. Lenin looked to me more like a wax statue, and the concert of patriotic songs was just a show of government propaganda. One major surprise for me was the Soviet women. I was expecting the see overweight women dressed poorly, but this is not what I saw on the street, in the subway, or in the laboratory. These were beauties with blue eyes, golden-red hair, nicely dressed. I still recall one such beauty at the Oncology Institute, a blonde who could have been cut out of any classical Hollywood movie.

My visit to Leningrad (St. Petersburg) was short but impressive. The city, the palaces, gave the feeling that it was a city of a past glory and extreme wealth. Everything that was modern was outside the city and not inside. One would have expected to see all the nobles and the czars walking on the streets, which were now populated with the working class citizens that replaced them after the revolution. The image of the Peter the Great summer palace is still with me, not only for its magnificent interiors, but also for its position on the sea. The view was just outstanding. Being May, the nights were already very short, and I had a strange feeling walking at 10:00 or 11:00 PM on streets that didn't need electric lights.

My guide was a nice young lady who spoke English and no Romanian. From what she told me, I got the impression that she was connected with the dissident movement that was growing in those days in the Soviet Union and throughout the satellite countries. The events in Prague, the so-called Prague Spring, were just developing, and its suppression by the armies of the Soviet Union and the Warsaw countries, with the exception of Romania, would follow shortly after my return to Bucharest. The scent of perestroika was in the air in Leningrad, as I was walking around with this nice Russian lady. My feeling was that the communist system was in a comatose state. It took another twenty years or so to have the Iron Curtain removed.

War?

By the summer of 1968, I had to finish my part of the book that I wrote with Professor Raicu and which was due soon. We sent Noël to Cluj to spend the hot days of summer there under the care of Sidonia's parents. It was a bright sunny day in June, and I was working at the academy library located on the main avenue crossing downtown Bucharest called Calea Victoriei (Victory Avenue). As it happened, around noon, I left the library and started walking home on Calea Victoriei. Several blocks down the street, I reached the large Palace Plaza, which had on one side, the Royal Palace, and on the other side, the building housing the central committee of the Communist Party.

A large crowd was in the plaza in front of the central committee building and was growing fast, spontaneously. On the balcony of the building, a little guy was talking, very agitated. There were loudspeakers throughout the plaza, and I soon realized that the man on the balcony was Ceaușescu, the president of the country. His talk was about what happened overnight, the invasion of Czechoslovakia by the armies of the Warsaw Pact led by the Soviet Union. Ceaușescu was expressing his opposition to this invasion in no equivocal terms, emphasizing that Romania was ready to militarily oppose any crossing of its border by any of these armies. People were listening quietly but getting the message; if they come, we are going to fight. For me, the message was clear; we were on the brink of war with the Soviet Union and its allies.

I went home in a hurry and discussed the situation with Sidonia. Noël was in Cluj, a city which was only less than one hundred miles from the border with Hungary, which was a Warsaw Pact country that would have been the first to move. Hungary was claiming for centuries that Transylvania belonged to it. Our decision was made; I would go to Cluj and bring the child back home. If anything happened, at least we could take care of him as best we could, and anyway, Bucharest was farther away from the borders than Cluj.

Next morning, I was on the train going to Cluj. The trip would take about eight hours. On the train, people were discussing and relating all kinds of rumors: Soviet armor divisions were assembled at the Romanian border, there had already been dogfights between the Romanian and Soviet fighter planes, Romania had a laser gun that could destroy any Soviet tank, etc. The truth is that, as our train approached Cluj, trains loaded with military warfare could be seen on the move, and this didn't make me less anxious.

I arrived in Cluj, where Noël was happily playing with some other kids. Next day, together, we returned to Bucharest. In the following days, the political situation remained tense, but then it dwindled down. Many years later, I learned that President Lyndon Johnson asked the leadership of the Soviet Union not to invade Romania. I guess it would be hard not to say that this worked, but at any rate, for Ceaușescu, this was the peak of his popularity with the Romanian people. I know honest individuals who enrolled in the Communist Party then, thinking that, at last, the party represents and defends the interests of the Romanian people. Naiveté and hope have no limits. Ironically in 1989, twenty-one years later, Ceaușescu delivered his last speech from the same balcony, but this time, he had to flee the crowds that were ready to take him down, and he ended up a few days later in front of the firing squad.

A Baby and a Car

By summer of 1968, our family life was getting back to normal. Sidonia was now away from the Oncology Institute, and was more relaxed, and we went for our seaside vacation at Tataia.

Fig. 5. Sidonia and Noël in a boat on Carol park lake, 1968.

Fig. 6. Sidonia and Noël on the Tataia beach. July 1968.

Fig. 7. Sidonia and Noël in Mrs. Popa's garden in Tataia. July 1968.

Sidonia and I had been discussing, for some time, to have another child, a companion for Noël, who was already the joy of our life. Being the only child after the death of my sister, I thought that having a sibling was very important. Since it had already been three years since Sidonia had the cesarean section for Noël, Fred Georgescu assured us that it would be safe for her to have another pregnancy.

Sidonia, being a faculty member, had more vacation time than me. Therefore, after the beach vacation, we rented a room in Azuga, a small town a few miles north of Bușteni in the Prahova valley, near the Bucegi Mountain. I took Sidonia and Noël there and returned to Bucharest. The following weekends, I spent walking with them around Azuga and taking Noël to the railway station so that he could enjoy watching the big engines passing by. On one of these weekends, when I joined Sidonia and Noël in Azuga, Sidonia gave me the good news; she was pregnant. We were ready to wait and hope.

Fig. 8. Sidonia and Noël in the mountain resort of Azuga. August 1968.

The fall of 1968 would also be important for another reason. We would acquire our first car. With the hope of having two children, the car was becoming a necessity. We learned that an official agency called Terra was selling imported cars to the public, more precisely to those who could pay in cash with foreign currency. Under the somewhat more liberal policies of the years 1960-1970, there were individuals such as artists or sportsmen, who would go abroad and be paid in foreign currency. By law, they were required to change it to the Romanian currency as they returned home, but now they could use it to buy things such as electronics or even cars.

The communist regime found out that Western currency, in particular the dollar, was good to have and was selling anything to get it. Most likely, the Terra Agency was a branch of the Securitate or under its supervision. The business that went on for years and was run by the Securitate was selling Jews to Israel and Germans to West Germany. There were hundreds of thousands of Romanian citizens who were of Jewish or German ethnicity, and the governments of Israel and, respectively, West Germany were willing to pay to get them out of Romania. These people were willing to leave their motherland that, under the Ceauşescu dictatorship, was becoming less and less motherly by the year.

For us, the opportunity to have foreign currency arrived through Uncle Willy. Uncle Willy was supporting his brother, Oscar, and his family by giving them a monthly allowance of $200. The way they did it was perfectly legal. Willy would come and spend a few weeks in Bucharest and would go to the National Bank, pay $2,400, the allowance for the following year, and get the Romanian currency in exchange. He would leave this money with Oscar. The official rate of exchange was one dollar for twelve lei.

By September, one of the nicest months in Bucharest, Uncle Willy arrived. We didn't waste any time and told him what our plan was. We would buy the dollars from him with the same amount of money in Romanian currency that the bank would give him. In exchange, we asked him to go with us to the Terra Agency and pay them the price of a Volkswagen Beetle, which was $2,400, the same amount that he would have changed at the bank. He accepted willingly. For him, it really didn't matter where the Romanian currency that he had to give Oscar came from, and everything was perfectly legal. The Oscar family was a little nervous since they had the impression that we didn't have the money, and therefore, their income would be jeopardized. We assured them that we had all the money. In reality, we didn't have all the money on hand, and we had to borrow some from Luiz, who was supportive of this action. We paid him back soon from our salaries that were quite good. And so we went to Terra, which was all business. Uncle Willy paid the price for the Volkswagen, and we were promised that the car would be delivered at the beginning of 1969.

Privacy

Another important event happened before the end of 1968; we moved. The story of why we had to move from the apartment in Bibescu-Vodă where I was born and spent thirty-five years of my life is long, complicated, and typical for the communist regime. This apartment consisted of four rooms arranged linearly like the cars of a train. As one entered the apartment through the foyer, there was a room that was used as a waiting room for my father's clients. My father's office was on the right side of the waiting room. On the left side, there was the dining room leading to the kitchen and through a double door to the last room, which was a bedroom. This was the only room that opened to the bathroom. During WWII, with my father gone, my mother rented out the office room to generate some much-needed income. When the communists took power, the building became state propriety, and the administration of the lodgings was run by the Office of the Inhabitable Space.

Over the years, a series of people occupied this room, the last ones being a couple, Mr. and Mrs. Cristescu. The Cristescu couple had been living in an apartment in the same building and had applied for immigration to Israel. For reasons that are beyond me, they decided to give up their apartment and to move in with us, renting the room that was available. When the Cristescu couple finally received their passports to leave the country, the Office of the Inhabitable Space, a government institution that regulated all the lodgings deciding who would live and where, awarded their room to a certain Mr. Trandafir. This was a young single man who came and took possession of the room. He was not allowed to use the bathroom since that would have meant passing through my bedroom so he used the small toilet near the kitchen. As for bathing, I assume he used the kitchen or he may have had some facility at his workplace.

After a while, Mr. Trandafir started a trial, claiming that he actually had the right to the bedroom I was using and, implicitly, the bathroom, because the Cristescu couple used to live there. The trial went to the court, and as lawyer, I had a former secretary of my father, Mr. Weinberg. Mr. Trandafir brought a friend of his as a witness, telling the judge that he saw me living in the room where Mr. Trandafir was now living. Obviously, he was a false witness. We won the case, but for me, it was quite an experience to have to defend the right to sleep in the bedroom where I had been born. This was the communist system at its best. Once this question was settled, our cohabitation continued peacefully. Sidonia moved in, we got married, and Noël was born.

Then Mr. Trandafir got married, and not too long after, he had a baby. One can easily imagine how this apartment was looking with two families sharing the kitchen and one having no access to a bathroom. At some point, we offered Mr. Trandafir money to move out. This was not unusual; there was even a term for it in Romanian, *filodorma*. He refused, saying that this was not enough; he wanted a full apartment.

With Sidonia expecting a baby, we decided to try a swap. We would offer our apartment of four rooms in exchange for two smaller apartments. We put a notice in the newspaper, and a miracle happened: we got a reply. Mr. Florin Mugur, a well-known writer and poet, wanted to move in with his father, Mr. Ghelerter, a widower. They lived in two smaller apartments; each had two rooms but were located at the opposite ends of the city. I went with Florin Mugur to the Office of the Inhabitable Space to ask for the approval of the swap. Mugur came armed with one of his books of poems. The inspector in charge of our space received us in his office and was flattered by the book (with a personal dedication) that Mr. Mugur brought with him and the swap was approved. I would never have thought that a volume of poetry could help with an apartment swap, but it happened. As they say in Romania, "The ways of the Lord are mysterious."

The move was planned and took place by the end of December. Just at that time, I had a bad case of the flu, but the movers came and started the move. The move lasted the whole day, mainly because we had my father's library of judicial books that had to be moved to the attic of the new apartment. At the end of the day, we offered the movers a bottle of plum brandy, țuica; they drank it and appreciated it. That evening, we slept in the new apartment. After years of living in a shared apartment, we were at last alone. The nightmare of living in a shared apartment was over, hopefully forever. Mr. Trandafir was history.

Fig. 9. Popa Tatu Street, No. 70 where our apartment was located and were we lived from December 1968 until October 1981 when Sidonia and the children left for the United States. The wooden gate led to the interior courtyard. The width of the gate and the tunnel was just enough to let a regular sedan car squeeze by.

The new apartment consisted of two rooms, a small foyer, a small pantry, a rather large bathroom, a toilet, and a large balcony. In all, there were 40 square meters (360 square feet) of living space. It was on the first floor of a two-story building, and there was also a garden with a fig tree and an apricot tree. There was room to park a car, an important advantage considering that we were expecting a new car soon. The building was located within walking distance to an open farmers' market and also about a 15-minute walk to the North Railway Station, something that proved very useful in the following years.

By February 1969, the VW Beetle arrived and was now sitting in the garden. For me, it was time to start learning to drive a car, something that I had never done before. I hired Mr. Iarca, who had been a race car driver and was now making a good living by giving driving lessons to individuals like me who needed to pass a driving test to get a driver's permit. I think I took about thirty hours of driving school.

I was driving a Soviet-made car called Moskwitch, which was very likely a copy of the old Opel car. At the end of the war, the Soviets had moved a number of German factories to the Soviet Union; Opel was one of those. The car had a stick shift on the steering wheel, something that I hated, and I would never buy a car with something like that. Until I learned how to use the clutch, the car was stopping easily when changing speeds. I have to say that Mr. Iarca, my instructor, taught me well. I passed the driving test, which was not easy, considering that for the test, one had to drive through the traffic in Bucharest, which was already becoming chaotic. Soon after I took the test, we all went to the mountain resort of Predeal. Coincidence or not, when I took the driving test in Columbia, South Carolina, I borrowed the Volkswagen Beetle from my colleague and friend Tim Sullivan. This time, the only difficulty with the test was the parallel parking.

West Germany

By the spring of 1969, I was invited to be part of a delegation of scientists to visit West Germany. The invitation was issued by the Zeiss Foundation. I don't know how I got on the invited list, but I suspect that Nicolaia Suciu-Foca, my colleague with whom I had collaborated closely at the Oncology Institute, played some role. She was part of the group along with several professors and scientists from other institutes. We were treated splendidly by the German hosts, with fabulous dinners in castles and visits of medical research laboratories in Ulm. The first evening, when I walked around the hotel, I was impressed by the shop windows. Compared with what I had seen until then, they were spectacular. They even gave us some money so I could buy Sidonia some small gifts.

The most impressive was the visit to the Zeiss factory in Oberkochen. We were told that there was a network of factories throughout West Germany employing thousands of workers. This was an extraordinary accomplishment, considering that the old Zeiss foundation that remained in the part of Germany occupied by the Red Army was shipped to the Soviet Union. At the end of WWII, the leadership of the Zeiss Foundation left this part of Germany and took refuge in the area that became the Federal Republic of West Germany. The only thing they took with them when they left the old factory were the blueprints of their products.

Alina

Back home, soon after my return, we got ready for the next big event—the arrival of our second child. Dr. Fred Georgescu had scheduled the cesarean section on a day when he was on call at the Filantropia hospital. It was April 8, a sunny and beautiful spring day. Sidonia was supposed to check into the hospital early afternoon. During lunchtime we went for a quiet walk in the park close to the hospital. The nature was in bloom. We were concerned but didn't talk about that. Like always, we tried to support each other. Everything looked normal but surgery always has risks.

By 2:00 PM, we went to the hospital and checked in. Within an hour or so, Sidonia was in the operating room, and I was allowed to assist. Fred gave her an intraspinal anesthesia shot and got started. It took a few minutes, and Fred pulled out the baby who turned out to be a girl. Holding her from her legs and with the head downward, his comment was, "Short and fat." The truth is that she was a beautiful newborn baby, looking exactly like a doll. The midwife who was in the operating room showed her to Sidonia, who was alert, and who remembered the midwife telling her what a beautiful girl this baby would be. By evening, everybody was soundly asleep, and I went home to take care of Noël. The following days went without anything remarkable, and soon, mother and daughter were home. Sidonia and I decided to name the girl Alina after my mother's first name.

Immediately after Alina's birth, the Ciugudean family moved to Bucharest and settled in our apartment. Tataie had sold his home in Cluj and, together with Mutis and Mimi, decided to join us in Bucharest. They were three, and we were four. All seven had to fit into the two rooms that were available. I have to say that overcrowding was not an overstatement. However, things went on quite smoothly; Sidonia and I went to work while Tataie and Co. took care of the children and the rest of the household charges. We hired a servant to help with the chores, and she lived in the servant room that our apartment had in the attic of the building.

In spite of Mutis being paralyzed and Mimi mentally handicapped, they helped Sidonia during the year that I spent in Houston, Texas, providing a warm family atmosphere. The bonding that developed between Alina and her grandparents was strong and long lasting.

By summer, we went for vacation to the Bucegi Mountains. We rented a room in Sinaia and spent the days sunbathing and playing in the field. This was our first vacation having a car and a few-months-old baby; it made a huge difference in our comfort and the possibility of moving around.

Fig. 10. Sidonia with Noël and Alina vacation in Sinaia, summer of 1969.

Houston I Come

By fall, an important event took place. I was awarded a fellowship by the International Association for Cancer Research (IARC) located in Lyon, France. This was the first fellowship IARC had awarded to anyone in Romania. It was, for one year, to be spent in Joe Melnick's laboratory in Houston, Texas, with the possibility of extension. I was expected to leave for Houston, Texas, USA, but there was still an important stumbling block to overcome. The Romanian government refused to issue me the passport and visa to travel to the United States.

As I was anxiously waiting for this to be solved, something quite unusual happened. The Securitate officer responsible for the Microbiology Institute, a young woman, called me to her office to fill out some papers. As I walked into her office, I saw on a desk, a handwritten paper with writing that I knew to whom it belonged. It was one of my closest colleagues and friend. While she was shuffling some papers, I had time to read it over; it was an information note, stating that if I was allowed to go to the United States, I would defect. Up to this day, I'm still trying to figure out if this officer had done this on purpose or if it was a coincidence. My gut feeling tells me that, for a reason that I cannot imagine, she did this on purpose. Maybe it was her way of telling me why I was denied the passport. What enraged me most was the fact that I was stabbed in the back by someone I trusted as a good friend.

I talked about it with the director of the institute, but there was nothing he could do. I had the feeling that, for him, this was an ordinary event, something that he was seeing often. I guess that a lot of my colleagues were using this to try to enhance their relationship with the Securitate and eventually be allowed to travel abroad or be promoted. I assume there was also a lot of payback going on. Fortunately for me, the IARC wouldn't let things go and informed the Romanian government that if they would not allow me to use this fellowship, they would not give any other fellowships to Romania, period. This blackmail worked, and I got my passport, no more questions asked.

By November, I left Bucharest. The excitement of going on such an important trip was lessened tremendously because I had to leave my dear ones behind and be separated for one year. Noël was only four years old, and Alina was just seven months old. Sidonia was left with a huge burden, having to take care of the whole family. It is true that Tataie and his group were around and willing to help, but they were not in great shape and needed assistance themselves. Still, for our family, this was a unique opportunity to improve our standard of living, not taking into account that, for my career this could prove to be a crucial event. This was the Iron Curtain at its best, punishing for achievements. I will never forget this ruthless way of holding my wife and children hostages. Unfortunately for us, this was going to be only the first instance of hostage taking.

My French Family

I flew to Paris and took a detour to Strasbourg. I had to go and meet my family who lived there, and above all, I wanted to visit the graves of my mother and grandmother. I was warmly received in Strasbourg; I felt like they were indeed my family. I stayed at Colette and Jackie, the same place where my mother and Mama Mare stayed before they died. Colette was my mother's cousin. The only one from Strasbourg I had met before was Jeanine, the sister of Jackie, Colette's husband. She had been in Bucharest sometime in 1960 or 1961, sent by the family to find out about me, being alone after my father's death.

After the death of my grandmother, Uncle Camille, the brother of my grandmother, had written me a very kind letter, telling me that he considered me like his son. He lost his only son, Raymond, in the war. Raymond was killed by the Germans for his work in the resistance, trying to get Jewish children out of the occupied France, where they were exposed to deportation in the concentration camps to be exterminated. Jeanine came to Bucharest, and we met in a little park to avoid the Securitate following her to my house or talking close to some microphone. We talked about my situation; she understood how things were in Romania and that there was no hope of me being allowed to leave the country and go to France.

In Strasbourg, I met Jeanine again. She was a very fine lady who had a very hard time during WWII when she was deported by the Germans to a concentration camp; I believe it was Buchenwald. She never mentioned that in our talks; I don't think she ever discussed this with anybody. It must have been something so dark and miserable that she kept it locked inside her for the rest of her life. She never married and lived her life close to her brother's family.

In Strasbourg, I went to visit Aunt Eugenie, my grandmother's sister, who spent many years in Romania, where she was married to Mr. Suliteanu, with whom she had a daughter who died very young in an accident. Aunt Eugenie now lived in a nursing home, and she enjoyed seeing me. She left Romania in 1935 or 1936, so she must have known me only as a very young child. My mother continued to exchange letters with her; I found two of them when I looked through my mother's papers. I was fortunate to have met her because the following year, when I returned to Strasbourg, she was no longer in this world.

I met also other relatives; they were all thrilled to see me there. Jean and Colette Gradwohl and their sons, Laurent, Joel, and Francis; and Claude and Claudine Meyer, cousins of Colette, received me warmly. I was taken to the synagogue to find out that I didn't understand what was going on during the service. Colette and Jackie followed the Jewish tradition and kept the Sabbath quite strictly. For me, this was all new; I had never been exposed to such a lifestyle. I passed the bar mitzvah when I was thirteen years old, after taking some lessons from Rabbi Gutman, but that was the only time I followed the rules. It was probably the only time I went to a synagogue in Bucharest.

Nonetheless, my relatives were very kind and understood my situation. Over time, they continued to take me to the synagogue, and when Sidonia came, they took her too, and showed her how to follow the rules. They loved Sidonia, who was Christian; they accepted her and considered her part of the family. I think that in their mind, because Sidonia married me, they thought that she became a little Jewish, and I don't think Sidonia detested that. Sidonia had a clear understanding of the universality of faith while keeping her Orthodox Christianity. She was a believer in what she was taught as a child, but she had no difficulty with other believers keeping different traditions.

I went to the cemetery and found the graves of my mother and grandmother Mama Mare quite close to each other since they died only two years apart. Following the Jewish tradition and putting a little stone on their graves, I felt like closing a chapter. Here was my mother and me at her resting place, me with my sorrow and my memories of her. When I left, it was like saying, "I'll be back, Mom," which I did as often as I could.

Fig. 11. This is the grave of my mother in the Jewish Cemetery, Strasbourg, France

Fig. 12. This is the grave of my grandmother – Mama Mare – in the Jewish Cemetery in Strasbourg, France.

From Strasbourg, I took the plane back to Paris and continued my trip to Houston. I landed in Houston late at night. While passing through the custom officers, I had a problem. I had brought with me cell cultures that we had developed in my lab at the Microbiology Institute that we considered valuable. These were living cells, and I thought we could use them in Houston for our research. Little did I know that you cannot bring some things to the United States. When I told the custom officer that I had these cells, he told me that he didn't know what the regulations were and had to call his supervisor. In the meantime, I had to step aside from the line of people checking in and wait. I recall a lady who was behind me wishing me "I hope you get in with your cells." I don't think she was referring to my cells in culture tubes. Very funny! Well, indeed I got in with my cells, all of them. The approval of the supervisor came quite soon.

Baylor College of Medicine

I took a limo from the airport to a hotel where I was instructed to meet a colleague from the Baylor Virology Department. He was Hans Ludwig, a German fellow at Baylor and was waiting to take me to the dormitory where I was going to stay. He was living in the same building with his family, a wife and a very young child. Since it was late, we shared a beer and went to a well-deserved but short night's rest. I will always remember the moment when I got out of the limo to enter the hotel. Until then, I had never felt the kind of tropical weather that I soon learned is typical for Houston, Texas. It was like walking into a greenhouse, and I didn't like it.

My living arrangements were very convenient. I was renting a studio in the student dormitory on the campus of the Baylor College of Medicine. This is a private medical school, quite notable, and the surrounding community is rich and charitable. I was receiving my monthly fellowship directly from the IARC into my bank, and it was around $900, tax-exempt. In those days, this was a good income; and over the year, I could buy lots of things. I decided to eat at home, both lunch and dinner. For dinner, I would follow the lessons that I got from Luiz and cook spaghetti.

I had my daily routine setup. I would come home and start making the sauce, adding into a saucepan meat, onion, bell pepper, tomato paste, and tomato sauce. I would let them cook while taking a shower. After the shower, I would put the spaghetti to boil, and in ten minutes, dinner was ready. Dr. Benyesh, Dr. Melnick's wife, loaned me a TV set. This was helpful because I could watch the news and then some TV programs that, for me, coming from a communist country, were quite unusual, to say the least. I was on the other side of the Iron Curtain, and the differences were significant. Once the novelty wore off and my work in the lab picked up steam, I used to go back to the lab after dinner and continue working, usually until midnight, when the cleaning crew would come.

The Department of Virology, led by Dr. Melnick, was very large. There were around fifty postdoctoral fellows from all over the world. When we had the department Christmas party, each foreigner was asked to produce something on the stage, and it was quite an international show. Very soon the international group had adopted me. I became friends, not only with Hans Ludwig, but also with John from England and Bobby von Essen from Finland. A group from Czechoslovakia included Dr. Vladimir Vonka, Dr. Macek, and Dr. Adam. Vonka, and Macek decided to return to Czechoslovakia, which, at that time, was under Soviet occupation, but Dr. Adam stayed at Baylor and was there for many years. Since I was the only one without a family, I was very often invited for dinners or for joining them around the pool for the weekend. Hans took me to Galveston and set me up fishing on the pier. We got enough fish to have a big cookout with grilled fish. There was a wonderful feeling of friendship and comradeship between all of us, and I feel grateful to all of them for the time we spent together.

At the beginning, I was assigned to Dr. Benyesh's group to work with Dr. Biswal. This was an Indian biochemist who had recently acquired the most advanced ultracentrifuge and was the only one handling it. The intent of Melnick and Matty Benyesh was to have me trained in using this machine. Dr. Biswal invited me for dinner at his home, and for the first time in my life, I tasted Indian food and liked it. However, a few weeks later, I decided to ask Melnick to move me to another group. The main reason was that, when I will return to Romania, it would be very unlikely to have access to such an advanced instrument, and therefore, all of my training would be wasted. It is likely that when Melnick put me in Biswal's lab, he wasn't thinking of me going back to Romania, but rather to have me in the department for some time. Melnick told me, "You stay here as long as you wish," a proposal that I was stupid not to follow.

There was also another reason for leaving Biswal, which I didn't tell Melnick. I didn't like the style of work of Dr. Biswal. It had something mysterious to it, something like he was performing some magic with his machine, and that didn't look right to me. In the lab, he operated like a wizard. After I left Baylor, Dr. Biswal published a scientific report with data that were obtained using his ultracentrifuge. It turned out to be false data, and he just vanished from science. Unfortunately, Matty got a black eye for this since she was his boss. She never recovered from it and had to leave research.

Following my request, I was assigned to the group led by Dr. Janet Butel. Janet was a young professor, very bright, and very quiet. She had been the graduate student of Fred Rapp, a famous virologist who, before I arrived at Baylor, moved to Hershey, Pennsylvania, to be the chairman of the Department of Microbiology. Both Rapp and Butel were well known for their contribution in the field I was working on—tumor viruses.

We immediately started working on several important experiments in this area. Her lab was well equipped, and my productivity was high. It was my field of expertise, and this helped make things happen fast. Within a few months, I had already three papers accepted for publication in excellent journals, and everyone was quite happy about that. The slogan of Melnick's group was "publish or perish," and I fitted their philosophy quite well.

It was rewarding to have my name in such a distinguished company, but there was a heavy price to pay for it. I was badly missing my family,

Sidonia, Noël, and Alina with whom I had not even had the time of bonding. By the time I left, she was just six months old. I wanted to go back home as soon as possible. Moreover, I found the climate in Houston to be unbearable. The warm air was a mixture of excess humidity and foul smell coming from the refineries that were not far, on the Gulf of Mexico. Of course I had the air conditioning in my studio, and the windows could be opened only in an emergency situation, but there were a few weekends when I tried to go on the roof of our building to get some exposure to sun, and it turned out to be just horrific.

Without a car, I had to walk to the nearest grocery, which was a twenty minutes' walk from my dormitory, and this was not fun under the hot sun and loaded with grocery bags. To go downtown, I could ride a public bus, and this was a convenient way to go shopping, usually for things that I wanted to take home, particularly for Sidonia. Looking back, it was unfortunate that I was not happy in Houston, which, for me, was the gate to America. The bad feeling did not promote any desire to stay over and accept the offer from Joe Melnick. I could have ended up being separated from my children for years, and Sidonia would have found this unacceptable, as she did years later.

While in Houston, I was shocked to realize the dependency of everyone's life on the car and implicitly on gasoline. For me, coming from Bucharest, where we used to walk to the market or to work, and rarely used the car, this life style was almost unbelievable. I concluded that one day, this would bring trouble, and I don't think I was wrong. By that time, the United States already had trouble that I was not aware of. While the Vietnam War was making big daily news in the US, in Romania, it was something totally marginal, an example of imperialist aggression, which we thought to be just another case of communist propaganda full of lies.

The only time I realized how serious this issue was, happened when I was invited to dinner by Dr. Janet Butel. Her husband, Dr. Graham, had just returned from his tour in Vietnam. After dinner, he showed slides from Vietnam, and they were not funny. However, I was still very far from these troubles, like they didn't belong to my world. After all, I was in the United States, and life was going on without problems.

In my viewpoint, I don't think I was far from many Americans except those who were going into the war. I was invited to a Christmas party at the family of a lab technician from our group. By the time gifts were shared, we were all invited outside the home to watch how the lady of the house, our lab technician, received from her husband, as a Christmas gift, a huge new car. For me, coming from Romania where nobody owned such a car this was striking. I remember this party also because it was the first time that I had shrimp with cocktail sauce. In Romania in those days, shrimp was unknown. I loved it and still do, although by now we rarely have it since it competes with many other treats. In those years, life in America was good for many, probably most people.

Fig. 13. A Christmas party with Joe Melnick (the guy sitting on the floor) and his wife Dr. Benyesh-Melnick, the lady on the far left. I am standing and smoking pipe.

In the spring of 1970, the international cancer congress took place in Houston. Luiz Graffe came for a few days, stayed in my studio, and we went together to several meetings. I met several former Romanian colleagues who were allowed to participate at the congress. Two of them, Nicolaia-Foca (now married Suciu) and Delia Beju, a biologist (cousin of Sidonia), told me that they were defecting. Both women had husbands in Romania, and Delia also had a daughter.

It was well known that Romanians had been defecting since the communists took power, but in this case, something was unusual. After all, in 1968, I was with Nicolaia in West Germany and she went back to Romania. Now less than two years later, she was defecting. Unfortunately, nobody bothered to tell me what was going on, and I had to find out for myself.

By 1970, Ceauşescu decided to implement a Stalinist type of personality cult. Things got worse when, in 1971, he went to visit North Korea and liked what he saw there. Returning to Romania, he started in earnest to apply the North Korean model to Romania, which had previously enjoyed several years of more liberal communism. It was the beginning of the Ceauşescu cult of personality inspired by the Korean example, that culminated in the years 1980, and ended up in 1989, when Ceauşescu and his wife faced a popular uprising, and were summarily executed after a brief trial.

In 1970, for intellectuals, the message became very clear; it was time to get out of the country as soon as you could. Run away, far and fast and this is what these ladies were doing. Unfortunately, I was totally unaware of what was going on in Romania. In my mind, there was still my group at the Microbiology Institute with whom I was hoping to extend my studies in collaboration with the Baylor group. Only after I returned to Romania, I found out how things had changed during the year I was away; of course, by then, it was too late.

I would say that, for me, the eye-opener happened as I went with Sidonia shopping to the Unirea grocery store. This was a store on the Bucharest main boulevard where, before I left for Houston, one could buy a bottle of Scotch whisky, French champagne, or some special cold cuts or cheese; basically, it was a deli store. Now it had empty shelves. This was only the beginning of the process that was going to end in 1989 with Ceausescu and his wife executed by a firing squad. It took me ten years to be able to defect, and this was a heavy price to pay for a major mistake. Still I consider myself very lucky to have had a second chance; it could have been much worst.

By summer of 1970, my decision to return to Romania was reached. In truth, I have never considered staying over. I could easily have obtained an extension of my fellowship, at least for another year, and Melnick offered me to stay for an unlimited time. I had not even considered that. Overall, the separation from Sidonia and children turned out to be unbearable.

Fig. 14. Sidonia and Alina, April 1970.

Fig. 15. Sidonia with Alina and Noël, April 1970.

At the end of my stage, I was going to try one last thing: to have Sidonia join me in Houston and then to travel together back home, visiting several places. Sidonia loved to travel, and for her, it would be a reward for her efforts to take care of children during this year. Her father was still strong enough to take care of the children during her absence. She applied for a passport, and we waited.

In the meantime, Sidonia has sold our Volkswagen. Since my salary in Romania was discontinued, she needed the money to cover her living expenses. I decided to buy a new car, and we agreed to purchase a Ford Capri. This could be done through Terra, the same agency where I have bought the Volkswagen. The price of a Ford Capri was $3,200, and that included everything, shipping and custom. And then something almost miraculous happened. As soon as I sent the money to Terra for the car, Sidonia received her passport. I will always be persuaded that the guys from Terra were hoping that we will defect, and they will have the car for themselves.

Sidonia arrived in Houston in September, and I met her at the airport. She needed an entry visa, and while I was trying to explain to the immigration officer that she intends to stay only a few weeks, he brushed me aside and gave her something like six or twelve months visa. He said, "I know better. She will stay." Unfortunately for us, we didn't listen to this kind man, and we returned to Romania.

Fig. 16. This is Sidonia's photo for her 1970 passport to travel to Houston, TX. No wonder the Custom officer told her to stay in Texas.

We left Houston by the end of September, and on our way, we stopped in Washington, New York, London, Paris, Strasbourg, and Vienna. We played the tourists in each of these cities. We enjoyed each one of them, visiting the famous tourist attractions that these cities harbor. The list is too long to recite, but I was happy that Sidonia, who carried the burden of taking care of our children, had the opportunity to see all these wonderful places. I think she really liked this trip. We found most impressive the Lincoln Memorial in Washington, the skyscrapers of New York City, and the view of the Parliament building in London. Paris had so many wonderful places to visit; we were overwhelmed.

Our visit to Strasbourg was important. Sidonia, who was a little worried meeting my family, she being Christian and they Jewish, was surprised and overwhelmed by their affection for her. Luckily for us, we got to meet Uncle Camille, who was very old. We spent one evening with him, and he kept asking Colette about Sidonia, "Who is this lady?" I think he knew who I was, but Sidonia was a new person, and he was intrigued by her. He died just a few weeks after our visit, like he waited for us before departing, hopefully, to a better world. Colette was still managing the family retail business, and she loaded us down with nice clothing for the children and apparel for our home. From Strasbourg, we bought a Kodak Carousel projector to be able to see the slides that we made on our tour, and an Italian-made refrigerator for our home.

Back to Romania

When we arrived at the Bucharest Airport, we were loaded with seven pieces of Samsonite luggage filled with everything we bought. When we got home, we were very happy. Noël was thrilled with all the gadgets that we brought him, including an electric train that he burnt in a hurry. However, Alina was totally confused about me. For her, I was a total stranger; for some time, she called me uncle. She was only six months old when I left, and obviously, she didn't remember anything from that age. She was now one and a half years old, and she recognized everyone, but to her I was a stranger. This was a heavy price that I had to pay for our separation. I think that this gap in our bonding persisted over the years. During childhood, she always preferred her mother, and this continued during her adolescence. Only after she got married and started her own family the relationship between us became more balanced, but she continued to have more affection for Sidonia than for me. I didn't mind it; Sidonia deserved all the love these kids had for her.

Overview

These were the years when our wish to have a family were fulfilled. We have accomplished our shared goal—to have a family. We were blessed with two wonderful children—Noël and Alina. For both of us, this was a dream come true. Moreover, in those years, our life improved significantly. We could live without having to share our living space with someone else. We had a place that was ours only; we had privacy. To have a car was beyond our dreams, and now we had a beautiful sport sedan that caught the eyes of a lot of people in Romania.

Professionally, these years were some of the most productive in my life. My previous training and research were now brought to fruition. I was recognized as a scientist, a researcher. I published my first professional book. I was awarded the first IARC fellowship in Romania, and I published papers in the most reputable medical journals. I have to stress again that all this was possible because during those years, the communist government ran a more relaxed policy. Sidonia and I were allowed access to top-level positions without being involved in the political system and disregarding our autobiography. The following twenty years, the regime ran an increasingly brutal oppression when people like us, not members of the party, were treated as second-class citizens, and any ties over the Iron Curtain were severely reprimanded.

I should add that I was naive or stupid not to see that the gates were closing, that the détente was replaced by the resumption of the brutal totalitarian communist dictatorship. Not recognizing these changes led to the major mistake of my life—returning to Romania from Houston. It took me ten years to correct this mistake, and I was fortunate to be able to do it. The Iron Curtain lasted another twenty years. For me, this was a bitter lesson to be learned and is something for everyone else to think about. This kind of mistakes can take their toll for a long time, sometimes for life, even over generations.

Chapter 9

Medical Schools: Craiova and Hershey 1971-1977

Sidonia at Cantacuzino Institute

Major troubles started very soon after our return from Houston. Sidonia went back to her university job to find out that she was fired. When she asked for an explanation her boss, Professor Raicu, the chairman of the Department of Genetics was honest and told her, "Sidonia, I am sorry, but I didn't think you'll come back." She went without a job for almost a year. At some point, the director of the Microbiology Institute, hired her on a temporary position and promised that as soon as a permanent Biologist position will open she will be moved to that one. After a few months, he told me that there is a permanent position open, and Sidonia will be hired. At the last moment, some bureaucrat from the Ministry of Finance called. His wife, a young biologist, was teaching in some small town and had to commute daily there. He had learned about the opening and was asking the director to hire her which he did. The result of this policy, was that the institute lost the old generation hired based on scientific capacity and interest for research, and was populated with individuals with connections but having no training or interest to do research. I should add that the institute survived to this day, and that may have been the price paid for its survival. Under the Ceauşescu regime, this may have been the right approach.

This turned out to be another example where destiny plays its role and one should never give up. Several months after Sidonia lost her job at the Microbiology Institute and her chances of getting another one seemed missing, I went to visit the Cantacuzino Institute. This institute was the backbone of the public health care in Romania. It was producing almost all reagents for microbiological tests for the hospitals and outpatient clinics in the country, and several vaccines and sera used for treatment. During my visit, I met the group that was in charge of the production of the polio vaccine, which included Andrei Combiescu, my classmate from the Gheorghe Lazăr lyceum and the medical school, Dr. Dina Sergiescu, and Dr. Nardi Horodniceanu.

As we chatted about all kind of topics, I mentioned the story of Sidonia's unemployment. That triggered an immediate reaction. Horodniceanu went to talk to the director of the Cantacuzino Institute, Prof. Vlad Bîlbîie, to tell him our story. Word came back that Professor Bîlbîie wants to talk to me. He was not a talkative guy, seemed to be careful of what he was saying. He asked me a few questions about Sidonia: education, where did she work, etc. It was an indirect job interview. We have never met before, and he was reserved but interested in hiring her. He took my home phone number and said that he will contact me shortly. I left without major hopes considering our previous experience. It turned out soon, I was wrong. The same day, in the evening, Professor Bîlbîie called me at home to tell us that Sidonia was hired, and she should come next day to fill up the forms. Sidonia went the following morning, and she was appointed as a biologist in the Tissue Culture Division headed by Dr. Gaicu.

From the time she was hired until she left Romania in October 1981, Sidonia was pleased with her job at the Cantacuzino Institute. For a couple of years she worked in the Tissue Culture Division under the direction of Dr. Gaicu. Her colleagues in this lab were Dr. Duldurescu, a young lady, and Dr. Voiculescu, a scientist mostly interested in writing poetry. After spending about two years with this group and acquiring the training for tissue culture, she was moved to the Division of Polio Vaccine. Here she was part of the team preparing the cell cultures necessary for the production of polio vaccine. These cell cultures were obtained from kidneys removed from monkeys imported from Africa. Sidonia and her team worked on the kidneys to produce the cell cultures necessary for the production of large batches of polio vaccine for the whole country. She enjoyed her work, was much appreciated, and, over the years, has built friendly relations with her coworkers, in particular, with Mrs. Ileana Brucker. When she left Romania, she missed her associates, and she was badly missed by them.

I cannot refrain from commenting about this episode in our lives. When Sidonia was fired from the university, we were concerned. When she lost the opportunity of getting a position at the Microbiology Institute, we were really upset. Then it turned out that totally unexpected, she was hired at the Cantacuzino Institute, and for the next ten years, she enjoyed her job there and left it only to join me in America. Isn't that another example when fate plays such a strange game? I believe that, except for the time when she worked at the Oncology Institute and we were together, she did not like any job so much as the one at the Cantacuzino Institute. Not mentioning the icing on the cake, the three years that we were together in the same lab! Destiny!

Craiova Medical School

As far as I was concerned, after my return from Houston, I went back to the Microbiology Institute. To my surprise and dismay, I found out that my closest collaborator, Dr. Nina Şahnazarov, was no longer in the institute. In my absence, she has obtained her doctoral degree (PhD) and was assigned as a general practitioner somewhere in the countryside. My other coworkers, Şerban Ionescu-Homoriceanu and Luiz Graffe, have graduated from college. Şerban (Tony) got a job in his native city, Ploieşti, while Luiz, after having visited me in Houston, disappeared without a trace.

I was assigned to a different department where the head was Dr. Nastac, a faithful party member. I was supposed to share the laboratory with two guys, Dr. Rosin and Andrei Iarovici, one crazier than the other. Notwithstanding, the laboratory had no equipment, nothing. Obviously, all my plans of developing the collaboration with the Houston group went through the window. This time, I didn't ask for explanations, there were self-evident. Nobody thought that I would be so stupid to return to Romania at a time when the general situation of the country was deteriorating so rapidly that everyone who could get out got out, never to look back. It didn't take me too long to figure out that I made a colossal mistake, and that I had to do everything to correct it as soon as possible. In fact, it took me ten years to do that, and I consider myself lucky that it worked out the way it did.

During the year I was at Houston, my old friend Albert Niculescu joined the Institute of Microbiology. After he got his PhD degree in East Germany and returned to Romania, he joined the Microbiology Institute and was appointed as team leader there. His national and international standing was above this position, but for reasons that I can only suspect, he was not involved in the administration of the institute, although I think that would have benefited the institute immensely.

Albert began planning the development of a new department at a recently established medical school in Craiova. He was thinking of starting a Department of Molecular Biology and Genetics, something that in those years was not set up in any medical school in Romania, and was to be found only in a few medical schools in the Western world. Albert shared with me this project, and asked if I would be interested to be part of it. I accepted his offer with some degree of optimism. At the Microbiology Institute, my fate was set. I had nothing to do but wait for my retirement or for an opportunity to leave the country. At the medical school, I was hoping to be able to do research, and teaching medical students seemed an interesting new challenge.

The major negative side was that during the weekdays, I would be away from my family, and Sidonia would have the extra burden of having to take care of everything in my absence. This could be partly compensated by the generous vacation time that professors enjoyed. Moreover, commuting between Bucharest and Craiova was not very appealing; there was either a three-hour drive by car, or riding the train for about the same time. In our preliminary talks, Albert mentioned the possibility that if this project is successful, we could move to Craiova with our families. For me this was sort of a plan B; I was still thinking about leaving the country but waiting for this without doing anything at the Microbiology Institute would disqualify me for taking a job anywhere.

> Wikipedia. Craiova (Romanian pronunciation: [kra'jova]), Romania's 6th largest city and capital of Dolj County is situated near the east bank of the river Jiu in central Oltenia. It is a longstanding political center, and is located at approximately equal distances from the Southern Carpathians (north) and the River Danube (south). Craiova is the chief commercial city west of Bucharest and the most important city of Oltenia. The city prospered as a regional trading center despite an earthquake in 1790, a plague in 1795, and a Turkish assault in 1802 during which it was burned.

I joined Albert on his first trip to Craiova to meet the dean of the medical school, Professor Neștianu, and the rector of the university, Professor Georgescu. Needless to say, driving my Ford Capri there was by itself an experience. In the university parking lot, the car was surrounded by students and attracted a lot of interest. It was not a common car in Romania.

At the beginning, the dean of the medical school raised some objections, which were, as we found out later, politically motivated. One of them, actually the most important one, was that the medical school needed a gym for the students. This was so far-fetched I almost couldn't believe. He was afraid that Albert's personality would diminish his hold on the medical school, which he considered his own domain. In the end, Albert won, and the main support came from the relationship he established with the party secretary of the region, a certain Comrade Băbălău. Under the communist system, the party secretary of a region was like a king; he could do anything as long as he stayed within the system.

In order to set up a department that could use modern research technology, we needed to purchase several big laboratory items among which an ultracentrifuge and a radiation counter were essential. Albert was successful in obtaining the financial support for these major acquisitions. One good example of his efficiency in this area is when he went to talk to the mayor of Craiova, a certain Mr. Bulucea, and convinced him to transfer the money that he had in his budget for expanding the electric network around Craiova, to provide funds to buy the ultracentrifuge and the radioactive isotope counter for our department. With his connections and power of friendly persuasion, Albert managed that in less than a year, the department had research equipment that would have made the envy of established research institutes in Romania.

Teaching Medical Students

By fall of 1971, we started our activity at the medical school in Craiova. We gave lectures and found out that the medical students were very receptive to our teaching. Soon we became one of the most favored departments by medical students. My stage in the United States gave me a special quality that was quite unique in the medical school and excited the interest of the students. They enjoyed having us as their faculty, we were bringing a breeze of fresh air, and they were ready for this.

The novelty of being exposed to the most recent acquisitions of medical science in genetics was exciting and highly appreciated. I developed special relations with some of the medical students: I spent several vacations at the home of one of the students, Ion Dagla, who happened to live with his parents in Tataia, the Black Sea beach resort. While vacationing with my family in the town of Piatra Neamț I was invited to visit Sorin Krumpholtz's parents.

In the first two years, we managed to set up the foundation of a department that was teaching the medical students the basics of genetics, and was able to start doing research with modern equipment and techniques. Albert has hired a former coworker, Costache Nedelcu, a physicist with good experience in using the sophisticated instruments that we had acquired for our department. Costache was fresh from a divorce that left his two children in charge of his former wife. A very pleasant person, with a huge appetite, split almost evenly between solid and fluid foods, Costache had a quiet personality apt to eruptions of anger that were violent but short in duration.

We even managed to have Joe Melnick, the famous American virologist, visit our department. I drove Joe from Bucharest to Craiova. On our way, we passed a column of horse-pooled wagons with gypsies. Since Joe was fascinated to see these people, I had to stop the car on the highway and he took lots of pictures. The gypsies were going home to Craiova after working during the summer in another part of the country, making bricks the old-fashioned way with mud and straw. With Melnick, we signed a collaborative contract that under normal conditions would have been a solid endeavor for research. Further events in Craiova prevented this to happen, not unusual for Romania of those days.

Albert

As part of the process of building up the new department in Craiova, Albert who was married to Anda, a nice lady that worked as a technician at the Microbiology Institute, organized a small party at their apartment in downtown Bucharest. Among others he also invited his sister, Mona, with her husband. This was the first time that Mona and Sidonia met. There were no words spoken, but I followed Mona's eyes looking at Sidonia. Then she glanced at me. Her look expressed what I used to read in earlier years as an approval. It seemed that she still thought that she has possession of me and has accepted Sidonia as my wife. Maybe she understood that there was not and will not be any overlap between the two of them.

A few years ago, Sidonia told me that she knew about Mona from the time I started dating her, and was concerned that she was interfering with a relationship that was rumored to be ongoing. Actually, by then, Mona was married to Mr. Costinescu for several years during which we have not met or talked. Fortunately, Sidonia decided not to listen to these gossips and to go ahead with our relationship, and the rest is history, our happy history.

While spending time in Craiova, Albert met Blondie and became romantically involved with her. Blondie was assistant professor in the Foreign Language Department. She was of German ethnic origin, and I wouldn't be surprised to find out that she knew personally Herta Müller, the Nobel Prize for literature winner, with which she shared many features: her ethnic background, her interest for literature, her wide cultural knowledge, and her desire to leave the country because of political beliefs. Among them, Albert and Blondie spoke often German and had in common the interest for literature, and most likely shared their view of the world that was not favorable to the Ceaușescu regime. In 1972, Blondie was awarded a fellowship at a German University. She left Craiova never to return.

Life in Craiova

With my move to Craiova, my life has changed drastically. I was commuting every Monday by train or car to Craiova and returned usually home on Friday. In Craiova, Albert and I were lodged for several weeks in the student dormitory where we learned how miserable student living conditions were. The city of Craiova was suffering from a chronic lack of water. In the intensive industrialization process pushed by the Communist Party, a huge petrochemical complex that had to use vast amounts of water was built on the outskirts of Craiova. When the Communist Party decided to build this complex, it did not take this into account. Water that was supposed to be used by the Craiova citizens was taken by industry.

After several months, I moved to a three-bedroom apartment close to the railway station, in a newly built complex of condominiums. My roommates were Dinu Tănăsescu, the chairman of the Department of Biochemistry, and Victor Voicu, the chairman of the Department of Pharmacology. Victor was spending at most two days a week in our apartment, but Dinu and I were there for the whole week.

Dinu, who was the chairman of the Department of Biochemistry, became my best friend in Craiova. Like many other faculty members, he was also from Bucharest and was commuting to Craiova weekly. As a student in Cluj, he has been involved in the student movement that occurred by the time of the Hungarian Revolution in 1956. He ended up in a political jail in Pitești, famous for the beatings that those imprisoned there were exposed regularly. He seldom talked about this experience. Because of that, he could not become a party member, and that greatly hampered his carrier. He was promoted to full professor only after the Romanian revolution of 1989.

A rather funny scene was taking place every time there was a general faculty meeting at the medical school. This meeting was always followed by the general meeting of the Communist Party. As soon as the general faculty meeting will end, the party secretary will announce, "Nonparty members are invited to leave the hall." Out of the two hundred faculty members, there were only three that were not party members: Dinu Tănăsescu, who has spent one year in jail for taking part at an anticommunist meeting, Professor Roșculeț, the chairman of pathology who, in his young age was a green shirt legionnaire, and me.

Fig. 1. Maurice wearing a tie is surrounded by medical students at Craiova School of Medicine. April 1973.

Family life

Those were the years when Noël and Alina were taken by Sidonia in the morning to Mrs. Banu that had a private kindergarten. After Noël started school, Alina went to a public kindergarten, which was closer to home. Sidonia made great efforts to cover for me with the family chores while I was in Craiova during the weekdays.

Fig. 2. Alina and Noël are showing their prize from school graduation with a proud mother behind them. June 1977.

Fig. 3. The Nachtigal family was reunited after seven years of partial separation. 1977.

One benefit of being on the faculty of the Craiova School of Medicine was the long summer vacation. We took full advantage of that. This was one way to compensate for me missing my family during the weekdays and leaving Sidonia in charge of taking care of the children during this time. During summer, we went to the beach. For the first several days it will be just me with the children. Sidonia was still following the advice she got from her breast surgeon that exposure to sun triggers breast cancer and usually will join us later, and those were the days when we really enjoyed the beach.

Fig. 4. Sidonia, Alina, and Noël, on Tataia Beach. This tent made by Sidonia was used for years when we went to the beach. July 1974.

Fig. 5. I bought this caravelle boat in France and brought it home when I returned from Hershey. It had to be registered (not to be used for defecting!). July 1974.

Fig. 6. Late afternoons we used to drive to Mamaia and walk on the sandy beach.

Fig. 7. Sidonia and Alina eating ice cream in Bușteni. 1974.

Fig. 8. Hiking was a family hobby; summer 1974.

Our beach vacation lasted about fifteen days and was followed by mountain vacation for the children. We took our children to Bușteni, where we had Mrs. Drăgoi as a host who would rent us a room. She was willing to take care of the children, and we trusted her. Noël and Alina have made friends with children in the neighborhood and were playing outside all day long. Mrs. Drăgoi's house was at the border of the woods. There was no traffic on the street, and it was totally safe. We would visit them over the weekend or join them to spend our vacation. Then we would go hiking in the surrounding Bucegi Mountains.

In one of these trips, we went hiking to the highest peak in the Bucegi Mountains called Omul (the man). We followed the Ram Valley trail, and when we arrived at the cabin, which is on the peak, there was a blizzard, not very unusual considering that it was close to the end of August, and we were at 2,500 meters elevation (7,500 feet). We had some warm food at the cabin, and we spent overnight sleeping in the common dormitory. Next day, the blizzard continued, and we decided to descend from the mountain.

We joined a larger group led by someone who claimed that he knew the trail. We started the descent following the larger group. At some point

I realized we were on a trail that is recommended only for summertime. It was one of those narrow trails on which you are squeezed between the mountain wall on one side and the deep cliff on the other. Now the trail was covered in many places with snow and ice, which made it very dangerous. It was too late to return, so we kept walking. In several places along the trail crosses could be seen; those were sites were people fell to their death. After about an hour of anxiety, we reached a rather abrupt descent through a wooden area.

The last part of the trail before the Diham lodge, which was our target, was hiked by climbing in mud under heavy rain. Exhausted we reached the lodge, but our kids were full of energy and they continued walking home with another family. We had lunch at the lodge, and the hot soup and the tea with rum provided new energy to take us home. As long as we were in Romania, the home of Mrs. Drăgoi was our place to spend summer and winter vacations. She was a trustful and honest woman that took motherly care of our two children and stays in our grateful memories.

Budapest Congress

In 1972, the World Congress of Virology was held in Budapest, Hungary, organized largely by Joe Melnick and his group. I had no trouble getting a passport and flew to Budapest. It was nice to meet again my friends from Baylor but, more importantly, to meet also Fred Rapp, who was there with his wife, Judith. Fred Rapp has been a professor at Baylor in the Department of Virology. He has been the mentor of Janet Butel with whom I worked at Baylor. Before I went to Baylor, Fred left for the position of chairman of the Department of Microbiology at the newly built medical school in Hershey, Pennsylvania. While at Baylor, I met him once as he was visiting Houston, and we had some small talk. Fred mentioned that he would welcome me at his department anytime, but at that time, I was stupid enough not to take his invitation seriously.

Now in Budapest, Fred asked me to join him and his wife touring the city. We went together to visit the old synagogue and a Jewish museum. He asked me if I would come as a visiting professor to his department at the newly founded Hershey School of Medicine. I accepted on the spot; I could not believe my lucky star. Unexpectedly, I had a chance to redeem my stupidity and to return to the United States. I was already dreaming that this time, it should be it, one-way ticket.

By now I lost interest in the congress; I was in a hurry to go home and start the process of getting a passport for Hershey, Pennsylvania. Back in Craiova, I started the paperwork to obtain the passport. Mr. Georgescu, the president of the university, approved without hesitation the invitation to go to the States, and Albert was all for it. This time, the University of Craiova was behind the process for obtaining my passport and visa, and the passport process was now run through the Ministry of Education to whom I belonged as faculty at the University of Craiova.

I was really catching the last wagon since by 1973, things have changed in Craiova for the worst. The party secretary, Comrade Băbălău, was removed and replaced with a relative of Ceauşescu's wife, Elena. At the university level, the president, Mr. Georgescu, was replaced with Comrade Nicola, a party operative. For us, these were bad signs, and I believe that Albert decided that there was time to leave town and join Blondie, who had no intention to return from West Germany to Craiova.

By September 1973, I had my passport and was ready to go. This time I was planning to do what I should have done in 1970, leave, and not return. I talked with Sidonia and told her about my plans. She agreed. She was the only person with whom I shared my intentions. I took with me just the clothing I could squeeze in my luggage. To buy the ticket, I was again lucky. Uncle Willy has just arrived in Bucharest, and I asked him to pay for the ticket. The airline didn't want to sell international flight tickets on lei, the Romanian currency. I never paid him back this money, but when we settled in the United States and the Mexican peso was devalued, we paid for his subscription to *New York Times* for several years. As a good-bye, I took Sidonia to the Seagull Restaurant, where we had a very good lunch. I was all cheerful about this chance, and to be honest, I had no idea what kind of trouble could be in store for us. We were both upbeat and didn't give a serious thought about what could happen.

Hershey, Pennsylvania

My final destination was Harrisburg, Pennsylvania. Fred picked me up from the airport and drove me to his home in Hershey, Pennsylvania. That night we had dinner at his house. I still remember the size of the steaks that were served. They were huge by the Romanian standards, and Fred tried to explain that these were regular-size American steaks. I slept at his house the first night, and the following day, I moved into an apartment that was very near the medical school. The apartment was very comfortable; it had two bedrooms and two bathrooms and a large living room.

Hershey Medical School has been developed with a large contribution from the Hershey Company. This little town of about ten thousand habitants was all related to Hershey Company. It was a very pleasant town with clean, tree-lined streets with sidewalks and nice houses. The medical school was built at the outskirts of the town and was surrounded by small hills harboring cornfields. The building was modern and nicely built. Fred's department was quite large and had several groups, and I was settled in a laboratory where I was supposed to do my research.

As soon as I got there, I loved the place. When I arrived in Hershey, it was fall with changing leaves. I could walk over the surrounding hills and enjoy the view, the fresh air, and the nature. Winter came, and I loved it. It was just as I knew it with snow and cold winds. By Christmas Eve a couple of Chinese fellows invited me to join them. I went with them to the church service and then to their home. It was a typical Christmas night as you see on greetings cards. So were the streets, the homes, and the trees. It was just awesome.

Jan

I shared the laboratory with Jan Walboomers, and he will be my laboratory companion for the duration of my stay in Hershey. Jan was from Amsterdam and was spending one year as a fellow in Hershey. He was there with his wife, Ellen, and two sons, Niels and Jan Marek, who were about four and six years old. Jan befriended me immediately. As long as I was in Hershey, Jan invited me for Friday night dinner almost every week. He also invited me to join them on some day trips around Hershey during the beautiful fall season in Pennsylvania.

I had many discussions with Jan trying to explain why I was considering not to go back home. Although he tried to understand the situation in Romania, he was of the opinion that I have a duty to my students to go back. It was almost impossible for me to make him understand how hopeless the situation was in Romania under Ceaușescu.

Jan was critical of the American system in general, and particularly, he didn't care about Fred. While Jan was a laboratory person attached to his bench, Fred was more of a political person. For as long as we were in Hershey, Fred was almost all the time away, giving talks, seminars, attending meetings, etc. Jan became one of my best friends, and I still mourn his premature death.

Another War

Soon after my arrival at Hershey, the Yom Kippur War in Israel started. At the beginning, nobody could know how long this war will last or how extensive it can develop. Within a few days, it became a confrontation between the United States and Soviet Union. This scared me seriously. I was considering what to do if the danger of becoming separated for my family for a long time would develop. This time, it was not only the Iron Curtain separating us; it was war and not of the cold variety. This thought really gave me goose bumps.

Luckily, this was a short war, and the only perceived major consequence at least immediately for the United States was the long lines of cars at the gas stations. Again, what I have seen when I was in Houston was this absolute dependence on oil. I could not understand how a country like the United States could develop a society that was vitally dependent on something that had to be brought from far away, and it didn't have control over it. In any event, my plan of not returning to Romania got a serious blow, considering that the whole situation showed how unforeseen events can develop rapidly with unpredictable consequences. Although I was willing to take the risk of being separated from my family for some time, being on the other side of an armed conflict would have been unacceptable.

Ștefan

Another important event occurred after the end of this war. I contacted my old friend and colleague Stefan Mironescu. Ștefan came to Philadelphia with an Eleanor Roosevelt fellowship in 1970. The fellowship was for one year. When this term expired, Ștefan asked for, and was granted, political asylum. He had left behind in Romania his wife, Karin, and his daughter, Jacqueline (Jackie). Because he left Romania with a so-called official passport and not a tourist passport, he was considered by the communist regime a deserter, and was put on trial by a military court. He was condemned in absentia to years of prison and confiscation of his fortune. By the time I arrived in Hershey, Ștefan was trying to put pressure on the Romanian government to release his family. He spoke at Radio Free Europe and went on a public hunger strike in front of the Romanian embassy in Washington DC, all without success. At Jefferson Medical College in Philadelphia, his research funding ran out. He was sustaining himself by doing some clinical laboratory work while searching for a position. Unfortunately, this was not effective as the economic situation in the country was not good. This was reflected also in the financial situation at Hershey. For me it was almost shocking to compare the situation as it was when I left Houston in the fall of 1970 and as I found it three years later when I arrived in Hershey. The truth is that living in Romania between 1970 and 1973, I didn't realize that USA was involved in a serious war in Asia. Years of war had burdened the national budget to the point that President Nixon had to cancel the convertibility of the dollar to gold.

Ştefan came to Hershey, and we talked about our situation and future. Judith Rapp, who was on the brink of divorcing Fred, was very kind and let him sleep at her house. The news that Ştefan brought with him were not good, and overall, his situation was not a model to follow. During the following months, we continued to see each other as I visited him in Philadelphia a few times. By 1974, he found a position with the National Red Cross in Bethesda, Maryland, and his situation seemed to improve. At least he had a steady income and was doing interesting research. Ştefan continued his fight to free his family from Romania.

By 1975, Ştefan got a breakthrough. It turned out that his supervisor at the American Red Cross was a friend of the Kennedy family and was willing to intercede on behalf of Ştefan with them. Ted Kennedy was a very influential politician, and his involvement opened the gate for the Mironescu family to leave Romania. Unfortunately, this resolution came too late to prevent the breakdown of the relationship between Ştefan and his wife. Five years of separation without any hope for speedy reunion took their toll. For the sake of Jackie, Ştefan and Karin tried to patch up their marriage; but this didn't work, and they ended up in a divorce, which was, as it almost always is, not friendly. Jackie stayed with her mom and visited her father during vacation time. Ştefan loved Jackie very much and was almost daily on the phone with her.

Bad News

A couple of months after I arrived in Hershey, I received a letter from Sidonia telling that her father had prostate problems. He was admitted at the Panduri Hospital and was seen by a certain Dr. Popescu, who was an associate of Professor Burghele, my professor of urology in the medical school. Sidonia informed me that he was diagnosed with prostate cancer and was given treatment with hormones. These were bad news because at that time, her father was still active in support of the household, and with this type of cancer, one never knows how it will progress. Some could last many years, and the patient usually dies of an unrelated cause, but some are real killers and inflict a lot of pain and suffering. So I was in Hershey, having to decide if I have to return home immediately or postpone my return at least for several months. I opted for the second option, but my original plan of defecting became even less attractive.

It was one day in March, in the afternoon, when I received a phone call from Ștefan. He was asking me if I knew that Sidonia had surgery, what for, etc. It came as a lightning stroke. I didn't know anything about it, and it was nothing planned. I picked up the phone and made a long distance call home. With the time difference, seven hours between the East Coast time and Bucharest, it was around 2:00 AM over there. The phone rang, and a totally confused, sleepy voice answered. It was Sidonia's father. He was followed immediately by Noël, who has figured out who was at the other end. Noël was a smart eight years old. He told me that, indeed, Sidonia had surgery and was at the hospital. He couldn't give me any detail about the surgery. I asked them to send me a cable next morning with full explanations, and I hung up.

I didn't have much sleep this night. The following day, I got a cable signed by Sidonia saying that she had uterus surgery and was well and recovering. I found out later that she went into surgery because some fibroids in her uterus kept bleeding. She hoped that she can do it without disturbing me, a good meaning, which obviously didn't work out. On the contrary, the fact that I had no warning scared me. Since I didn't know the nature of her surgery, it could have been for cancer of the uterus, I started planning for my return home. Under these circumstances, there was no way to leave her and our children alone. The following day, I learned more about the situation home, and I decided to stay and continue my research in Hershey. However, by then, I realized that I would not be able to defect this time; therefore, I applied to the Romanian government for a three-month extension of my visa. This was granted without difficulty. It was for them a clear sign that I intend to return to Romania.

A Small World

It was May 1974, when the American Association of Microbiology had its annual meeting in Chicago. Fred decided to send several of his researchers to the meeting to present papers. I was one of them, and together with Jan, we boarded a train in Harrisburg to travel to Chicago. It was a rather long trip, but I found my first experience with Amtrak, the American railway company, wonderful. Although we had ordinary seats, the trip was very comfortable. We arrived in Chicago, and Jan and I shared a room in the old Hilton Hotel, on the border of the lake north of the city. The meeting went well; I presented our papers and enjoyed Chicago very much.

One of the days of the meeting happened to be May 17, my birthday. To celebrate it, Jan and I went to a restaurant nearby our hotel and had dinner. At the end, Jan ordered a glass of Hennessy cognac for my birthday. As we were enjoying the cognac, I noticed a lady entering the restaurant and being seated at a table. As she was busy ordering her dinner, I looked at her and was impressed how close she resembled my medical school classmate and short-time girlfriend Noemi Rosenfeld. I knew that she has married Harry Ioachim, a pathologist, and left Romania long time ago and were living in New York. Since we graduated from the medical school, I have not seen or talked to her. I thought to myself that this was a close resemblance. Any possibility that this lady would be Noemi seemed out of question. What were the chances? Not even one in a million. Jan and I left the restaurant and went back to our hotel.

The next day I went for dinner alone, and as I was returning to the hotel, at the entrance, I just bumped into this lady. This time, we instantly recognized each other. It was indeed Noemi, and my sight the previous evening didn't mislead me. She invited me to her room, and we had a long chat over a late supper. She was in Chicago for some medical course. She told me that she had two girls, and that her sister was still living in Bucharest. When I told her that I will return soon to Romania, she asked me if I would be willing to take with me a dress for her sister, which I did.

We said good-bye to never see each other again. I am still awed by this meeting. I wonder what the chances for this meeting to happen were. She came from New York, me from Bucharest, and we were at the same time in Chicago, in the same hotel, and we ate in the same restaurant at the same time. One in a billion? Since then, I have never been back to Chicago, and probably she never went back either. None of us were world travelers, but still this meeting has occurred. Strange things happen, and I think this could be listed as one of them. After all, we live in a very small world.

A Failed Breakaway

Back to Hershey, it was time to prepare my return to Romania, which had to be by the end of June. Fred wanted to have me in his department for a longer time. I asked him to give me a written offer, a contract for three years, which he did. I was not hopeful, but at least I had something in writing to show my superiors, and ask for permission to leave the country for this contract. There were instances where Romanians have been allowed to go and work for several years in African countries like Libya or Algeria.

A few days before leaving Hershey, I got a phone call from Albert. He was in Washington and told me that he is not returning to Craiova. He asked me not to return and to join him in Houston at Baylor, where he would go along the contract we had with Joe Melnick. I told him that my family situation is such that I cannot afford a separation that could be long and very damaging. The most important factor was that my passport was official one issued by the Ministry of Education. This meant that if I defect, I will have Ștefan's fate, being judged and sentenced for treason by a military court. My family would suffer the consequences, and we could be separated for years, something that I considered unacceptable.

Ștefan came to Hershey to say good-bye, and we decided to stay in contact by any means possible, and he to try to help me to leave Romania. Both of us were thinking that there was little chance to see each other again. I left Hershey with sadness. The time spent there was wonderful. I did excellent research, I got several new friends, and I loved the place, the hills covered with cornfields, the tree-lined streets with pretty homes, and the weather. I would have given anything to be able to stay there, but I knew very well that this was not possible. Having a semiofficial Romanian passport exposed me to the same retaliation as that of Ștefan, who was still separated from his family. And in so many years, so many things could happen. Sidonia and our children that were very young could be exposed in Romania to all kinds of pressure. There was no way to abandon them.

My first attempt to break free from the Iron Curtain failed. I was not sorry, for I knew that the price I would have to pay was much too high. Professionally, it would have been a major success; I already had excellent job offers. But then I would have lost my family, and for me, this was unacceptable. However, I was not abandoning the idea and the hope. Ștefan would help me in any further attempt of escaping from Romania and he kept his word. It was due to him that I moved to Columbia, South Carolina, in 1980. But we were only in 1974, and the future was totally unpredictable.

I left Hershey, and flew Icelandic Airline from New York to Luxembourg. From there I took the train and arrived in Strasbourg just in time for the wedding of one of my relatives. The bride was Liliane, the daughter of my cousin Colette. It was a big Jewish wedding with hundreds of participants like I have never seen before. My family was quite happy to have me. They introduced me to their guests as "our cousin from Romania who comes from America." Not a very common occurrence in those days!

Return behind the Iron Curtain

During my stay in Hershey, I managed to have some savings. I wanted to buy a car and drive it to Romania. That would save the cost of the air ticket from France to Bucharest, and also would replace our car that Sidonia had to sell to cover for the lack of my salary while I was away. It was July, and in France, that means vacation time for everyone. In Colmar, not far from Strasbourg, I found a Ford Taunus, exactly the car that I wanted. José, the elder brother of Liliane, took me to the dealer. The price was better than I expected; very likely, the salesman just wanted to get rid of the last car on his lot, and leave for his summer vacation.

The evening of one of those long days of July, I took off from Strasbourg. The trip to Romania would take me through West Germany, Austria, and Hungary. As I left Strasbourg, I was expecting to reach soon the border with Germany. Actually, I had some items that I bought in France and planned at the border to try to recover the VAT taxes that I paid for them. As I was driving, I soon realized that I am in Germany. I have crossed into Germany without noticing the border. The highway was jammed with people eager to go to their summer vacation. My Ford Taunus was pushing to 120 kilometers per hour (about seventy-five miles), but on the German highway, it felt like it wasn't moving. The other cars were passing me, and the trucks that were in the same lane with me were pressing on me all the time.

Night was coming, and by 10:00 PM I just took an exit, went off the highway, and I ended up in a small town. It was now almost 11:00 PM, and I parked in front of a "restaurant-hotel." It was still open, and I entered the restaurant. I asked if they can feed me and if I can have a room for the night. I was told that they can offer whatever food I would order, but all rooms were booked. However, I was told there was a family that would be willing to rent a room for the night.

To reach the house, one of the men that was drinking beer with a party, proposed to take me to this home if I would bring him back to the restaurant. It turned out that he was the policeman of this little town. I accepted his offer, and we went to the house. The host was an elderly lady who showed me the room. The room looked very clean and comfortable, and it had a large bathroom. An open window was letting the fresh air of the night come in. The bed was covered with a heavy-duty comforter that could stand the cold mountain air. I returned with the policeman to the restaurant where he resumed his beer party, and I had an excellent schnitzel with beer. When I finished my meal, it was past midnight. I returned to my room and slept without dreams.

Next morning, I woke up rather early, but it was already daylight. In the dining room, the lady told me that her husband has already left for work. I understood from her that he was a carpenter, but her English was not very good. My German, well, you know the story; Mitzy didn't accomplish much. Anyway, the breakfast was ready and delicious, with boiled egg, ham, coffee, etc. I asked how much I was charged, and it was so little that I was almost embarrassed to take advantage of such a nice lady.

I hit the highway and kept driving. My next stop was Vienna, where a colleague of mine was working for the Atomic International Energy Agency (AIEA). After I left Germany and entered Austria, the traffic on the highway became so low that I almost fell asleep driving. I managed to survive (another miracle) and reached Vienna in the afternoon. I found the house where Ovidiu Chita and his wife lived. They were glad to see a fellow Romanian, and I had a nice dinner with them. Chita was associate professor at the University of Craiova and the dean of the Faculty of Biology. He was a pleasant guy trying to be in good terms with an influential person such as Albert and, implicitly, his associates. I didn't tell him that Albert had no intention to return to Craiova; he will have plenty of time and opportunities to find out. I spent the next day walking on the main street of Vienna and I bought some gifts for Sidonia.

The following day was Sunday. I left Vienna early morning, when the streets were almost empty. I took the highway going to Hungary. It was deserted, I was the only car on the road. It was not long when I realized I was approaching the border between Austria and Hungary. Houses along the road were sparse and looking modest. Then I saw the Hungarian border. It looked exactly like the enclosure of a concentration camp as you see it in movies. It had barbed wire all over and towers with soldiers carrying guns. I drove through some barriers that opened and then closed behind me. I had the tangible feeling that I entered a jail. I knew I have just crossed the Iron Curtain and not in the direction I would have preferred.

There were many cars and an office building. I stopped my car, and soon a Hungarian officer came and took my passport. He left me in my car, and I had to wait. It took a few hours of waiting, and I became impatient. I was planning to reach Craiova that day, and I still had to cross Hungary. At last, the officer came back with my passport, and I was allowed to leave this mini-concentration camp and free to drive through the large one, the socialist camp.

It took me several hours to cross Hungary. The only remarkable stopover was for having lunch. Early afternoon, I reached the Romanian border at Nădlac. This place looked less threatening than the border between Hungary and Austria. After all, Romania and Hungary belonged to the socialist camp, whereas Austria was a capitalist country, on the other side of the Iron Curtain. The Romanian border soldiers were friendly, they seemed happy to have something to do. I was the only one crossing the border. I filled the custom forms and drove away. Around 8:00 PM, I reached Lugoj, the first important Romanian city, and I parked close to a bar-coffee place. Being Sunday evening, it was crowded. I found a table and ordered a large cup of coffee. I still had to stay awake to drive several hundred miles to reach Craiova.

As night was falling I started my last leg to Craiova. I was alone on the two-lane highway. In those years there were few privately owned cars in Romania. I knew I was on my right track when, under the moonlight, I saw the Danube river. I have reached Turnu-Severin, the town bordering this large river. There were less than a hundred miles to Craiova which was reassuring since it was already well past midnight and my car was getting low on gas. Running out of gas would have meant to be stuck somewhere in the middle of nowhere for the whole night. This night luck was on my side; by 3:00 AM, I arrived at Craiova, my final destination.

Dinu Tănăsescu and Mihai Oțoiu, my colleagues received me warmly. They were waiting emptying a bottle of Scotch, for my return celebration. The two were among those that at the medical school believed in my return from America. There were many in the medical school that were betting that I will not come back.

The next morning, I went to the medical school and confirmed that I was back. Then I drove to Bucharest. When I arrived in front of our house, Noël came out first, followed by Sidonia and Alina. The joy of our family being reunited made up for this long separation. After paying a huge custom tax for my new Ford Taunus, we went to our beach vacation at the Black Sea. We rented a room at Mrs. Popa in Tataia and had a wonderful time. From France I bought an inflatable Caravelle boat. On the beach this became Noël's favorite toy. The funny thing about it was that I had to have it registered with the coast guard office. The communist regime thought that it could be used for defecting. I was back to square one.

Textbook

By fall, I was back in my department in Craiova. Due to Albert's defection, I had to take charge of the department. Not being a party member, I had no chance of being appointed the head of the department. Nevertheless, the department had to function, and I would have to take care of it. One of my colleagues, Ion Rogoz, could help with the teaching. I had also a part-time appointment at the laboratory of the Municipal Hospital, which was affiliated with the medical school.

The Medical Genetics course that we were teaching had no textbook, and that made it difficult for our students. I started writing such a textbook and within a rather short time, I finished it. It had also contributions from Rogoz and Chita, and we had it printed at the University Press in Craiova. This continued to be the textbook for this course years after I left the University of Craiova. When I was in the United States a physician who graduated from Craiova School of Medicine, contacted me from New Zealand, inquiring about a residency in pathology. He asked me if I am the person who wrote the genetics textbook that he used as a medical student in 1985 at the Craiova School of Medicine.

Dinner with a Securitate General

Being a professor at the medical school in this provincial city was a special social position. My colleague and friend Dinu Tănăsescu was often invited by different families, and many times, I joined him. The dinners were usually quite formal, and the dishes were almost always sophisticated. One of the most interesting dinner that we were invited to was at Comrade Simion's house. Comrade Simion was Professor of so-called scientific socialism. This was supposed to be the course of indoctrination of the young generation with the communist ideology so that they understood the political scene both inside the country as well as around the world. Simion was concerned about the intellectual competence of our medical students including knowledge of the political world. I wonder if someone listening to radio Free Europe would have been acceptable, but I have a hunch that he or she would have scored better than one that would have ignored this information.

Comrade Simion was too smart not to see what was going on with the country, and maybe just because he was raised by the system, he was concerned how the whole system will survive. In this respect, he must not have been alone, and I suspect that the 1989 revolution in Romania was based on this background. It brought to power what could be termed capitalist communists that figured out that their regime was doomed. Comrade Simion invited Dinu and me to have dinner at his house in the company of his godfather, General Sprîncenatu, the head of the Securitate for the county of Dolj, which included Craiova as its capital.

For me it remains a mystery, why out of the two hundred or so faculty members of the medical school, Simion decided to invite just those two individuals that were not party members, one who spent one year in jail for political subversion, and the other the only Jew. The dinner went on in a friendly atmosphere; the general seemed to be at home in our company, we never touched any political subject, but jokes were appreciated. Like a good chess player, was the general anticipating the following three or four moves, and testing potential future partners?

Ceauşescu Visit

In those years, Ceauşescu was the absolute power in Romania. After his visit to North Korea in 1971, where he was received with a colossal ceremony, he adopted the way of the Korean leadership. This personality cult included so-called working visits. Ceauşescu will visit different regions and will be received like an absolute leader. A demonstration would emphasize how revered he was by a people grateful for his leadership. A significant goal of such a visit was to show him how the economy was reaching new peaks due to his leadership. During these visits, he will give his opinions that would become directions to be followed no matter if they made sense or not. No one would dare to argue about this advice.

Craiova had one of these visits, and the School of Medicine was included as an objective. Very likely, we, the faculty, were screened by the Securitate. In my department, I received the visit of the head of the University Securitate, Colonel Predoiaşu. The Securitate agents were very concerned about our radioactive laboratory reagents. In our research, we often used radioactively labeled chemicals. Securitate agents took these reagents that we stored in a refrigerator in the laboratory where they were currently used, and removed them under their supervision two floors away from where the leader will visit. This confirmed the rumors that were running in Romania after the death of Gheorghiu-Dej, the previous leader of the Communist Party, that he was killed for his independent policy from the Soviet Union by means of irradiation, by the KGB. Since then, protection of the Romanian communist leadership included careful screening for any potential source of radiation; and in our case, that included our laboratory radioactive reagents.

The supreme leader came, descended from his limo like a hurried businessman, entered the School of Medicine building, and was received in the hall by the dean, Professor Neştianu, and a chorus of medical students that serenaded him with some patriotic songs. After the leader was shown a laboratory where some research was on going and given explanations by the dean, he left with the same hurried pace. The whole visit lasted probably fifteen minutes. He left no advice to be followed.

Looking for a Killer

Soon after my return from Hershey, I started establishing a group of students that would be interested in doing medical research. I had a good response; several students volunteered to join the group and started coming to the laboratory on a regular basis. The Scientific Student Group was spending some time in my laboratory and was enthusiastic in learning something about medical research.

On a different level, an important event happened soon after my return to Craiova. Dinu Tănăsescu, who was the chairman of the Biochemistry Department, Dr. Nae Constantinescu from the Department of Internal Medicine, and I, decided to set up a research team to investigate a disease that involved villages in a certain area of the Dolj county near the Danube river. This disease called Balkan nephropathy was killing the inhabitants of certain villages that, with time, became deserted. We submitted a grant proposal and it was funded by the National Council for Scientific Research. The grant amounted to one million lei (the Romanian currency), which was a large sum of money considering that the monthly salary of a university professor was no more the four to five thousand lei.

Having the team set up, we decided to examine the inhabitants of a village for signs of the disease, and to collect samples for laboratory analysis. Children attending the village elementary school were surveyed to see if they had kidney changes and how early they occurred. Memories of this visit are still vivid because what I saw was impressive. There was one thing to read and learn about how deadly this disease was, and something else to walk on the unpaved, dusty dirt roads of the village and to see homes vacant because all family members were killed by this disease.

We examined a good number of adults that were already affected by the disease. One could see the mark of the disease on their face; they were pale but with a yellowish taint. They were going to die; the only way to keep such a patient alive was to have a kidney transplant. In those days in Romania, this was not available. One lucky case managed to travel to United States and have the kidney transplant. He survived, a testimony for the argument that kidney transplantation would save these sick people.

Walking on the village road, our group was stopped by some residents who invited us in their home to share with them their celebration. It was a certain saint day, and as was common, the peasants will celebrate it by cooking some special meals, and drinking their wine and țuica, the Romanian plum brandy. It was a quiet moment because we didn't know the nature of the disease, and there was a strong suspicion that the disease was transmissible. If such, we had no idea how it was transmitted. On the other hand, the hospitality of this people was outstanding, and it would have been a major offense to refuse their kind invitation. We accepted the invitation, went into the home, and tasted the food and the drinks.

The way the disease came about involving husband and wife led us to suspect that it was caused by some environmental agent. There were cases when a woman from a village without the disease, married a man from the village with the disease and moved into his home. Within several years, they were both dead because of the kidney disease. Suspecting a transmissible environmental agent we collected water from springs and wells that were used by the villagers for their drinking water.

When we exposed cells in culture to the spring water, the cells showed clear damage. It was proof that whatever was in the water could damage human cells. A medical school classmate of mine, Alexandru Gaşpar, who was working at the Cantacuzino Institute, volunteered to examine these cells under the electron microscope. It took several weeks, and Gaşpar came back with photos that showed viral particles in these cells. It was an interesting beginning of a long road that could lead us to identify the potential killer.

Party Member?

By the time this research was going on, the search for filling the position of chair of the Department of Microbiology was started. I thought I was qualified for this position and decided to apply. I filled up the papers and went to see the president of the university, Comrade Nicola. He told me that the university and the local party will support me, but he warned me that not being a member of the Communist Party was a major handicap. The search procedure involved a step in which the candidates files were submitted to the central committee of the party. It was thought that Ceauşescu's wife, Elena, was screening the files. This was the preliminary step of the search process, and it was without recourse. You made it through or you failed. Another candidate for the position was Dr. Voiculescu, a researcher from the Cantacuzino Institute. He had no major scientific contributions but has written some patriotic poems and was a faithful member of the Communist Party.

After a few months, Comrade Nicola called me and told me that my file was rejected by the central committee of the Communist Party. He was kind enough to tell me that the only way to become competitive was to become a member of the party. I thanked him for his advice and told myself that I knew a better way to become competitive, and that was by leaving the country with its Communist Party behind.

Earthquake

By March 4, 1977 around 9:20 PM, Romania was hit by a strong earthquake, rated 7.2 on the Richter scale that lasted about one minute. The earthquake primarily hit Bucharest and the Danube plain. It completely destroyed a small town near the Danube River and spared Transylvania. The Ceaușescu government did not report the true figures of deaths so that the system could not be blamed for the disaster. Many of these people just vanished in the rubble. Officially, the earthquake killed about 1,570 people and wounded more than 11,000. About 35,000 buildings were damaged, and the total damage was estimated at more than two billion dollars. Most of the damage was concentrated in Bucharest, where 33 large buildings collapsed.

It was Friday evening, and I was on the train coming home from Craiova together with my friends and colleagues Dinu Tănăsescu and Mihai Oțoiu. We were alone in the compartment and were relaxing after a week of lectures, meetings, and research. Each one of us was looking forward to a weekend of time spent together with family and friends. The train arrived on time in the North Railway Station at 9:20 PM. We went off the train and started walking along the train to the exit. Within a few seconds, I felt the earth underneath me starting to roll and saw the ceiling lights swaying. I became dizzy. My first thought was that I was having a stroke. Then the lights started flickering and went off. In the darkness that followed, I saw the exit lighted by outside light. I rushed outside the station. There were no street lights, but the sky was illuminated by a sort of luminous haze that was filling the air. My thought was that an atomic explosion has occurred, and I am seeing the radiation in the sky. I didn't bother to think where the explosion could have come from, and I didn't realize that this was dust from the crushed buildings.

I started walking fast to go home. Luckily, my home was only a fifteen— to twenty-minute walk from where I was. I crossed the large square in front of the station and started to walk on a boulevard. Here there was a lot of glass on the street from the broken shop windows. I passed a group of people, and I picked up some words among which "earthquake" were significant. I fathomed that in most likelihood, this was what happened, a strong one. I panicked thinking, what could have happened to my family, and I walked even faster. In fact, I was so immersed in my thoughts that I didn't even notice that I passed by the big modern building of the National Railway Center that has crushed to the ground.

Within minutes, I reached my home and was relieved, to say the least, it was standing. As I entered the courtyard, I heard Sidonia's voice talking from our balcony with some neighbors. Apparently, everybody was fine. Alina was sleeping at the time of the earthquake, so she had no memories of it, while Noël was awake and told me how he stopped the fall of a large China cabinet. There was no electricity, no phone, no radio, or TV; everything seemed just dead.

I appreciated that the only way to find out what happened to our loved ones was to take the car and make our way through the town. All four of us went into the car, and we started driving through the city to check out Sidonia's family. They were living close to the center of the city, and our home was in the northern part of it. We took the large boulevard crossing the city from north to south. It seemed that everybody was out on the street, either by foot or by car. The traffic was very heavy, but in spite of the lack of stoplights, or any lights, or police, the traffic went on smoothly. Although everyone was rushing to reach some family or friends, there was no fender bender; everyone was behaving at their best. We reached the home of Sidonia's parents, and were relieved to learn that they were just fine. There were some cracks in the interior walls, but no major damage has occurred to their rather old house.

From there, we continued our drive on the north-south boulevard, to reach the high-rise condominium where Carmen and her father lived, at the south end of the city. When we arrived there, we climbed the ten floors to their apartment, but we didn't find them home. Like everyone else, they were somewhere outside, too scared to return to their apartment. By chance, we met their neighbors, the Dinu Tănăsescu family, and thus found out that they were fine.

We started driving back north to see Uncle Oscar and his family. At some point, when we had to stop the car because of the traffic, a couple knocked at the window. They were asking us to take them to their relatives. We squeezed them in our car, and we dropped them at the place they wanted to go. This was quite close to the high-rise condominium where Uncle Oscar and his family lived. We climbed the six floors to find out that everyone was fine, but the outside wall of their bathroom, which consisted of a single large piece of reinforced concrete, was hanging out in the air still held by the steel wires that were supposed to keep it in place. It took months to have this wall repaired, but on this night, everyone was happy to be alive and well. We got home around four or five in the morning. The kids behaved wonderfully, and we got a few hours of sleep. Early morning, Carmen came with Alex, her future husband, to spend the day with us. She was afraid to go home; at the tenth floor, the shaking must have been frightening.

The following day, we decided to go and see some of the crushed buildings. The first one that impressed me most, was the Scala Building, a high-rise condominium, twelve or fourteen stories high, with a famous coffee shop on the ground floor. My father used to live in this building for many years; now it was just a mound of debris with God knows how many people buried in the rubble. It turned out that the demise of the building was probably related to the coffee shop. By remodeling the ground floor to make room for the coffee shop, several pillars that were important in maintaining the structure of the building as it was initially projected, were removed. A similar situation probably happened with the Nestor Building, a high-rise condominium with a fancy coffee shop on the ground floor. Now it was just a mound of rubble.

Troubles with Securitate

As the country was trying to recover from this major disaster, I went back to Craiova. An international symposium has been planned to be held there, and Dinu Tănăsescu was the chairman of the organizing committee, and I was the secretary. In spite of the earthquake, we decided to go ahead and to hold the meeting since we had a good number of foreign scientists that wanted to come. The symposium was organized in conjunction with the immunology group from the Babeş Institute in Bucharest led by Victor Gheție.

We had about two weeks to prepare, and everything was ready to go. The foreign scientists came mostly from Sweden, France, and Germany. The meeting was good, and everyone seemed satisfied. We took the foreign scientists to visit the former royal vineyard from Segarcea and have a wine tasting. By the end of the day, everybody was happy. In my capacity as secretary, I had to meet all the foreign scientists, and my English experience was helpful in communicating with them.

As the guests left, I went home to Bucharest for a few days of rest and recovery. As I was home, I received a phone call from Professor Neștianu asking me to come to Craiova for "an important meeting." Reluctantly, I accepted this invitation; and the next day, I drove to Craiova. As soon as

I arrived there I was invited to the meeting hall. A long table was there, and around were the dean of the medical school, the secretary of the party, Professor Neştianu, and two Securitate officers that were in charge of the medical school, colonel Predoiaşu and a captain whose name I don't recall.

I was seated in front of these officers, and the colonel started with questions: Is it true that I met foreign scientists? Was it true that I met them without witnesses? What did I discuss with them? Did I know that I had to write notes about my meetings? Well, my answer was that I met all those foreign scientists in my official capacity as secretary of the symposium, and as such, I don't believe that I needed third party witnesses. We just had casual discussion, presentation of the laboratory, and coffee. In particular, I had coffee with one of the Swedish scientists in my office, and we discussed the research we were doing. No specifics were mentioned as is customary between scientists.

The list of accusations didn't stop there. Was it true that I listen to Radio Free Europe? What a question? Everyone in Romania was listening to this radio, including very likely themselves. Obviously, some of my neighbors were Securitate informers. Was it true that I supported Goma? Paul Goma was a dissident writer who had recently expressed his criticism of the Ceauşescu dictatorial regime and was badly abused by the Securitate. In a discussion with some students, I said that he should be allowed to express whatever he thinks about the country. Very likely, one of the students was one of the numerous informers of the Securitate that were roaming everywhere, piling up tones of informative notes.

And finally, the last accusation came: Was it true that I see Karin Mironescu, the wife of a traitor? Of course it was true; I didn't hide that we, Sidonia and I, continued to meet Karin. Being separated for years from her husband, she needed more than ever the support of friends. They finally reached the conclusion that I broke law number 22, which was regulating the relationship of the Romanian citizens with foreigners. They decided not to send me to trial if I would sign a statement in which I will promise not to do the same mistake again. I signed the paper and left the room.

I knew then that my time in Craiova School of Medicine was coming to its end. Professor Neştianu told me just that. I have no proof, but my strong suspicion is that he played a significant role in triggering the whole Securitate inquest. Neştianu was power hungry, and Dinu Tănăsescu was his opponent, and I was wholeheartedly in his camp. I could have applied anytime to become a member of the party and had good chances to be accepted. The red card member in my pocket would have opened the door to become the chairman of the Microbiology Department, and my ascension to a position of influence in the medical school would have been fast. On top of that, the positive results that we had in our research project on the Balkan nephropathy would have given us a very important advantage. Neștianu knew that if that would happen, this would not be good for his power play. With my removal, the whole project would be dead, and he proved right on that.

I was ready to move to Bucharest not only because Craiova was a dead-end road for me professionally, but also because I felt that my chances of getting out of the country were better from Bucharest. It was obvious that my relationship with the local Securitate was so bad that they will view with a lot of suspicion any application for a passport. A very significant role in my decision was a discussion that I had with Sidonia, who was no longer willing to put up with the hardship leaving her with all the troubles of our household and taking care of children. In this case, the decision was to choose between moving my family to Craiova or just end the commute. Although I would have considered moving to Craiova if I would have been appointed chair of Microbiology under the present circumstances with the troubles that I had with the Securitate, any promotion was unlikely.

I went to Comrade Nicola, the university president and I told him that my family does not stand anymore our separation, and that I think Ovidiu Chita can replace me and he agreed. Chita wanted the prestige to teach at the medical school, and for him, this was a unique opportunity.

Looking for a Job

Now I had to find a position in Bucharest. I went to talk to my former director at the Microbiology Institute. He received me at his home, listened to me, and told me that there is no position at his institute. By then I was no longer surprised by his decision. Things have changed at the Microbiology Institute from the time when Niculescu was director, now the survival of the institute was based solely on political connections. The more and higher-up the connections, the better chances of survival. I was not a good connection provider and could be even a potential troublemaker. Looking back, I was lucky I was not hired. In life, sometimes losses can turn out to be big gains.

My next stop was at the Babeș Institute. I went and talked with Victor Gheție a scientist that I had a great deal of respect for. He appeared supportive of the idea of having me join their group. Then I discussed the issue with the director of the institute, Professor Moraru. I knew him since he was assistant professor in the Department of Physiopathology, and I used to have laboratory practice with him. He was sent for postdoctoral training to Moscow, and when he returned to Romania, married with a Soviet lady, he was appointed director of the Institute of Forensic Medicine. Next, he became director of the Babeș Institute, a prestigious scientific institute focused on pathology and with a strong research group. Moraru was genuinely interested in medical research and used his political influence to promote it. When I approached him, he did not refuse me upfront but referred me to the Ministry of Health to get some bureaucratic approvals that were rather dubious and difficult to get.

Being back to square one, I decided to try the Cantacuzino Institute, where Sidonia was quite happy with her position. I asked for an appointment with Professor Bîlbîie, the director of the institute. Professor Bîlbîie received me kindly, and after asking several questions about the administrative situation, told me right away that he is pleased to hire me. It was just a matter to file up the paperwork, and the secretaries will take care of that. That was the end of my Craiova experience and the beginning of my new working place at the Cantacuzino Institute.

I am grateful to Professor Bîlbîie for his unreserved support, first hiring Sidonia and then I at a time when we were outcasts of the political regime, and the only thing we could offer was our professional skills. I am sorry I had to leave the Cantacuzino Institute the way I did. My defection had nothing to do with the institute itself or its administration; it was a matter of survival for me and my family caught in an oppressive, totalitarian regime. Lately, we watched the demise of the Cantacuzino Institute, and Sidonia and I were sorry for it.

Wrap-up

I looked recently at the web site of the Craiova Medical School, and to my surprise, under the Department of Medical Genetics, I found the following:

> Formed as a subject within the Faculty of Medicine of Craiova, in 1971 under the name of Biology, Department of Genetics will operate under various names: Biology-Genetics (1974-1987), Medical Genetics (2003), is associated with Cell and Molecular Biology. Since 2003, the discipline of Medical Genetics is independent, so that title, as well as functionality, the syllabus is currently in line with that of similar departments around the world. Having as founders two outstanding teachers: Professor Albert Niculescu, and Professor Maurice Nachtigal, currently professors in Switzerland, and respectively the U.S., people with an avant-garde vision, an entrepreneurial mind and a spirit eager to see more than here and do more than for today, the discipline of Medical Genetics was born shy, but grew naturally decisive in the context of a global "Life Genetisation."

This unsolicited acknowledgment of my contribution to the development of this department is a reward for the struggle and the effort of those years in Craiova. Besides the troubles that I had there with the Securitate, it was not their fault that the Central Committee of the Communist Party under the direction of Ceaușescu's wife has rejected my application for the position of chair of the Department of Microbiology.

I know that the students enjoyed very much my lectures, and among them there were at least a few that along with me were looking forward and further. After I defected, one of my scientific group students, Mândrescu, visited Sidonia and brought her some wine as an expression of support. My former colleague Ion Rogoz did the same thing. In those days, such expression of support for families of defectors was considered by the communist regime as treason. As far as I was concerned, I knew that the circumstances were such that individuals could do very little to improve the overall situation.

By then I was aware that for me and my family, there was only one desirable solution—to leave the country for good. I tried to do it legally when I came back from Hershey and submitted the contract that I had from Fred Rapp to the president of the Craiova University. I have never received any reply; it was totally ignored. For me, the conclusion was clear; I had to get out of the country by any means.

Once again, destiny played its game and showed its power. What appeared as a personal disaster, conflict with Securitate, and forced out of job, turned out as a blessing. In the short run, I had a position in the most prestigious medical institute. Moreover, I was again together with Sidonia at work. What could have been better? We always loved to be together all the time. Still in the long run, rejection by the communist regime enhanced my determination to leave this country that was closing all avenues of my professional advancement. And this turned out to be a blessing for me and my family!

Chapter 10

The Cantacuzino Institute 1977-1980

By the time I joined the Cantacuzino Institute in 1977, this was the most important medical institution in Romania. It was covering all major areas of public health, producing reagents for laboratory testing, immunizations, vaccines, sera, etc.

"Dr. I. Cantacuzino" Institute of Sera and Vaccines was founded in 1921, but Cantacuzino had created and run the Experimental Medicine Laboratory since 1901, when this laboratory prepared, for the first time in Romania, anti-streptococcal and anti-dysenteric sera (1904). The foundation law for „Dr. I. Cantacuzino" Institute of Sera and Vaccines was published in the Official Gazette of Romania on July 16, 1921, voted by the Parliament and promulgated by King Ferdinand on July 13, 1922. In 1924, the institute was moved into a new building, located close to „Victor Babeș" Institute. In the last 85 years, research in major fields of microbiology and related sciences has been developed, a number of vaccines and therapeutic sera have been prepared, and specialists have been involved in public health, epidemiological surveillance of the Romanian territory and professional training. http//jurnalul.ro/viatasanatoasa/stareadesanatate/institutul-de-seruri-si-vaccinuri-45455.html

Polio Vaccine

I was assigned to the Division of Enteroviruses, which had, as a main goal, the fight against polio in Romania. This unit had to make sure the country had the necessary amount of polio vaccine, and this vaccine was distributed correctly in the population. It would also survey the country for any case of polio or related disease. The head of the division was Dr. Andrei Combiescu. The group that was involved with the production of the polio vaccine included Dr. Maia Fâciu, Dr. Irina Ionescu-Matiu, and Dr. Mihai Zamfirescu, Sidonia, and several technicians. A separate group of the division was involved with the diagnostic of polio and related diseases and was led by Dr. Mariana Combiescu, the wife of Andrei Combiescu. There were other biologists and technicians, altogether a rather large group, probably thirty to forty individuals.

When I became part of the division, I was left independent and allowed to continue my studies on herpes viruses and their effects on chromosomes. After all the years spent mostly teaching at the medical school in Craiova, this was, for me, like a return to the good old days when I was doing research almost full time. In a rather short time, I was able to start doing some interesting experiments and to publish again in scientific journals.

After two years, I was asked to take charge of the control of the polio vaccine for so-called adventitious viruses. These were viruses that could contaminate the cells used for the production of the polio vaccine. Most of these undesirable viruses would come from monkeys that carried these viruses in their kidneys. Dr. Irina Matiu, who was in charge of this task when I joined the Cantacuzino Institute, defected to the United States while being a visiting scientist at Baylor College in Houston, Texas.

Our life during these years at the Cantacuzino Institute was quite tranquil. In the morning, Sidonia and I rushed to sign in no later than 8:00 AM. This was considered essential by the administration, unrelated to how much work would follow. In the laboratory, we were doing our work separately, but we were still together, and this was a blessed thing for both of us. I know Sidonia was happy, and for me, it was a dream comes true. After all these years of separation, we were again working together with the happiness brought by the knowledge that we were close to each other.

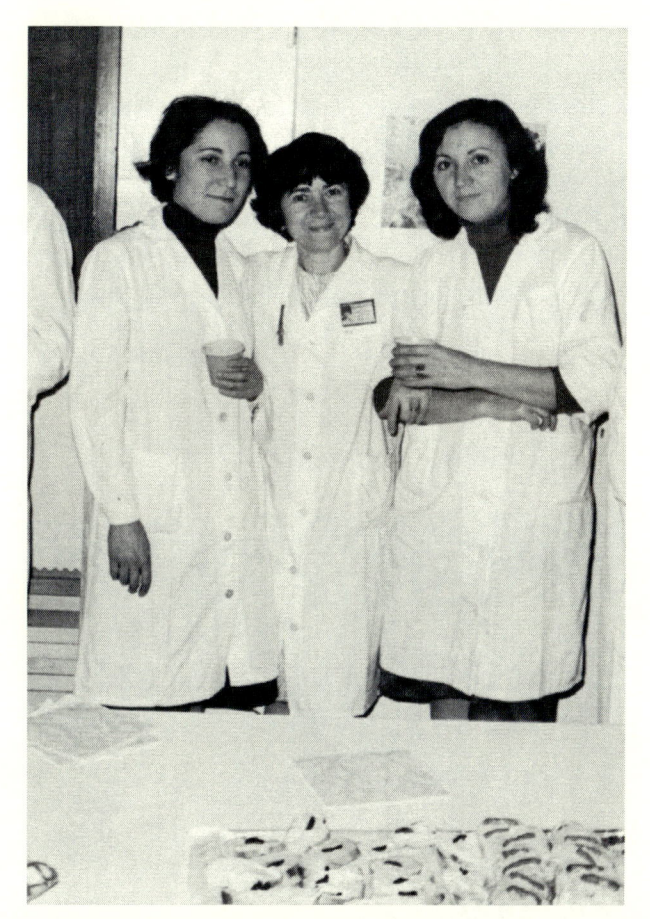

Fig. 1. Sidonia is in the middle, flanked by two of her technicians, Valy (right) and Jenny (left). 1978.

At midday, we would get together often joining other colleagues having lunch in the laboratory. The schedule was from 8:00 AM to 3:00 PM without a break for lunch. Actually, there was no eating place in the institute. Usually, Sidonia will leave at 3:00 PM and go home where the children were by themselves, hopefully not fighting. I will stay overtime doing some more work till 4:00 or 5:00 PM. Many times on my way home, I will stop to do some grocery shopping. Those were years when we had a pleasant family life.

In the group, I made friends with Dr. Mihai Zamfirescu, a tall man with white hair and a young-looking face. He was maintaining an atmosphere of academic quality to our group. By 3:00 PM, when everyone was leaving, he would make tea in his office and share it with me, or other colleague, over some interesting discussion. He has been an assistant director of the institute, but not being a member of the Communist Party was no longer in the administration. However, his wisdom was highly appreciated by everyone, and even the party secretary for the institute, Dr. Arion, was sometimes seen having tea with Mihai over a friendly discussion. Another person with whom Sidonia and I became friends was Mrs. Ileana Brucker, a woman endowed like her husband, Jean, with a lot of common sense and life experience. We all got along very well, and the whole atmosphere was that of a large family.

Fig. 2. Christmas party at the Cantacuzino Institute. December 1978. Sidonia is second to the right; I am the first to the left. The tall guy in the middle is Dr. Mihai Zamfirescu. Mrs. Ileana Brucker is on his right.

This environment was encouraged by our manager, Andrei Combiescu. I knew Andrei since we were classmates in the lyceum and in the medical school. He was always among the top of the grade, largely because of his intellectual abilities. Andrei was the nephew of Professor Combiescu, one of the founding fathers of the Cantacuzino Institute. Andrei lost his mother at the 1940 earthquake, when he was rescued miraculously from the rubble. His father, a professor of internal medicine, remarried and moved to Timişoara. Andrei was brought up in Professor Combiescu's household and probably was looked upon as his successor in the Cantacuzino Institute.

Mariana was Andrei's second wife, after he divorced his first wife, the sister of our medical school colleague, Daniel Constantinescu. While Andrei was more of the scientific type, Mariana was more interested having an active social life, which implied spending late hours with friends. Andrei was showing up signing in at 8:00 AM, and surviving the rest of the day on multiple cups of strong Turkish coffee. By afternoon, after work hours, he would have a nap and then social life till late night. This schedule did not prevent him from being a kind and friendly chief, and the work of the team kept the polio vaccine production going.

Andrei was a member of the Communist Party. Without this attribute, it is unlikely that he could be in a leadership position. Andrei is a typical example of the way the system worked. Very likely, he became a party member while he was practicing medicine somewhere in the countryside where the government sent him after graduation. There is no doubt in my mind that he became a party member knowing very well that the system was rotten and worthless. The party membership was the mandate for any leadership position. Professional qualities were of secondary importance. It happened that Andrei had excellent professional qualities, but they would have been ignored if he wouldn't have been party member. I am convinced that in those days, there were no more individuals thinking that communism is a superior system, except maybe a few of the old guard, and even they knew that their paradigm was not working. The party members were interested only in the benefits that the little red card could bring.

Job Offers

A few months after I joined the Cantacuzino Institute, I received a phone call inviting me to a meeting with Dr. Nicolae Simionescu, the director of the Institute of Cellular Biology. As a freshman in the medical school I knew Dr. Simionescu as associate professor of anatomy and supervisor of the dissection laboratory. He was a good-looking man, very professional. My good friend and colleague Ștefan Mironescu did research with him and they became friends.

Dr. Simionescu moved to the Endocrinology Institute in the Pathology Department, and Ștefan followed him there. In 1969, when I was struggling to get my passport to travel to Houston, Texas, Ștefan told Dr. Simionescu about my difficulties, and he offered to use his connections to facilitate my departure. This was not necessary, but I remembered this friendly deed. As it happened, when I was at the Oncology Institute, I reviewed a book written by Dr. Simionescu on thyroid cancer and my review was not very kind. I had a lot of criticism for many parts of the book. According to the editor, my criticism was transmitted to Dr. Simionescu, and instead of him being upset, he was grateful for the work I did. It improved his book that was translated in English.

In the meantime, the career of Dr. Simionescu has markedly changed. He and his wife and coworker, Maya, were invited by George Palade, a Nobel Prize winner, to his laboratory at Rockefeller Institute. The Simionescus entered a new field of research related to blood vessels and atherosclerosis and, in a few years, had a favorable reputation in this field. Rumors claimed that Palade persuaded the Ceaușescu couple to build a new institute of biology to be run by Simionescu. Nicolae and Maya Simionescu could have stayed in the States and would have had no problem having excellent appointments and funding for their research. However, they decided to return to Romania and to run this research institute. I went to the opening ceremony of the institute and the number of Nobel Prize winners attending this event was unique for Romania.

So here I was having an appointment with the famous Dr. Simionescu. He received me kindly and told me that he has learned about my predicament in Craiova and was troubled by this story. He offered me to join his institute. At this juncture, my scientific interest was not even close to what they were doing, but I was honored by his offer and grateful for it. However, at that time, I was planning to leave Romania, and I wouldn't want to hurt him by leaving the country as I was determined to do, being employed at his institute. Leaders of the institutions where defectors worked were blamed for the defection since they must have approved the passport application.

He insisted, and offered to use all the facilities they had at the institute, which, in those days, was more than any other place in Romania. I thanked him and left. I could not even imagine then that years later, I would be deeply involved in atherosclerosis research, which was what he was doing, and I will return several times to his institute, give talks, and even try to help them financially. Destiny, how uncharted is your ways!

I was already established at the Cantacuzino Institute, when one day I had the surprise visit of Professor Chiricuță. Dr. Chiricuță knew me as a medical student, when he was an adjunct professor of physiopathology. When I was starting my pathology training, he was at the Oncology Institute, but left to become the director of the Oncology Institute in Cluj. Professor

Chiricuță was one of the best surgeons in the country, and was also interested in cancer research. When he came to visit me, he sounded quite distressed because the head of the cytogenetic laboratory of the Oncology Institute, Dr. Dorin Olinici, has left to become chairman of the Pathology Department at the Cluj Medical School. Dr. Chiricuță was offering me this position at his institute. He was laying down all he could offer, such as a nice apartment in Cluj and a fellowship in America.

I have to say the offer was very attractive; one couldn't ask for more. Sidonia loved Cluj, the city where she grew up and would have been happy to return. But I had in my mind something else. I wanted America but not for a fellowship; I already had that. I wanted America for good because by then, I figured out that Romania as a whole was sinking as fast and as hopeless as the Titanic. So I respectfully turned him down. I felt sorry for him, but . . .

The irony of the fate is that in 1992, I went to Cluj invited by Professor Olinici, who was the chairman of the Department of Pathology and also consultant at the Oncology Institute. I presented a seminar and talked to the medical students. In the meantime, Professor Chiricuță has died, and I was invited by the new director of the Oncology Institute to audit the pathology laboratory that included the cytogenetic laboratory.

Having these jobs offers were a good sign. I was still considered competitive, and my skills were valuable. In spite of the fact that I was not a party member, these people were willing to hire me, because they were trying to make their institution working. I appreciated their interest, but I was decided to leave the communist regime behind. I knew that we were on a sinking ship, and I had to get me and my loved ones away from it. I was fully aware that not being a party member will continue to be a serious obstacle to any further promotion. Years later when I returned to Romania and visited these institutes, I realized how right I was in my decision.

Balkan Nephropathy Again?

The following event that occurred while I was at the Cantacuzino Institute is probably relevant for the general environment we were living in those days. One day I was invited to attend a meeting with our director, Professor Bîlbîie. This was unusual, and I was wondering what will happen. In the institute library, there were twenty to twenty-five persons attending this meeting. We were not told in advance what the purpose of the meeting was. As soon as we were seated, Dr. Bîlbîie walked in accompanied by a man that we didn't know. Dr. Bîlbîie introduced him as Dr. Gajdusek. I was in shock! This was the world-famous Dr. Gajdusek that I read about years before. According to Wikipedia, Daniel Carleton Gajdusek (pronounced GUY-dah-shek) was an American physician and medical researcher who was recipient of the Nobel Prize for work on kuru, the first human prion disease demonstrated to be infectious. Like the mad cow disease, kuru is caused by a transmissible protein, called prion, which kills brain cells. To have such an outstanding scientist visiting the Cantacuzino Institute was a stunning event.

What brought him there? The answer came from him: Gajdusek has learned about the Balkan Nephropathy and was interested to do research on the cause of this disease because he was suspecting that it was caused by a transmissible agent, possibly similar to kuru and mad cow disease. Gajdusek wanted to know if there was anyone among us interested to be involved in this research project. When I was at Craiova Medical School, I was actively involved in such a project. I had to leave the medical school because I was accused by the Securitate that I passed secret information about this matter to a foreign scientist. For me it would have been a unique opportunity to collaborate with such a famous scientist on an exciting project. I would have been a perfect coworker; I knew the disease and the environment. But now I was decided to leave Romania, to get me and my family out of the quagmire that this country was. Moreover, I had already in my Securitate file the statement that I will not contact a foreigner unsupervised. Collaboration with Gajdusek was impossible unless I would become a Securitate informer on Gajdusek. So I kept my head down and so did everyone else to the relief of our director and to Gajdusek's disappointment. A wonderful project that may have solved the killing of people living in those villages never happened. The Iron Curtain worked well, too well.

Warnings

In spite of the comfortable life that we were enjoying, several things happened that were enough to remind me, if it was necessary, that Romania was not a place to keep my family. One day my friend from Craiova, Prof. Dinu Tănăsescu, came to my lab with a newspaper. It was the newspaper of the Ministry of the Interior, the one that included the Securitate along with the police (called militia). In the newspaper, it was the story of a certain professor at the University of Craiova named (fictitiously) Mihai Nacu, who had a foreign scientist visiting his lab and stealing from him some very valuable and secret scientific material. The story had a happy ending because the Securitate intercepted and recovered this material before leaving the country. It was not hard to read through the lines of this story that this was the case against me starting with the fictitious name. It was published now so that everybody should know what the Securitate wanted everyone to know; their account of what happened and how watchful they were.

Another episode in my conflict with the Securitate was soon to follow. Professor Lima-de-Faria, a famous scientist, came to Bucharest as the official representative of the Swedish Academy to sign some agreements with the Romanian Academy and to give a seminar. He was scheduled to visit the Cantacuzino Institute, and I was asked in advance to receive him in my laboratory, and to discuss with him my research. I was pleased to meet this person who has published one of the most famous textbook of cell biology in the world.

Professor Lima-de-Faria came accompanied by Ms. Ileana Cârnu, the party secretary from the Babeș Institute who was likely assigned to watch his every step. Ileana has been one of the biologists that worked in my genetics laboratory at the Oncology Institute. She sat through our discussion, which went very well. I had no doubts that she would report in writing our discussion to the Securitate. This was the law.

When our discussion ended and Lima-de-Faria left, I accompanied him to his car that was waiting at the institute gate. It was November, and it was a beautiful sunny fall day. I asked him if he had the opportunity to travel outside Bucharest to see the landscape, and he said no, but he would like it very much. I took this as a request and asked him if he would like to go and see the Carpathian Mountains, a trip that would take only a few hours. He said he would love it, and he had the afternoon free. I offered to drive him there, and he immediately accepted. All this discussion was done in front of the party secretary as I thought I learned the lesson from my Craiova experience.

Lima-de-Faria went back to his hotel where I was supposed to pick him up, and I turned to the party secretary and asked her to provide a third member for our trip so that I wouldn't be alone with him and be exposed to accusations the way it happened in Craiova. She found a coworker and most likely party member, Mrs. Constantinescu, willing to accompany us on this trip.

Around 2:00 PM, I picked up Mrs. Constantinescu from a bus station and drove to the Athénée Palace Hotel, where Lima-de-Faria was waiting for this trip to the mountains. We took off and drove for about two hours until we arrived at the Cota 1400 Hotel in the mountains surrounding Sinaia in the Prahova valley. It was indeed a gorgeous day, and the fall colors were on display. We had coffee and cake at the hotel, took pictures, and started our way back to Bucharest. We got back to Bucharest around 9:00 PM. I dropped Dr. Lima-de-Faria at the Athénée Palace Hotel and Mrs. Constantinescu at a bus station and went home.

Fig. 3. Lima-de-Faria (left) and I visiting the Cota 1400 Hotel near Sinaia. November 1979. The Swedish geneticist, Antonio Lima-de-Faria, has been knighted by the king of Sweden for his scientific achievements and was professor emeritus at the University of Lund, Sweden.

The next morning, I went to the institute as usual and headed immediately to the Babeş Institute, which was in the vicinity, to attend the seminar that Lima-de-Faria was supposed to give. From people that were already there, I found out that the talk was canceled. Apparently after I dropped him at the hotel, Lima-de-Faria found out that in his absence, his luggage was searched, and some of his slides were missing. He got all upset and decided to leave Romania immediately. Next morning, instead of delivering a talk, he was at the airport catching a flight back to Sweden. Obviously, the Securitate has overdone its job.

A few days passed and I got a phone call in my lab. I was invited to the Securitate officer of the Cantacuzino Institute. I had a strange feeling of déjà vu and went. This time, the Securitate captain was polite and restrained. He told me that I repeated the same mistake as before, thus showing me that I have my file well established. However, having Mrs. (comrade) Constantinescu with me I had an alibi and that cushioned the accusation. Nevertheless, this time, the crime was that I did not report to them this trip and, of course, all the small talk that I had with Lima-de-Faria. My reply was that I considered that Comrade Constantinescu will do it, but this answer didn't satisfy him. I got a new warning, and my file with the Securitate definitely got thicker.

A few months after I started working at the Cantacuzino Institute, I was hired as an adjunct professor of microbiology to help teaching medical students of the Bucharest School of Medicine. I enjoyed having again interaction with medical students, but this was not going to last. After a few months, I was told that my contract was cancelled. Confidentially, the chairman of the department, Prof. Mărăşel Georgescu, asked me if I have a relative abroad. I told him that I have an uncle in Mexico, but he has left the country fifty years ago. No, there was no arguing with the personnel service that functioned as an appendage of the Securitate. The order must have been clear; everyone with a relative abroad had to be kicked out. This was the end of my teaching activity in Romania.

And then one more thing happened. I received an invitation from my friend and former colleague, Marius Ianconescu, from Israel to attend a scientific meeting there, all expenses covered. With this invitation, I went to Dr. Bîlbîie, the director of the institute, to ask permission to attend this meeting. He told me that this is not a good time to ask for a passport to travel abroad. It was clearly another door that was shut in front of me. The message was clear, stay inside the communist camp and be happy.

In light of these events, the following story may be interesting. One day I received a call from a man. He introduced himself as Mr. Văleanu, and he told me that he has an important discussion to have with me. We set up an appointment. I become curious and went to meet him. The man, a middle-aged individual, older than me, looked like an accountant or a clerk. He invited me to go to a place not too far to sit down and talk.

I accompanied him to a high-rise condominium in a rather fancy neighborhood of Bucharest, close to the Armenian Church. We got into a flat that looked well taken care of, but uninhabited, furnished efficiently but not elegantly. We sat down, and he opened the talk. It was an offer to give me and my family passports to migrate to Israel. There was one condition: Sidonia and I would have to sign contracts to become officers of the Ministry of Interior. We will be paid full salaries by the Ministry of Interior, and the salaries will be deposited in our bank account and could be collected by us anytime we return to Romania.

This offer that came out of the blue took me by surprise. I knew that there were many Jews migrating mainly to Israel, but usually, they had to wait years to get their passport. As far as Sidonia and I were concerned, we were decided to leave the country, but we didn't want to go to Israel. We had to take with us Sidonia's family, who were not Jews, and they may have problems with their social support which they needed. Also, I had my understanding with Ştefan Mironescu for USA. For us, the question was: Did *they* know anything about our plan? How did *they* pick us up?

Obviously, the major problem of this offer was about being recruited as Ministry of Interior officers. In my view, this sounded more like becoming a spy. He was talking about salary but nothing about what had to be done for these salaries. I told him that I have to talk to Sidonia about the whole project, and he should call me within several days. I went home and told Sidonia the whole story. Her reply was short and straightforward: not interested, period. After several days, Mr. Văleanu called. My answer was that of Sidonia: We are not interested. Still he wanted something from me: Can I give him names of people that he could contact with this offer? This gave us part of the answer to the question that bugged Sidonia and me: Why us? Obviously, someone has given these guys our name. Who? We'll probably never know.

Altogether, looking back, we realized that this was a win-win situation for the Securitate; they will get paid several thousand dollars for providing Israel with new citizens, and on top of that, they will get a few spies there, that they could use for whatever were their interest, all for free. Salaries in Romanian currency were worthless outside the country. Not a bad deal.

The dark shadow of the communist regime reached Sidonia again. For several years, she was working to get her doctoral degree, the equivalent of the American PhD on a topic related to infection of cells in culture with mycoplasma. These are some little bugs that are common contaminants of cells in culture and create a lot of confusion for those who use these cells. She has reached the final stage, which means that her thesis was ready to be presented to the committee in charge of scientific evaluation and, after their approval, to defend it publicly. But the new rule imposed by Ceaușescu was that before the scientific committee, the thesis was to be approved by the Communist Party. At this stage, Sidonia's thesis was rejected. In her file, it was the fact that her father has owned land that was taken by the communist government; therefore, she had a rotten social origin. Not good for a PhD degree. Now we shared one more thing: the party rejected me to be chairman of Microbiology and rejected her to have a doctor degree. Surely for the communist regime we were second class citizens.

Family Life

With my move from Craiova to the Cantacuzino Institute, a major change occurred in our family life, and it was all for the better. We were again together, and being with Sidonia all the time, at home and in the lab, was a blessing for both of us. Work in the lab was not very intense; it was more work during the period of polio vaccine production and less in the intervals between. The companionship in the lab was pleasant, and Sidonia had three colleagues that were her best friends, Dr. Rodica Mihăilescu, Ms. Eugenia Lungu, and Mrs. Celli Pop. Like Sidonia, Celli was originally from Cluj. Very likely, they attended the same biology faculty, and they became very close friends.

By the summer of 1979, I was invited by the graduating class from the Craiova School of Medicine to their banquet, which was to be held in a hotel called Valea de Pești, "The Fish Valley," somewhere north of Craiova in the Jiu valley in the Carpathian Mountains. This was a nice gesture from my former students since I was no longer a faculty member, and moreover, everyone in the medical school was aware of my conflict with the Securitate. I accepted gratefully their invitation and embarked my family for a rather long drive. The celebration was enjoyable, lasted late into the night. Noël got up from our hotel room where he was sleeping and joined the party.

Fig. 4. Graduation banquet held at Valea de Pești Hotel for class of 1979 from Craiova School of Medicine. I am talking to a former student of mine, Sorin Krumpholz, presently a physician in Israel. Sidonia is on my right. Next to her is Dr. Zaharia (with the white beard) and his wife, parents of Dr. Bogdan Zaharia, assistant professor of pathology at the Craiova School of Medicine.

All in all, we had a delightful family life. We had a few weeks' vacation in the summer when we enjoyed going to the beach at Tataia and to Bușteni in the mountains. Having a car we could drive to Mamaia beach and meet there our friends. We and our children loved to spend the winter holidays in Bușteni. Those were years when Sidonia was a happy woman. She really enjoyed her life and missed it when she was exposed to our separation ordeal and left the country.

We had as good salaries as we could have for our positions. In addition, I started mentoring students for the admission examination to the medical school. Being a member of the admission commission at Craiova Medical School for years, I had a good knowledge of this field, and people were ready to pay good money for having their children prepared for this tough examination.

I had three students, and one was admitted at the medical school. It turned out that she became the family doctor of my cousin Mariana and her family in Bucharest. Ms. Eugenia Nițu wrote me a letter dated September 20, 1981, when she was already starting her second year at medical school. After thanking for my teaching, she ended her letter, saying, "At the end of this little letter let me thank you again and wish you and your family that I hope with all my heart is with you now, much, much happiness and good health. With much gratitude, your student Eugenia Nițu."

For me this was not a very exciting activity, but it brought a substantial increase in our income. It has allowed us to offer private lessons of English and French to Noël, and piano lessons to Alina. Our kids were doing very well. Noël was the first or second in his grade every year, and Alina was making promising progress with her piano training at the George Enescu School of Music. Her outstanding piano teacher, Ms. Camelia Pavlenko, was pleased with her and pushed her toward a musical career.

In spite of this enjoyable and comfortable life, I was feeling increasingly uneasy about the situation in the country. Under Ceaușescu's dictatorship, the country was going down, and going down fast. Although by that time there were not yet the problems of lack of food or energy, including heating, that occurred later, there were times when some items such as meat, eggs, or butter will disappear from the market. Why? Years later we found out that Ceaușescu was paying off the Romanian foreign debt of about three billion dollars in natural products. We learned from the wife of a Canadian engineer who was involved in that deal, that to pay for a nuclear reactor bought from Canada, Ceaușescu exported the whole harvest of strawberries. Moreover, there were major troubles in Poland, with threatening talks from the Soviet Union about occupying this country.

From what happened to us, we felt that we were in fact second-class citizens. We were kept in our positions because the regime needed people with our expertise, but we were clearly told that any attempt to move to an upper step on the professional ladder will be restricted. Without doing anything wrong, I run into trouble with the Securitate twice. I was refused to attend international meetings and I was driven out of the competition for a higher academic position; Sidonia was prevented of obtaining a postgraduate degree. What else was in store for us?

Fight for Passports

In 1977, when Uncle Ovidiu visited us, he sought to have a discussion with his brother Marius, my father-in-law, and with Mutis, about leaving the country. He was enthusiastic about the United States, and the way he and his family have been treated there, and thought that we should move to America. I drove him to Marius's house, and waited outside, while Ovidiu debated this issue with Marius and Mutis. I will remember this afternoon vividly, because it played an important role in our life.

Dusk was falling, when Ovidiu came out from the house, and Sidonia, I, and him, stood around our car and talked. Ovidiu told us that Marius was opposed to the idea of leaving Romania, but, Mutis would accept such a move. His advice was that I should leave the country, go to America, and pull out the rest of the family. This was the time when Sidonia and I decided that this was the plan we were going to follow. For us, it was important to have from a Ciugudean family member the green light for leaving the country. Sidonia was very close to Uncle Ovidiu, and his advice weighted heavily in her decision making.

In my previous plans for leaving Romania, Sidonia's family has been a major concern. Essentially they were two elderly people, one of them paralyzed, and her sister, mentally handicapped. Which country would take them? Moreover, I could not ask Sidonia to leave them in Romania, I don't think she would have done it. Now we had a plan that may be acceptable to Sidonia. Once established in the United States, Sidonia and I could support them financially. The Ovidiu plan had to be tried and executed. Unfortunately, this was the last time we saw Uncle Ovidiu. He died in California, and we never made it to see him again. He was a fine man, and we kept his good memory. We are grateful for his advice and support in leaving communist Romania.

I decided it was time to try to get out of the country. There was no more time to waste. My decision was boosted by a visit of Dr. Nicolae Ciobanu, also called by his nickname Culiță. He was a young MD that has done PhD work in my laboratory in Craiova. He joined us often on our family Sunday morning long walks. Culiță married an American lady and was thus allowed to leave Romania for the United States. Culiță came to visit his parents in Bucharest, and he brought a message from Ștefan Mironescu, who, by now, has been appointed professor in the Department of Pathology of the newly founded medical school in Columbia, South Carolina. The message included an announcement in *New England Journal of Medicine* offering two teaching positions in this department. Ștefan was asking for my resume. Although it seemed peculiar to apply for a position in the United States from Romania before even asking for a passport, I was happy to provide. This was the first step on our flight from Romania.

By late fall of 1978, Sidonia and I started the proceedings to apply for a passport to travel abroad. We decided to ask for visas to travel to France to visit my family and the graves of my mother and grandmother. We were going to try to take advantage of the fact that Romania has signed the Helsinki Accords, which specified that people should be allowed to travel abroad for family visits.

> Wikipedia. The Helsinki Accords, Helsinki Final Act, or Helsinki Declaration was the final act of the Conference on Security and Co-operation in Europe held in Finlandia Hall of Helsinki, Finland, during July and August 1, 1975. Thirty-five States, including the USA, Canada, and most European states except Albania and Andorra, signed the declaration in an attempt to improve relations between the Communist bloc and the West. The Helsinki Accords, however, were not binding as they did not have treaty status.[1] According to Ford, "The Helsinki documents involve political and moral commitments aimed at lessening tension and opening further the lines of communication between peoples of East and West" . . . "We are not committing ourselves to anything beyond what we are already committed to by our own moral and legal standards and by more formal treaty agreements such as the United Nations Charter and Declaration of Human Rights" . . . "If it all fails, Europe will be no worse off than it is now. If even a part of it succeeds, the lot the people in Eastern Europe will be that much better, and the cause of freedom will advance at least that far."[6] The civil rights portion of the agreement provided the basis for the work of the Moscow Helsinki Group, an independent non-governmental organization created to monitor compliance to the Helsinki Accords (which evolved into several regional committees, eventually forming the International Helsinki Federation and Human Rights Watch). While these provisions applied to all signatories, the focus of attention was on their application to the Soviet Union and its Warsaw Pact allies, including Bulgaria, Czechoslovakia, the German Democratic Republic (East Germany), Hungary, Poland, and Romania.

The first step was obtaining the approval of the institution where we worked. This was easy to obtain since Andrei Combiescu had no doubts that for us this would be just a nice vacation trip. We seemed and actually were a happy family. When I was younger I have already been in the States twice, and I have returned on time. I was reaching an age when chances to get a position elsewhere seemed negligible. Life for us was good; why leave? Judging from his reaction when Sidonia told him that I defected, I am convinced that he has been certain I will return to Romania from this trip. It is likely that others were thinking like him.

The next and essential step was to obtain the approval of the local chapter of the Communist Party. This proved to be a difficult and tricky step. Their decision to our application was negative, a big no. I was not ready to give up, and I asked for an interview with the party committee. I was granted an appointment, and I was met by Dr. Lemnete, a man that I knew being one of the communist activists admitted to the medical school without the admission examination. He was probably one class ahead of me. I presented my case, stressing my desire to meet my relatives in France and visit my mother's grave. He listened quietly and bored to my story, and by the time I finished, he looked at me and asked if I was a classmate of Ioan Costică. Ioan Costică was one of the Communist Party members admitted to the medical school and was, by far, the brightest one. I answered affirmatively, trying to guess what his point was. He told me to leave a memo with him and to wait for the decision.

Miraculously, the decision came positive; the party committee allowed us to apply for a passport. I will never know what made them change their mind. I could only speculate that Lemnete may have asked Ioan Costică his opinion about me, and he got some good references or, that in his mind I was somewhat connected with Ioan Costică, who was an influential guy preferably not to fool with. Anyway, this was not my major concern as Sidonia and I went to the passport office in December 1978 and filed up the forms requesting passports and visas to travel to France.

By May 1979, Sidonia's mother passed away. Mutis had high blood pressure probably since young age and survived two strokes. Her family history was just terrible. Both her parents died young with heart problems, and one of her two brothers, Mircea Ignea died, before fifty years of age of heart disease. It was a wonder she survived to reach the age of seventy-six without any treatment, which, at that time, was not available. Sidonia was hurt by the loss of her mother to whom she was especially attached, and Mimi understood that she lost her guardian.

We buried Mutis in the town of Alba-Iulia, in the grave where other members of her family were already buried. Tataie, Sidonia, Alina, and I drove to Alba-Iulia following the van with her coffin. The burial followed a traditionally Romanian Christian Orthodox ritual, including a get-together with food and drinks after the funeral so that the memory of the deceased becomes a happy one.

The year 1979 went on with us waiting for the reply to our passport applications. Summer came, and I went with the children to the beach, renting a room in Tataia. Sidonia, who avoided sunbathing, following some medical opinion saying that exposure to sun increases risk of breast cancer, remained at home. She went every week to the passport office to inquire about our passports. She never got a reply; she was always told to come back. Finally, she joined us, and we had a wonderful time at the beach.

By fall, we got a postcard telling that our application for a passport was rejected. I was not ready to give up, and this refusal made me even more decided to press. I asked for an appointment at the Passport Office, and I was granted one. I went to this office trying not to be intimidated by walking in lion's den. The Passport Office of the Securitate on Nicolae Iorga Street was located in a very fancy old house that undoubtedly before the communist takeover belonged to an aristocratic wealthy family. The owners, if they were smart and lucky, fled the country, if not, have died in one of the regime's jails.

I was invited by a secretary into a room that looked more like a pleasant sunny and large living room. I was seated in a comfortable chair and waited a few minutes. A tall well-dressed man walked in the room and greeted me politely. In his elegant well-tailored suit, he had an air of self-confidence that spelled trouble. He sat down at a table, having in front of him a manila folder at least one inch thick. Most likely, this must have been my personal file from the Securitate.

He started softly, saying that he is aware that Sidonia and I have requested passports to travel abroad. However, he told me the government was very concerned about the welfare of children. Did I know that my wife was paying child support to a daughter from her previous marriage? What will happen to this child if my wife will not give her support? This was the reason to reject our application.

I let him give this talk without interrupting. And then I told him that, I was fully aware of the humane policy of the government toward children, but the child he was talking about, Carmen, was already married, had just finished her studies, and was already employed. Therefore, I thought that she can survive without our support at least for a while. I have never seen a person having a stroke, but there he was: his face got congested, and he was almost unable to talk normally. This high-ranking Securitate officer made a fool of himself since he didn't bother to check the file more rigorously and come up with a better reason to support the rejection of our passport application. I stood up said drily thanks and left the building, thinking that this was the end of the road.

Fall came, and life in Romania went on an interesting pathway. By November, a major political event occurred—the congress of the Communist Party. This time the opposition to Ceauşescu's policy reached the party leadership. A party member veteran, Constantin Pârvulescu expressed his condemnation of Ceauşescu in front of the congress. An open debate between him and Ceauşescu took place, inadvertently televised for all the people to see. The country was shaken and, I assume, so was the Ceauşescu leadership.

After that happened, I had a talk at the laboratory with Jean Brucker. He was the husband of our colleague Ileana and had some connections with Securitate officers, sharing with them a glass of wine, a good meal, and possibly more. He strongly advised me to write a letter to the higher-ups of our government and the party about the rejection of our passport application. What did I have to lose? I decided that there was nothing to lose; at least I could vent a little our frustration. I set up at my typewriter and wrote a letter in which I mentioned several arguments; I have been in the West three times and returned home each time; as a Jew I can always apply to migrate to Israel; my goal was to visit my family in France, which was a right supported by the Romanian Government. I sent copies of this letter to Ceauşescu's office, to the Ministry of the Interior, and other three high-ranking officials. This was November 1979.

About that time, I received from Ştefan a picture of him getting married to Donna in Columbia, South Carolina. Although it didn't say anything that could raise the suspicion of the censor, I took it as a signal that he is there in a stable position, waiting, and willing to help.

Winter holidays came, and we went to Bușteni, where we spent Christmas and the New Year hiking in the snow. The last days, a winter storm arrived; by the time we were ready to drive home, the car was well buried underneath a thick blanket of snow. We managed to get it out and going, which was not easy. I always had battery problems with that car. We got home safely, and the following day, the first working day in January, we went to work. The blizzard was still going on, and the roads in Bucharest were covered with snow. Public transportation was absent, and at the institute, we were asked to get out and clean the snow from the alleys surrounding the buildings.

Close to noontime I was called to answer a phone call. An official-sounding voice asked to talk to me and told me that I should come to the Passport Office to pick up our passports. My reply to him was, "Man, this is not a good joke." Undisturbed, the guy repeated his message, and I hung up. I went back to the lab and told Sidonia about the phone call and how some individuals have nothing better to do than this type of jokes. I could not believe that this was true.

Sidonia had a different approach. She said, "I'm going." I told her that this is going to be a long walk in the snow-covered streets of Bucharest, and she may be disappointed. She insisted, and I let her go. After a few hours, Sidonia came back. She managed to walk through the snow to the Passport Office, identified herself, told the officer why she came, and after a short while, the officer told her to prepare to pick up the passports. She told him that we were not ready to leave, that our children were in school, and that when we applied for the passports we planned our trip for the spring vacation, when children were out of school.

I can only imagine the amazement of this officer. Usually, people would take the passports as soon as they were available, like some hot pancakes, and leave the country as fast as they could before Securitate changed its mind, which happened quite often. But here was someone willing to wait for months to use this passport; the officer certainly thought this is a crazy lady. The truth is that we were not prepared to leave. We have been waiting for almost a year for these passports and we have lost hope we will ever have them. We had no one to take care of the children. After all, Noël was fourteen years old and Alina ten. Mimi was very sick and living with Tataie in their home. We could leave only when we have covered the care for them and for the kids.

Mimi's Death

The death of Mutis in May 1979 has brought a major disruption in the life of the Ciugudean family. Tataie, who was suffering of Parkinson's disease, has been taking care of all three and particularly of Mutis, who was paralyzed after a stroke. Now he became reluctant to take care of Mimi and even of himself.

By December, Mimi started showing signs of advanced Parkinson's disease. Treatment was started without much success. By January, Mimi developed pneumonia. She was admitted to the hospital and died after a few days. She was buried in a cemetery in Bucharest, but after seven years, Mimi's remains had to be removed from the grave. They were moved to Alba-Iulia to the family grave where her mother was buried. For me and anyone else, Mimi remains a medical mystery, which is most unfortunate.

One of the strangest stories of my life is related to Mimi's burial. In those days in Romania, there were no funeral homes. Everyone had to make all the arrangements on its own. So I went at a shop to buy the coffin. When I arrived there, the small office room was filled with people. I was told that there were no coffins available. A truck loaded with coffins was supposed to come from the northern region of the country, but the snow and the deep freeze were the reason for the delay.

Everyone in the shop, and we were about fifteen, was waiting for the coffins. Obviously, there could be no burials without the coffins. In those sad moments, instead of mourning the loved ones that have just passed away, we had to wait for their coffin, not knowing if or when it will arrive. Finally, a happy ending: after we waited anxiously for a few hours the coffins came, and there were enough of them for all of us, the buyers. Romania proved that there could be happiness even in death. What a country!

How to Set Up a Breakaway

After Mimi's death, we decided to move Tataie with us. He sold his home to an orthodox priest that during the filling up of the papers was telling me how the Jews were guilty of all the evils of the world. I was listening patiently to this canard that has been repeated for at least the last two thousand years, and was glad when the paperwork was over. Obviously, he couldn't even imagine that I was a Jew and would have been shocked to find out. By then, most of the Jews have left the country. Tataie moved with us just before we were leaving Romania. Although we were tight with our space, at least he would be together with the children and provide some supervision, and we could take care of him.

The only offer for help came from Andrei Vermont. Andrei has been a student at the Craiova Medical School in 1975. He then transferred to the Bucharest Faculty of Medicine. By fall of 1977, I received a call from him asking to come and visit me. I didn't know what this was all about because in Craiova, we never had any interaction outside class. Nevertheless, being a former student of mine, I invited him to come.

Andrei came and told me that his late father, has been a medical doctor and Jewish, and his mother was a Christian living in the city of Galați, about three-hour drive from Bucharest. Andrei was asking my opinion about leaving the country as a Jew. He wanted to know if he qualifies as a Jew and if he should do it. This was a difficult question. Clearly, he could qualify as a Jew for the state of Israel and for the Romanian government anxious to sell as many Jews as possible for dollars. However, giving him the honest advice, "leave the country," could be easily interpreted that I was also interested in leaving the country. This information transmitted to the Securitate would mean that we would never receive a passport.

At that time, I didn't know Andrei and he could very well have been a Securitate informer. On the other hand, he could have been just a trustworthy young man that was seeking advice on a very important life decision from a professor that was Jewish, most likely the only one he had. I don't remember the kind of advice I provided, but in all likelihood, it wasn't very clear or straightforward.

But this turned out to be the beginning of a friendship based on trust. After this first visit, Andrei returned quite often, and we returned his visits. However, we didn't tell him about our passport application until we got the passports. When he found out that we have the passports, he insisted that we make arrangements not to return to Romania. He took us to Galați to meet his mother, Ileana, hoping that we can make provisions so that she could take care of the children while we were away, which, according to his opinion, should have been permanent. It was a nice try but a dubious solution. It would have been a major disturbance in everyone's life to move from one city to the other. So basically, we couldn't find a solution to this problem, and for us that proved to be the cause of major troubles.

March 1 is a special day in Romania, when women receive from friends a little trinket hanging on a thread with white and red colors made exclusively for this day. We decided to send such a gift to Ştefan Mironescu's wife, Donna, with the mention that we hope to see her soon. It was meant to be a coded message to Ştefan that we are close to leave the country. For the censorship, it would have meant nothing, just a nice act on our part.

We bought our international railway tickets without any trouble. The tickets were for traveling through Hungary, Austria, West Germany, Holland, Belgium, France, and Switzerland and back to Romania. I went to get the visas from the Austrian and French consulates. These were the only countries with which Romania had no visa waiver agreements. The visit to the Austrian embassy was uneventful, but after I left the French embassy, I walked to a nearby open market, Piazza Amzei. Walking through the stalls, I was stopped by a policeman. He asked to see my identification card to check if I had my blood group inscribed in it. Each Romanian citizen was compelled to have an identification card and to have his/her blood group inscribed in it. While looking at my card, he was repeating my name and address in a loud voice, and he asked me where I worked. In fact he was talking to a walkie-talkie, probably linked to a Securitate office nearby, and assigned to verify the identity of those who enter the French embassy.

We were getting close to our departure date, which was set for April 4. At the institute, our colleagues were happy for us. We were going on a wonderful vacation, and we played the game of letting everyone know how we planned to come back. However, an unusual act came from my colleague Mihai Zamfirescu. Without saying much, he gave me a personal card with a written message for André Lwoff, a Nobel Prize winner who worked at the Pasteur Institute in Paris. In the message, Mihai was asking Lwoff to give me assistance. This came as a surprise to me. I have never mentioned to anyone my intention to defect; that would have been suicidal. With Securitate informers roaming around, it would have meant the loss of any chance to leave the country. Nevertheless, Mihai's appeal to this influential scientist was asking him to help me and the only help that I would need to be able to defect was getting a position. This would be my first requirement if I would defect.

Having a position as soon as possible was essential for a defection that had to be followed by family reunion. It would be very hard to ask the Romanian authorities to allow a family reunion without having the financial means to support it. It seemed obvious that Mihai was thinking that I was going to defect, and I will have to find soon a position, but these words have never been spoken by us. Even if I didn't consider defecting, this card may have been an invitation to do it. I can speculate that this was a form of support within a worldwide brotherhood, but this may be just my imagination. Nevertheless, after her return to Romania and during the time that followed, when Sidonia was exposed to vicious harassment, Mihai was by her side with moral encouragement and advice, and we remain forever grateful for his unreserved support. In her letters Sidonia often referred to him as "the big Z." All her letters went through censorship, and she didn't want to expose him by mentioning his name.

We wanted to go to Paris, and we thought that we could meet there our friends Vlad and Mira Pauker. I knew Mira since she was a good friend of Mona. It happened that Mira's mother was a classmate of Aunt Jenny, Uncle Oscar's wife, at the Pharmacy College. Mrs. Millo remembered how Jenny, a Christian, walked out with the Jewish students when the legionnaires chased them out of the college.

Mira married Vlad Pauker, the son of the famous (according to many Romanians, infamous) Ana Pauker. Vlad was a down-to-earth and easy to befriend guy. By that time, his mother, Ana Pauker, was having major troubles with the leadership of the Romanian Communist Party; actually, she escaped prison and probably death because of her relationship with important foreign communist leaders. After Mira's wedding, I went to her apartment and Ana Pauker showed up. I was introduced to her, and she started a small talk with me inquiring about my father, who in 1935 has been her lawyer at her trial in Craiova.

Vlad and Mira left Romania and moved to France. I don't know the details, but Vlad's sister, Masha (Maria), and her husband, Martin, have been previously allowed to leave Romania. Masha has been fostered by the wife of a leader of the French Communist Party. Maybe her intervention got them out of Romania.

We went to visit the Millo family. Mr. Millo was sick, but Mrs. Millo was as active as ever. She gave us Mira's phone number and her address; she volunteered to let Mira and Vlad know we are coming, and she openly advised us to leave Romania and not come back. It was noticeable that this opinion came from a person that has been a supporter of the Communist Party by the time it was outlawed, and after WWII, was an active member of the women's organization, one of the umbrella organizations related to the Communist Party. This came if it was necessary, to boost my decision to defect, but we did not mention anything about our plan. It would have been foolish on our part to jeopardize our chance.

One of the last, but not least things that we had to take care before living, was the children. They were getting close to the spring vacation, and we arranged to take them to Bușteni, and have them there in the custody of our host, Mrs. Drăgoi. This would cover the first two weeks of our absence.

Alina, who was in the fourth grade, was the first one to start vacation. I drove her to Bușteni. After we arrived there, I took her for a short walk in the woods behind Mrs. Drăgoi's home. There was still snow on the ground, but the spring undergrowth was already coming out. I felt that I had to say farewell to those places where we spent many vacations, and we loved them. I knew then that I will never see these places again.

Fig. 5. Alina in Bușteni. April 1980. We got together again in October 1981.

Alina was unaware of what was going on, and was ready to start playing with Violeta, a girl from the neighborhood with whom she used to play for years. I told her good-bye, wondering how long it will be until I will see her again. Not a happy feeling, but I was starting to get used to these thoughts. I felt a growing commitment to put up the fight for our freedom and win it. When you know that there is a now-or-never situation, a lot of fighting spirit comes along, and this is what it was for us. As far as Noël, he will be driven to Bușteni by Paul, Mariana's husband, and it will be also Paul that kindly agreed to drive them back to Bucharest at the end of their vacation.

Out of Romania

Back in Bucharest, Sidonia and I were getting ready to leave. Our departure was scheduled for April 4. The train was leaving around 7:00 PM. Andrei Vermont came to escort us with Noël to the Railway Station. We tried to get a taxi, but this proved to be an impossible task. One of our neighbors gave us a ride to the North Station, which was just a mile from where we lived. Finally, we got to the station and got on the train. We had seats in a sleeping car, and we were only the two of us in the compartment. The train departure was late. We took a casual good-bye from Andrei and Noël, like people that leave for a short vacation. However, I took Noël aside and told him about our plan. I asked him to be confident that he will join us, and he seemed to enjoy this prospect.

The train took off, and we settled in our compartment and prepared for sleeping. Sidonia, who was always a good sleeper, had no problem sleeping, and I followed her example. We were awake around 4:00 AM by light and noise. We were reaching the border with Hungary and it was the Romanian custom inspection. An inspector came to our compartment, and he was as asleep as we were. He looked around in our luggage, but we had nothing to interest him. The only useful things were a few papers on which I had some important phone numbers and addresses and also some of my results from my research, which I was hoping to resume and possibly publish. He saw them but was not interested, and finally asked if I have some cigarettes for him. He was hoping for some Kent cigarettes, which were, by that time, used widely for bribes in Romania. I told him that I was sorry, but I was a pipe smoker, and therefore had no cigarettes. He seemed disgusted and left.

A few hours later, we entered Hungary. The management people changed at the border, and when we went to have lunch at the restaurant wagon, the waiters were all Hungarians. To my surprise, Sidonia started talking with them in Hungarian. I didn't know she can speak Hungarian. In her childhood at Cluj, she had Hungarian kids in her neighborhood, and she picked up their language. The waiters were absolutely thrilled to have a Hungarian-speaking lady to serve, and we had a delightful lunch.

Crossing the Iron Curtain

The train went through Hungary as we were having lunch and arrived at the border with Austria. The Hungarian border guards checked our passports.

Since there were very few people crossing the border, the whole procedure lasted just a few minutes. The train moved on, and we were on the other side of the Iron Curtain. It all seemed so easy. It took us more than a year just to get passports to be there, but we were only the two of us. Our children were still on the other side of the fence. The fierce battle to get everybody out was still ahead.

Around 4:00 PM, we arrived in Vienna. There were several hours until the train will take off for West Germany. We decided to leave our luggage locked in the wagon and to walk around Vienna. As soon as we left the station, it started snowing; actually, a blizzard was over Vienna. As we were walking in the snow, we saw a McDonald's place. We entered there and ordered hot chocolate. I had a few dollars that I have saved from my previous visit to the States. We were on the old-age side; most customers were teenagers, but nobody paid attention to us. For us it was a beginning; to be together at McDonald's was looking like we took our first step toward freedom. After warming up, we went back to the railway station and boarded the train. Outside it was cold and damp, but in our compartment, it was nice and cozy. We went to bed and slept very well while the train was going west, farther and farther away from the country we were ready to leave. This was our first night on the other side of the Iron Curtain.

The next morning, we arrived in Köln. It happened to be Easter Sunday, and we left our luggage at the station and went to visit the famous cathedral. The Easter service was going on, and we saw the cardinal arriving at the cathedral. For us, walking through the streets of Köln and looking at the nice shop windows was another start. I have been in West Germany before, but for Sidonia this was the first sight.

We went back to the station and boarded the train for Amsterdam. A small incident occurred on the train. When the controller came, he told us that we should have taken another train, and we have to pay a fine. He was a little agitated, probably expecting trouble from us. The German lawfulness was in danger from people coming from the other side of the Iron Curtain! Fortunately, I had enough dollars with me and he had no problem taking them.

Jan in Amsterdam

Jan Walboomers was waiting for us at the railway station in Amsterdam. Sidonia was meeting Jan for the first time, and they got along very well. Jan had such a warm and friendly personality, and he really enjoyed having us visiting him. Jan drove us to his home, which was in a suburb of Amsterdam. It was a nice modern home, and Jan, Ellen and the two kids have received us with friendly and open arms. We were put in a bedroom that was at the upper level, very nice and cozy. I was impressed when for the first time I used liquid soap. For Sidonia, it was the first time she visited a Western-type suburban house, and she liked it and later, remembered it.

In the following days, Jan and Ellen showed us how wonderful Holland is. They took us to a village close to the North Sea where we saw the famous dikes that protect the land from the sea. Also, we visited Kokenhofen, a wonderful park full with flowers, among which tulips were predominant. We also visited Madurodam, a miniature replica of the main places in Holland. We also called on the Knollenburg family. We met this family on the beach in Mamaia, and Sidonia loved them, and they loved her.

As we spent time together, I told Jan about our plan to defect from Romania. Jan took me to his laboratory to meet Dr. Van der Nordaa, a virologist and good friend of Fred Rapp. We exchanged some pleasantries and nothing else. Several years later, Jan told me that he approached Van der Nordaa about providing a position for me and was turned down. Lucky me!

Fig. 6. Sidonia, Jan, and Maurice, Amsterdam, April 1980.

From Amsterdam, I mailed Ştefan Mironescu a postcard giving him the exact date when we were scheduled to arrive in Paris, and the phone number of the Pauker family, where he could reach us. It was like preparing a blind date. I had no idea if the postcard will reach him and what will happen next.

The visit to Jan and Ellen went fast and was very pleasant. Jan was as good a friend as one can be. Unfortunately, his family life will be badly shaken in the following years. He will divorce Ellen, and this was not a friendly separation. The two sons, Jan Marek and Nils, were given to Ellen, and Jan was very unhappy about that.

Ellen will remarry soon after, and Jan will also later remarry. My understanding is that Ellen was not happy being the wife of a researcher that was spending most of his time in the laboratory. She was interested in having an active social life, and Hans, the new husband, provided that. Ellen and Hans visited us, and we met them once in Atlanta as I went to attend a meeting. They were planning to return to Holland, and as they did, they discontinued our relationship. We continued our relationship with Jan until his unexpected death.

Paris and HIAS

We left Amsterdam and took the train to Paris. We arrived there around 6:00 PM and were met at the station by Vlad Pauker. He drove us to their home located in Bièvres, a suburb of Paris. We met Mira, his wife, and were impressed by the house they build, a modern villa with woods behind it. We settled down and went to bed for a well-deserved sleep.

It was probably 1:00 or 2:00 AM when the phone rang. Everyone got up, and Mira called me to take the phone. It was Ştefan calling from South Carolina. He has received our postcard from Amsterdam and was telling me that I had a position in the Department of Pathology of the medical school in Columbia, South Carolina. He told me to go to the American embassy and apply for a visa to travel to the States.

There is no doubt in my mind that this has been the most important phone call of my life. My decision was instant. Our plan for defecting, the Ovidiu plan, was working. I would join Ştefan in Columbia, South Carolina. I have never heard of South Carolina, but I didn't care, Ştefan was there. Having a position in the United States meant that I will find enough political support to get our children out of Romania, and this was my priority goal.

The following morning, Mira drove us to downtown Paris, and Sidonia and I went to the American embassy. There were many people there, and the marines were trying to keep some order. We managed to talk to someone and the conclusion came out very clear and very soon. Our way to the USA was not going to be easy and, in any case, not through the US embassy. We went home, and the Paukers advised us to go to HIAS.

The Hebrew Immigrant Aid Society (HIAS) has had an extraordinary impact on millions of Jews. HIAS has provided essential lifesaving services to world Jewry through its mission of rescue, reunion, and resettlement. The HIAS Paris office was directed by Mr. Swarcz, an elderly gentleman. Mira drove us there, and he received us kindly. We discussed with Mr. Swarcz our situation, emphasizing the problem of our two children left behind in Bucharest. There was nobody there to take care of them. Moreover, there was the eighty-six-year-old Sidonia's father. Mr. Swarcz told us that if neither of us returns to Romania, with help from the International Red Cross, it may take nine months to get the kids out of Romania. For Sidonia, the thought of leaving her children without her care for so long was unbearable. Sidonia felt strongly that she had to go back to take care of the kids and her father. The only person that foresaw this problem was Andrei, and he tried to provide some assistance. Unfortunately, his mother, Mrs. Ileana Vermont, was not living in Bucharest, and moving to Bucharest for an indefinite period of time would have been for her a major disruption. Moreover, she didn't know our family, the children, and my father-in-law, and the interaction between them was unpredictable.

As far as I was concerned, I understood that having Sidonia going back will be a major problem. The Securitate will no doubt construe this as a split in our family and will make it even harder for Sidonia and the children to leave, thus putting more pressure on all of us including me. However, I was reluctant to take the responsibility to tell her to stay. I would have to deal with her relentless concern about the kids and her father, and risk that at the minor trouble to have her jump on a plane to Bucharest. Moreover I couldn't trust the Romanian Red Cross to take care of our children.

At this point, we decided that Sidonia will return to Romania and fight from there to get out, and I will be assisted by HIAS to get to the United States as soon as possible, and press on from there for their release. This was a fateful and very hard decision for the two of us. I was fully aware of that, but I didn't see another option. I knew that having Sidonia back in Romania and being separated from her for an indefinite period of time, would be a punishing burden for me. I also knew that leaving the children and her father by themselves in care of strangers was very risky. My only hope was that once in the States, I will be able to gather enough political support to make this step as short as possible.

The next day, we went to the Pasteur Institute to meet our former colleagues from the Cantacuzino Institute, Dr. Nardi Horodniceanu (Horaud) and Dr. Radu Crainic. They were working at the Pasteur Institute, and Nardi had a leading position in his group. Nardi asked what our plans were, and when I told him that my next step will be to go to the United States, he told me that I should consider remaining in France, where he can arrange for me a good position in the city of Nice on the French Riviera. I told him that my decision was already taken, and I will pursue it with the necessary formalities.

Nardi offered to let me work on a small project in his laboratory for the time I was supposed to wait for the American visa. Moreover, he talked to Dr. Luc Montagnier to give me some work and provide some funding and Dr. Motagnier accepted it. A few years later, Luc Montagnier was the Nobel Prize winner for AIDS research. I will always be grateful to these people for their unsolicited assistance during these very difficult days for me.

Strasbourg Family

After having started my paperwork for the entry visa to the United States with HIAS, Sidonia and I took the train to Strasbourg. We spent the next several days at Colette, debating our plan with her and her husband Jackie. They were extremely supportive and expressed regrets that we have decided to move to the States instead of remaining in France. They even put me in touch with some professors at the Strasbourg Medical School to check if there was some job opening. Indeed there were some, but I was not interested. I was absolutely decided to move to the States. The main reason was that I was counting on the pressure that American politicians could exert on the Ceaușescu regime to release my family, and this was my priority.

From these relatives, I got immediate help. Uncle Oscar has given us a check of six hundred Swiss francs to be credited to his account in Switzerland funded by Uncle Willy. Liliane's husband, Claude Hohnel, offered to cash this check, which otherwise would have been useless.

The other support that proved to be vital was that Colette and Jackie, through their connections, found an apartment in Paris where I could live without paying rent. HIAS had assigned me to stay in a hotel attic room for thirty-five francs a day. I went to see the room. It was very small, and it had a bed, a wardrobe, and the smallest sink I have ever seen. Not an attractive place to say the least. The owner of the apartment was a professor in Israel, and he was pleased to have someone trustful living in his apartment. When I met him, he was even willing to let me drive his car, which he kept in the garage in the condo basement. I turned down this offer; this would have been costly (gas, parking), and driving in Paris was not the first thing on my mind. For me this apartment proved to be a heaven.

Separation Ordeal

Our Romanian visas were due to expire May 1, so Sidonia had to be back in the country by then. The day of our separation came, and it was the saddest day in our lives, a day imposed on us by the communist regime that will really live in infamy.

I remember this night as one of the most horrific I ever had. We went to bed and tried to have a few hours of sleep. We were awoken by Jackie, who took us to the railway station. In Strasbourg, the train stopped around 4:00 AM. Sidonia was very quiet; she didn't utter a word. As far as I am concerned, I was profoundly shaken and tried hard to cover it.

We got to the station, and the train came soon thereafter. Sidonia had a sleeping car site, and Jackie went to help with the luggage while I was waiting on the side, feeling miserable. This was a terrible separation, and the whole scene was like a funeral. There were no kisses or hugs. We didn't talk because there was nothing to say. The train left, and I went home, pondering if I was doing the right thing inflicting so much pain on us.

Sidonia, in her letter of June 28, 1980, reflects on this hardship: "In this situation when one of the two of us had to be sacrificed, had to return—because I am becoming more and more convinced that it could not be otherwise—fate found to pick me, arranging things in such a way that it was normal and obvious that it was I and not you. Logical and rational. I accepted this fate choice, moreover I assumed the responsibility to do everything to get things right, to take all the blows so that nothing would reach the kids and my father." She accepted the choice that fate imposed on her, but she resented what was actually an unfair selection preference. As she mentions in her letter, there was no other option for us.

Sidonia the Brave Fighter

According to Sidonia, her trip to Bucharest went on smoothly, and having the comfort of a sleeping car for such a long trip helped to improve her mood. However, when she reached the Romanian border, this is how she describes her reaction: "When I returned I got a terrible fear (you can laugh) when entering the country, the officer who checked passports stamped mine hard and with force, likely to see clearly the date and I don't know what else! From that moment and just like only then, I realized that my fate is sealed factually and figuratively, and I got a terrible fear of what lies in wait for me, how much time will pass before I will have a passport in hand." This anxiety lasted about a month until as Sidonia wrote: "Then literally with an iron will, this time I recovered, and I moved to the other extreme of total indifference and belief that I am more than Achilles, I have nothing vulnerable!"

It was June 7, 1980, when Sidonia went to the local police and filled up the first papers requesting passports and visas for all four of them to join me in the United States. She was told then that there will be three months until they may be called to be judged by a commission. In fact she was summoned at this commission only in April 1981, nine months later. This was the communist regime at its best, and no wonder that Sidonia called them pigs and beasts.

In her letter of June 28, 1980, Sidonia wrote: "In this time there were a few people who encouraged me, to whom I cannot ever thank, especially the last letter of the alphabet that how big he is, fretted all to help me, he was impressed with my situation and kept advising me, he was often seeking me, I think he was afraid that I'll throw myself out the window." Sidonia was referring to Dr. Mihai Zamfirescu (the last letter of the alphabet) avoiding uncovering him to the censorship that was screening every letter. However, she discovered soon that postcards went through much faster than letters. Understandably, the communist government didn't want the tourists from Germany, Holland, or Sweden, to find out that a postcard mailed from Romania takes a month to reach their friends or relatives at home.

The worst for both of us was the separation without a deadline. We have been previously separated, in 1969 and 1973 when I was in the United States, but we always knew the day when we will be together again. We could count the days. This time, it could be years of separation, an unknown number of years. On our anniversary on June 27, 1980, Sidonia wrote: "For us, many happy returns of the day! With health, happiness and many accomplishments and I say as much as possible together, and as little separated. I kiss you with much love and embrace you."

In my letter of July 2, I told Sidonia, "My loved and adored, this is a letter just for you. It is not a response to letter 4 who wanted to be sentimental and succeeded in part, but comes from an earlier desire that began on the night of 30 April. I hope there is nothing unusual at our age to write and receive declarations of love. The truth is that from that night, when I watched you, I got into a passionate love that does not leave me at all. I do not know, but, it seems, I love you more than 16 years ago, and definitely I love you differently, and it is very serious, especially as we're apart. Here my Love, please receive this serious and profound statement of love, and know that I'm waiting only for the moment when we'll be together and try to make you appreciate how real and serious it is."

In the same letter I said, "My Adored, please believe me, that although both you and I go through difficult days, I have the belief that is everyday confirmed, that for all of us, but absolutely for all of us, I took the best decision, I chose the only way achieving it. It couldn't be done otherwise, and to deceive you with regret that it would have been possible otherwise is delusional. That is the price to pay for a future that is quite quickly approaching, and which promises to be good for us." The letter ends saying, "I love you in a special way as I cannot wait to have you near me, and I can receive you in a new world, expecting you with open arms, and, I am sure that you will feel so good that you will forget the nightmare of the past. I kiss you a lot with much love and longing, I love you." This was my response to what she wrote me in a previous letter that some people have told her that I could have asked to leave the country from Romania, implying that I submitted her to this ordeal which could have been avoided.

In her reply letter Sidonia said, "Burşi, my love, I received your letter/letters, and I was very pleasantly impressed reading them, I should say, they have made me happy, but I'm afraid of this word mostly because of the difficult moments through which our family is going through. From the depth of the soul, I must say that I love you very much; I think that I had a fantastic chance to meet you, hitches are few and meaningless, and children very successful and endowed by nature, develop so beautifully just because of our caring and harmony. We have a very successful and happy marriage, but if you sit and make a balance sheet of those 16 years, we have gone through enough tough times, we've struggled a lot to rise above mediocrity, to accomplish something, and I hope that with this last effort, of our separation, the problem would be greatly solved. I have complete confidence in you, I do not doubt for a moment, that for you the problem solving our family reunion is your priority, and I feel, I do not know by which extra sense, and by what mechanisms, that you help me, that we are joined together in this common effort."

These few lines actually summarize not only our happy life together blessed with two outstanding children, but also our sacrifices including this final struggle for a better life. Sidonia ends this letter, which was the last one that I received from her before leaving Europe, saying: "I assure a wonderful climate for the rear guard, and conduct military operations here like a genius. Anyway for none of us it is easy, and the sooner together the better it will be. We kiss you with all our love, trust us, we keep our strength, and we are not overcome by anything, we think about you all the time. Țuțu."

The tough times that Sidonia is referring to were the result of the communist regime policy forcing us to be separated whenever we tried to get to a better situation. Both times, when I had the opportunity to go to the US, I had to leave her and our children behind, hostages to the communist government. In order to survive professionally, I had to get the Craiova position and to commute there for years. As Sidonia said, we managed to keep a successful and happy marriage only because we were so closely bonded by our love. We felt like one, and we were joined together in this effort, and in everything else. Nothing could separate us, not even the Iron Curtain. We were now engaged in a battle to have everyone on the other side of the Iron Curtain, and as Sidonia rightly expressed in her letter, we were in a state of war with the communist government. We were fighting for our lives.

During these early months after her return to Romania, until she was allowed to leave the country, Sidonia acted bravely. This struggle went on from May 1, 1980, the day when she returned to Romania, until October 3, 1981, when together with her eighty-six-year-old father; Noël, sixteen years old; and Alina, twelve years old, she landed in New York.

During this time, we, Sidonia, the children, and I, have exchanged a large number of letters; fortunately, I stored almost all. The letters that she wrote in these difficult times are a record of the fight she had to put up facing the communist authorities. The story of Sidonia's fight for our family reunion will continue in the next part, which starts after my move to America.

This wonderful daughter, mother, and wife, fought the fight for a free life for all of us, willingly and courageously carrying the burden of her cross against all the adversities she had to encounter, keeping her sense of humor and unabashed optimism. It was a huge sacrifice on her side to return to Romania, without any guarantee if and when she will get out. Returning to Romania meant that she had to take care of our children and her old father, all by herself. On top of that, she knew she would be exposed to all the harassment that a vengeful totalitarian regime was able to gather to punish her for my defection. What will be the worst was the unknown length of our separation: There were only hearsay, and people were talking about years. Our children and I will never be able to express our gratitude for her unselfish sacrifice, so that we can live in a free world. She was an awesome brave fighter!

Life in Paris

I left Strasbourg and returned to Paris. Nardi invited me to spend a few days at his apartment in Meudon, a suburb of Paris, while his wife was away. I went there, and almost immediately developed a bad case of flu. I spend several days in bed in Nardi's apartment, lying with high fever and chills. I used to have such flu before, but this one was horrific, maybe following the dramatic stress of all these decisions and the separation from Sidonia.

Finally, I got up and was ready to move to my apartment. Taking the subway at rush hour, loaded with all my stuff made me an easy target for the pickpockets. I felt a couple of youngsters that were working my pocket while I had my arms holding my stuff, and there was no room to move standing up in the crowded subway. By the time I arrived at destination, my wallet, including $200 and the photos of Sidonia, was gone. I learned the lesson and how to avoid further losses.

I was glad to take over my new lodging. It was a two-room apartment in a condo, very quiet and, apparently, safe. It was a different world from the hotel attic room, and in addition, I didn't have to spend 35 francs per day. All the expenses for me living there turned out to be around 1,800 French francs, which covered the maintenance of the place. I don't know when Jackie and Colette covered this expense, but on my first visit to Strasbourg, I was glad to reimburse them. The apartment had a kitchen that would allow me to cook some meals, another way of saving on the little money I had. It was a ten minutes' walk to the subway station that would take me to the Pasteur Institute or downtown.

In the meantime, I had to take care of my separation from Romania, so that the whole process would not antagonize the feelings of the government that after all was holding my family hostage. I wrote a letter to Dr. Bîlbîie, the director of the Cantacuzino Institute, asking for my resignation and saying that I decided to leave in order to be together with my family in France. The same reason was presented to the Romanian embassy in Paris, where I applied for the status of Romanian citizen with residency abroad.

The Romanian government was very sensitive not to have defectors, and preferred therefore to grant a special passport to people like me. For them it was face-saving, considering the increasing number of Romanian citizens that were fleeing the country, one way, or another. In principle, they will release the hostages, my family, in exchange for me asking and getting this special passport, and therefore preventing me to claim political refugee status.

Between the assistance from the Paris Jewish Community and the compensation from Dr. Luc Montagnier, I was surviving financially quite well. Not having to pay rent was a major help. Offer of financial support came from Jan Walboomers and Mrs. Maria Motz. Jan and his family stopped at my apartment on their way back from a vacation in Spain. We had lunch, and he told me that he could lend me $200 a month until I will have normal income. I found it very generous from him, but I refused. I really didn't need this money.

American Visa

HIAS took me under its wings. A gentleman, who I believe was doing volunteer work for the society, took me to the police station to get a visa on my Romanian passport, so that I could extend my stay in France waiting for the American visa. We went there and found a large crowd. Apparently, my man knew well the ladies that were behind the desks. He approached one, and from nowhere, produced a box of chocolate candies that he graciously handed to the lady, who swiftly took it. After that, the formality of putting a visa stamp on my passport took just a few minutes. At the HIAS office, my case was in care of an elderly lady, Ms. Hannoun, who was very matter-of-fact and efficient.

An important event occurred soon thereafter. I received an official letter from Ștefan, stating that I have a position in the department, and he would like to have me there as soon as possible. A similar letter was addressed to

HIAS. This letter was followed by an official letter from the chairman of the department, Dr. Jim Caulfield, with an offer for a one-year contract for a position of lecturer in the Department of Pathology with a salary of $30,000 per year, starting August 1, 1980.

UNIVERSITY OF SOUTH CAROLINA

SCHOOL OF MEDICINE
Veterans Hospital Enclave
Columbia, S. C. 29201

Department of Pathology

May 19, 1980

Hebrew Immigrants Aid Society
4 bis Rue de Lota
Paris 75016
France

Dear Sirs:

This is to inform you that we are delighted to offer Dr. Maurice Nachtigal the opportunity of joining our research team here at the University of South Carolina School of Medicine in Columbia, South Carolina, U.S.A.

Dr. Nachtigal's internationally recognized expertise and accomplishments in the field of cytogenetics will fit perfectly in our group and augment the present existing potential. He will be responsible for carrying out important investigations, such as chromosome banding and sister chromatid exchanges, which appear as indispensable tools for both our present ongoing and planned studies.

Our annual budget will offer him considerable freedom in exploiting and implementing his capabilities and creativity. Additionally, others on campus, should he so desire, are most anxious for collaboration with him on both basic and clinical studies. Moreover, we contemplate utilizing his unique abilities and expertise for the teaching of Sophomore Medical Students, as well as participation in Graduate and Post-Graduate Continuing Medical Education Courses.

Because the South Carolina Legislature is in the process of finalizing its budget for the FY 1980-1981, I cannot tell you now the exact amount of Dr. Nachtigal's salary. However, I can assure you that it will be a competitive stipend, well in the five-figure annual range, which can comfortably support him and his family.

Again, we will be very glad to have Dr. Nachtigal with us, starting on July 1, 1980, or sometime thereafter, and we are looking forward to a mutually rewarding and productive association.

Sincerely yours,

Stefan Mironescu

Stefan G. D. Mironescu, M.D., Ph.D.
Professor of Pathology

SGDM/dpm

Fig. 7. The letter on my behalf, addressed by Ștefan Mironescu to HIAS.

These letters put pressure on HIAS and the American Immigration and Naturalization Office (INS). This was not the routine case of immigration to the USA, that was usually handled in about seven to nine months, and where the main problem was to make sure there is a sponsor willing to assume the responsibility of the immigrant. Almost none of the refugees had a job waiting for them in the States. For me there was a definite job at the end of the road, and missing the starting day could, in theory at least, jeopardize everything. To my great satisfaction the paper processing including the unavoidable red tape started moving faster. In my mind, the sooner I would be in the US, the better my chances to start the process of rescuing my family from Romania. Also, according to my communication with Sidonia, I knew that this will definitely boost her morale.

I passed a medical exam in a French doctor's private office, making sure I didn't suffer of tuberculosis or syphilis. Next, I went for the critical interview with an INS officer at the American embassy. The officer was as nice as it can be. He asked me the reasons for defecting from Romania and listened to my stories that you already know: my encounters with Securitate in Craiova and Bucharest, my rejection based on political discrimination from job applications that I was qualified for, the horrendous obstacles in traveling abroad, etc. The guy told me something about the South of the United States, which for me at that time didn't matter. For me it was the USA that I cared for, south, north, east, or west. I don't know where from, but I got the impression that he knew a lot about me. We separated on friendly terms, and I felt that I am almost there.

After my arrival in Columbia, South Carolina, I found out that the paper process was not completely smooth. Ștefan Mironescu has asked Columbia Jewish Community to sponsor me. After all, I was Jewish, and HIAS was a Jewish organization. According to Ștefan, the community was hesitant to sponsor me, the reason being that the position job offered by the University of South Carolina was for one year only, and they were afraid that after this year expires, they will have me in charge. I ended up being sponsored by Ștefan and his wife, Donna, and I was never in charge of anybody. I should mention that after I arrived in Columbia, South Carolina HIAS was helpful in supporting my efforts to have my family released from Romania.

My American visa application was progressing very well, and HIAS and the INS were doing their best to have me in the States by August 1. This date was approaching fast, and I was already preparing my departure. I didn't want to have with me too much luggage, so I mailed two pieces on Ștefan's address. The departure date was set from Paris on July 30. I was to board a train in Paris and travel overnight to Brussels, Belgium, where I would be transferred to the airport and board a plane for New York around noontime.

Nardi gave me a ride to the North Railway Station, where I joined a large group of immigrants of different origin. We were probably twenty or thirty of us, and I met a young couple that was Romanian. All of them were much younger than me. I felt rather old: I was forty-seven years old. We slept as we could on this overnight trip and arrived as planned the following morning (July 31) in Brussels. We were transferred immediately by train to the airport and waited until noon for the takeoff.

I was ready and anxious to leave Europe and to start a new life in a new world. My breakaway was successful, but the intense fight to get my loved ones out from behind the Iron Curtain was just beginning. For the following fourteen months, I will have no respite until I will see them on the American soil.

Edwards Brothers Malloy
Thorofare, NJ USA
February 26, 2014